FARMING WITH THE WILD

Enhancing Biodiversity on Farms and Ranches

Written by Daniel Imhoff   Designed by Roberto Carra

Foreword by Fred Kirschenmann

A Watershed Media Book

Sierra Club Books

The Sierra Club, founded in 1892 by John Muir, has devoted itself to the study and protection of the earth's scenic and ecological resources–mountains, wetlands, woodlands, wild shores and rivers, deserts and plains. The publishing program of the Sierra Club offers books to the public as a nonprofit educational service in the hope that they may enlarge the public's understanding of the Club's basic concerns. The point of view expressed in each book, however, does not necessarily represent that of the Club. The Sierra Club has some sixty chapters throughout the United States and in Canada. For information about how you may participate in its programs to preserve wilderness and the quality of life, please address inquiries to Sierra Club, 85 Second Street, San Francisco, California 94105, or visit our website at www.sierraclub.org.

A Watershed Media Book
Produced and Copublished by Watershed Media
451 Hudson Street
Healdsburg, CA 95448
www.watershedmedia.org

Published by Sierra Club Books
85 Second Street
San Francisco, CA 94105
www.sierraclub.org/books

Distributed by University of California Press
Berkeley and Los Angeles, California
University of California Press, Ltd.
London, England
www.ucpress.edu

Printed in Canada on New Leaf Reincarnation Matte text, archivally coated, processed chlorine-free, 100 percent recycled paper containing 50 percent post-consumer waste.

ISBN 1-57805-092-8

First Edition

07 06 05 04 03

10 9 8 7 6 5 4 3 2 1

Library of Congress Cataloging-in-Publication Data

FARMING WITH THE WILD: Enhancing Biodiversity on Farms and Ranches
written by Daniel Imhoff; designed by Roberto Carra; foreword by Fed Kirschenmann

184 p.; col. ill.; c 22 x 31 cm.

ISBN 1-57805-092-8 (paper)

Includes bibliographical references (pages 174-176) and index. 1. Sustainable agriculture–Case studies. 2. Sustainable agriculture–United States–Case studies. 3. Agriculture–Environmental aspects–United States–Case studies. 4. Agrobiodiversity–United States–Case studies. 5. Agricultural conservation–Case studies. 6. Agrobiodiversity conservation–United States–Case studies.

S494.5.S86 I455 2003   2002735568

Front Cover photographs:
Cranes in rice field, Cosumnes River Preserve, California, Robert Payne
Apple harvest in the Anderson Valley, California, Roberto Carra
Mountain lion via trip camera in Sonoma County vineyard, Jody Hilty
Desert wildfire, Gray Ranch, New Mexico, Steve Smith

Back Cover photographs:
Buffalo herding at Ladder Ranch, New Mexico, Pat O'Brien
Hay fields in the Champlain Valley, New York, Gary Randorff
Pacific tree frog in heirloom lettuce, Occidental Arts and Ecology Center, Doug Gosling
Union School Slough, Winters, California, John AndersonAll other photographs by Roberto Carra and Daniel Imhoff

ACKNOWLEDGMENTS

On and off over the past two years, Roberto Carra and I have driven the nation's backroads, following the trail of farming with the wild. It has been an exhilarating and sometimes humbling project that took us far longer than we anticipated or could afford, but one that we will ultimately remember as one of the most satisfying efforts of our 12-year-old collaboration. This book is dedicated to all those people who possess the courage and the insight to strive to make Aldo Leopold's conservation ethic a reality on the ground in this present day and age. We hope that these positive examples may provide inspiration and encourage more communities around the country to join the movement to create agriculturally vital communities integrated within a continental network of protected wildlands. We are greatly indebted to the foundations who shared our enthusiasm for this project and graciously supported us to see it to completion. Our heartfelt thanks go to Doug Tompkins, Quincey Tompkins Imhoff, John Davis, Melanie Adcock, and everyone at the Foundation for Deep Ecology. Your leadership and vision are unparalleled. We thank the Wallace Genetic Foundation, the Garfield Foundation, and the Winslow Foundation for their generous contributions. Without our champions, Rick Reed and Beeline Associates, this couldn't have happened. For reviewing the copious drafts of the book and invaluable words of encouragement, research, leads, and advice, I am indebted to our project editor, Jo Ann Baumgartner. John Davis and Sam Earnshaw also provided valuable editorial assistance. Wild Farm Alliance discussions and research, including Paula MacKay's writings, were extremely helpful. To my wife, Quincey, for her unfailing support including line editing, and to Claudia Carra for her tedious work on photographs and patience—*grazie mille*. Fred Kirschenmann, you are a legend; thanks for an out-

standing Foreword. Danny Moses, of Sierra Club Books, helped bring the book to the mainstream, while Jeff Medelsohn of New Leaf Paper made sure it had maximum post-consumer content for a coated sheet. Finally, we extend our sincere appreciation to all the photographers who donated images to help illustrate the stories and points made in the book, and to everyone who reviewed individual sections of the manuscript. Onward!

—Daniel Imhoff and Roberto Carra, December 2002

We would like to additionally acknowledge the following individuals and organizations as well as everyone else who played a role in making this book possible:

Miguel Altieri	Randy Gray	Gary Nabhan
John Anderson	Ed Greaves	Pat O'Brien
Jo Ann Baumgartner	Dan Guenther	Robert Payne
Janet Reed Blake	Seth Hadley	Pam Porter
Ben Brown	Roseann Hanson	Gary Randorff
Alan Buchman	Tex Hawkins	Paul Robbins
Bob Bugg	Greg Hendrickson	Tom Schott
Anna Bullard	Dave Henson	Ellen Smith
Claudia Carra	Jody Hilty	Helen Sweetland
Eliot Coleman	Quincey Tompkins Imhoff	Doug Tompkins
Barbara Damrosch	Dana Jackson	Kim Vicariu
Ellen Davenport	Dan Kent	Peter Vogt
John Davis	Paula MacKay	Tom Waddell
Sharon Donovan	Jennie McCann	Peter Warshall
Sam Earnshaw	Dan McGrath	Becky Weed
Mick Erickson	Skip and Kerry McKallip	Keith Whitener
Terry Evans	Jeff Mendelsohn	The Wild Farm Alliance
Wendy Glenn	Karen Morton	Wren Wirth
Doug Gosling	Danny Moses	Dawit Zeleke

CONTENTS

Diagram of states in which site visits were conducted. Over the two-year research period, an attempt was made to document as broad a base of operations in various regions as time and resources would permit. We apologize that we could in no way include all of the important work being done throughout the country, but look forward to learning about your efforts.

FOREWORD

By Fred Kirschenmann

As a farmer, my relationship with wild things has been fraught with ambiguity. I grew up believing that wildness was the enemy of agriculture. I didn't like blackbirds eating our sunflowers, coyotes attacking our calves, or weeds robbing our crops of nutrients and moisture. So I had an almost instinctive inclination to tear all the wildness out of our farm. I was ready to use all the tools or scientific management tactics available to eradicate wild things from the farm.

A part of me even felt morally justified in harboring that attitude because it is deeply entrenched in our culture. The early Puritans who settled on New England's shores considered it part of their manifest destiny to "tame the wilderness" and "build the Kingdom of God" in this "new land." Cotton Mather (1663-1728) considered the wilderness to be the "devil's playground." It was, therefore, part of his God-given responsibility to urge his fellow Puritans to replace the wilderness with nice, neat rows of corn. For good or ill, that Puritan ethic shaped much of the culture in North America once Native Americans were driven from the land. I am a product of that culture.

Like the generations of farmers and ranchers before me, I have lived, in part, by this wilderness eradication ethic and caused devastating harm to natural ecosystems. Meanwhile, conservationists have adopted a countervailing ethic in order to protect the wilderness. In response to centuries of abuse, conservationists decided to preserve wilderness in its natural state by designating certain regions as Wilderness Areas that are to be protected from human activity. Only with great difficulty have wilderness advocates managed to keep a small proportion of our country (approximately 5 percent) free from industrial intrusions (though not free of livestock). But by quarantining humans from certain parts of the landscape to preserve it, we have also inadvertently consented to humans using the rest of the landscape without any regard for its wildness.

We now know that this dual approach to land use is dysfunctional on both counts. Wildness cannot be "maintained" in the form of isolated pieces of the landscape, and farms cannot be productively managed without wildness. Just as wild organisms need the connectivity of natural ecosystems to thrive, so agriculture needs the wildness of soil organisms to maintain soil quality and pollinators to grow crops—both necessary elements for productive farming. So in the interests of both productive farming and robust wilderness, we need to revisit our dualistic mentality.

Since producing as much as possible in one part of the landscape while preserving everything in its natural state in another part of the landscape is not working, and the real goals of conservation—preserving the integrity, stability, and beauty of the biotic community—have been betrayed, we are now forced to come to terms with our fundamental role as *Homo sapiens* within the biotic community. The essential fallacy in our dualistic thinking is that in both cases—wilderness and agriculture—we had assumed that humans were separate from Nature. Isolating wilderness areas from human activity assumes that wilderness thrives best without human intervention. Indeed, large areas uninhabited by people such as the Brooks Range of Alaska provide powerful testament. That assumption, however, while probably true in the modern, industrial context, serves only to deepen the schism between humans and wild Nature. Isolating wildness from agricultural landscapes presumes that humans, acting separately from Nature, can control production systems purely with human ingenuity and technology. Neither assumption encourages the sort of healthy reintegration into the biotic community that humans must achieve—for our own sake and the sake of all life on Earth. Behind that dualistic fallacy lies another, namely that Nature is a given, that it has evolved into a state of equilibrium (that it will remain essentially the same) and that we can either manipulate it at will (agriculture) or preserve it in a natural stasis (wilderness). Again, there are no empirical data to justify such assumptions. And this both encourages the alienation of humans from Nature and represents a serious underestimation of Nature.

Fifty years ago Aldo Leopold attempted to overcome this flawed dualistic thinking by introducing a new paradigm—an "ecological consciousness." The role of *Homo sapiens*, he suggested, had to be changed from one of "conqueror of the land-community to plain member and citizen of it." This way of thinking, he suggested, transforms our relationship within Nature. It "reflects the existence of an ecological conscience, and this in turn reflects a conviction of individual responsibility for the health of the land. Health is the capacity of the land for self-renewal. Conservation is our effort to understand and preserve this capacity."[1] When our understanding stems from this perspective, the boundaries between domesticated agriculture and wilderness begin to soften.

Our society's failure to appreciate the need for an ecological consciousness is evident not only on industrial farms, but on organic farms as well. We have, unfortunately, come to think of organic farms as isolated enclaves that have little or no connection with the ecology of the landscape in which those farms exist. Organic farms, treated as isolated enclaves, cannot maintain the rich biodiversity necessary for a healthy farm, any more than an isolated wilderness can preserve the biodiversity of a healthy ecosystem. If we hope to create an agriculture that ensures the land's capacity for self-renewal, or a wilderness that perpetuates the native biodiversity of a region, then humans who possess an ecological consciousness need to be part of the landscape.

It is, in part, our dualistic thinking that has led us to believe that the "environment" exists of its own accord. It is just "out there." In truth, however, the environment is constantly being constructed by the organisms (including humans) who live in it. As Harvard evolutionary biologist Richard Lewontin reminds us, all organisms "are in a constant process of altering their environment. Every species, not only *Homo sapiens*, is in the process of destroying its own environment by using resources that are in short supply and transforming them into a form that cannot be used again by the individuals of the species." In other words, if it were not for the activity of organisms in nature modifying their environment–and in doing so, destroying part of it–there would be no environment.

It is the process of one species destroying part of the environment that creates opportunities for other species. Cows eat grass, thereby destroying part of the environment. The by-product of that activity is manure, which provides food for dung beetles and other organisms, who in turn destroy the manure, and in so doing create nutrients for the soil to produce more grass. As Lewontin goes on to say, "...every act of consumption is also an act of production."[2] The appropriate role of humans, then, is to engage in a dance with other species in the biotic community in a manner that enables the community to renew itself–both its wild and domestic parts.

Applying such a view to 21st century agriculture will require a radical shift in our relationship with Nature. First and foremost, we must reclaim our solidarity with the ecosystems in which we farm through "place-based reinhabitation." As David Abrams has written: "It is only at the scale of our direct, sensory interactions with the land around us that we can appropriately notice and respond to the immediate needs of the living world."[3] Our mission as farmers and ranchers then, must evolve from providing adequate, affordable, nutritious food and practicing good conservation to taking direct responsibility for the "health of the land." Our conception of science must change from one that invents technological innovations to solve human problems to sciences that engage in locally based conversations with Nature. Our notions of organic farms must change from enclaves of purity to habitats within ecosystems. The certification of individual farms must give way to standards and monitoring systems for certifying entire watersheds. At that point, agriculture's relationship to wildness will move from production enclaves to wild farm alliances, and as the author of this book argues, restoring interconnected healthy ecosystems.

On our own organic farm in North Dakota we have begun to appreciate the role of wildness in productive farming. We now use livestock breeds that have retained some of their "wildness" and as a result our beef cows possess the instinct to protect their calves from coyotes until the youngsters are old enough to fend for themselves. We have discovered that maintaining a suitable habitat for pollinators and beneficial insects increases the productivity of our cropping system. By mimicking the "succession" inherent in wild systems with crop rotations, we have eliminated the need for costly herbicides to control weeds. We hope that someday perennial polycultures will replace annual crops, eliminating the need for annual disturbance of agricultural lands. We are convinced that many additional benefits lie hidden in the vast resources of the prairie ecology in which we farm. Despite decades of research and education devoted to controlling Nature, we have a lot of catching up to do. We first need to comprehend how the prairie ecology functions so that we can better understand how to farm by accessing Nature's free ecosystem services while improving the land's capacity to renew itself. Once we achieve that understanding, our farm will become more profitable and more sustainable.

Given the depletion of fossil fuel resources, the inabilities of our farming regions to sustain any further agriculture-related degradation, our expanding human population and its impacts on biodiversity, many of the above changes will take place. But this will require that we abandon our dualistic thinking, adopt an ecological consciousness, and erase the hard boundaries between tame and wild in our minds.

THE CASE FOR FARMING WITH THE WILD

On a rural roadside just north of Winters, California, with the summer sun so hot the air shimmers like a mirage, we stand between two radically different farming philosophies. Miles away to the west are the tawny and creviced hills that drain the wetseason rainfall of the Pacific Coast Range. Those waters eventually make their way to the Union School Slough, now actually a volume-controlled ditch, which meanders eastward through the irrigated row crops, orchards, and livestock pastures of Yolo County. On the western side of the road, you get a sense of time travel, a feeling of what the land may have looked like in a former era. The bunch grasses and sedges that line the canal banks are bushy, tall, and luminous. Farther out, above the understory, rises a canopy forest of willow, cottonwood, and oak. In the water, a paddle of young mallards shadows their mother as she zooms for cover behind a curtain of grass.

original oak savanna and local ecosystems and began to establish seasonal wetlands and tailwater ponds to filter runoff. Eventually, some 50 species of native perennial grasses, forbs, rushes, shrubs, and trees were planted around field borders, roadsides, riparian areas, and other unused strips of the farm. Two decades later, beavers, carnivores, dozens of bird species including three types of owls, and up to ten threatened or endangered species find haven there. What he didn't realize at the time, was that he was also sowing the seeds for a change in agriculture itself. What looks like a move backward in time allowed him to move forward as both a farmer and lover of the land. Due in large part to his initiative, a community of conservation-minded farmers, local agencies and extension officers, and nonprofits has slowly been building the expertise, resources, and momentum necessary to forge a new approach to farming in the region.

Directly across the road to the east is a scene more typical of industrial agriculture in California's Central and Sacramento Valleys. The 180-degree shift is so dramatic that it almost takes your breath away. Between the field edge and the slough, a distance of perhaps 20 feet that includes a single-track dirt lane, the soil is sprayed and scraped bare and, in contrast to the scene just on the other side of County Road 89, looks like scorched earth. Both sides of the road are working farm operations that depend upon the Slough's water for production. It is early summer, and both farmers are in high production mode, weeding, irrigating, and managing a hundred tasks. Just a few decades ago, I am told by the farmer on the west side, he too practiced "clean" farming and viewed weeds and noncrop vegetation as mortal enemies of modern agriculture. But as a Boy Scout leader he had studied conservation principles, and as a wildlife veterinarian he had visited hedgerows in England during a trip abroad. Not long after, he and his wife decided to begin improving wildlife habitat on their 500-acre farm, bringing its edges back to life. He devoted himself to studying California's

Across the country throughout the 1990s, similar discoveries, similar commitments, similar reversals of vision were occurring in widely separated areas. The essential role of native pollinators in local ecosystems and in agriculture and the crisis of their rapidly vanishing habitat were being researched in the Arizona desert. Native plant aficionados were seeking out remnants of prairies and beginning to collect, save, and grow out seed for local restoration projects. After decades of clearing, draining, and attempting to render marginal lands suitable for cultivation to "feed the world," federal agencies were working with farmers to return those same fields to wetlands, grasslands, and bottomland forests through perpetual easements. Partnerships between farmers, rod and gun clubs, land trust organizations, and environmentalists were forming to carefully time farming practices with the migratory pulses of waterfowl and fish. Natural processes of flood and stream flow were being reintroduced into a few select riverside agricultural areas in California while lightning-ignited wildfires were being welcomed on a million-acre tract of grasslands in the New Mexico-Arizona-Mexico

Bootheel region—both as means of regenerating the land. A few ranchers were making peace with large carnivores, while some dairy and beef farmers were bucking the livestock feedlot model and perfecting the art of small-scale rotational pasture systems. A Kansas geneticist was pursuing a vision of creating, through classical plant breeding, a self-seeding prairie of perennial grains that would require little fertilizer and no tilling, ideally adapted to its place on the land. The reassemblage of former free-roaming grassland species such as the bison, prairie dog, ferret, wolf, and elk was beginning to take nascent shape in fragmented areas of the Great Plains. Throughout the mid-elevation coffee farms of Central America, biologists were discovering the critical link between habitat remaining on forest shaded coffee farms and declining populations of migratory songbirds. There are more examples, many more, of people tuning in to both the small picture of their own farms and ranches and to the broader landscape, working in partnership with, rather than against, the surrounding natural world. It is time to give a name to what can only be described as a gathering movement: *farming with the wild.*

This book has been the result of a multi-year research project to document and chronicle on-the-ground efforts to restore wild habitats within farming and ranching regions across the country. My interest in taking on such a challenging topic came from various personal experiences and sources of inspiration throughout the 1990s. As the owner of a remote 100-year-old apple orchard in Northern California's Anderson Valley, one frequented by wild turkeys, bobcats, screech owls, gophers, pileated woodpeckers, black bears (who eat fruit by the limb and must be discouraged if harvests are to be sustained), as well as an additional cast of wildlife too numerous to list, I was naturally inclined. As a freelance writer who reported on the organic industry for many years, I ultimately became convinced that the standards set for organic farm management had not necessarily taken into account a farm's impact on its watershed and surrounding ecosystems. One particular assignment for *Whole Earth Magazine* triggered a host of questions that led me to write further articles in *Sierra* and *Orion Afield*. Finally, as a part-time activist who had attended numerous presentations about the need for wildlands connectivity across the landscape, I encouraged John Davis and Mark Ritchie, program officers at the Foundation for Deep Ecology, and Paula MacKay of the Wildlands Project to help me organize and host a conference on the topic. Held in January 2000, the small retreat resulted in the formation of the Wild Farm Alliance, now led by a nationally placed steering committee and advisory board of farmers, naturalists, educators, writers, gardeners, and others that spend copious hours each month discussing the successes and shortcomings of promoting agricultural

systems that are truly compatible with the full range of wild Nature. The need to produce a book that could help further the establishment of conservation communities across the country emerged as key tool for the organization. I eagerly volunteered and convinced my longtime collaborator, photographer and graphic designer Roberto Carra, to join me. Our hope was to assemble a vision of what interconnected, fully functional ecosystems and healthy farming communities might look like. We wanted to focus on positive examples rather than problems, and we wanted to keep our standards rigorous. Two years, twenty-one states, and two countries later, we present what we hope is a unique yet inspiring view of the American landscape.

Industrial Agriculture and the Biodiversity Crisis

At first glance, the phrase "farming with the wild" may seem contradictory. Agriculture, by its very nature, has been and remains the relentless process of selection and minimization, one that now blankets billions of the earth's acres with a mere handful of crops. Farming and ranching activities are consistently identified as the primary cause of habitat loss, the arch foe of the biodiversity crisis. Some 10,000 years ago, out of the cereal-bearing grasslands of the Fertile Crescent, out of the apple forested mountains of Kazakstan, out of the planet's 200,000-plus wild plant species and nearly 150 large wild mammalian terrestrial herbivores and omnivores—slowly and yet almost all of a sudden—there emerged the beginnings of what we now know of as the domestic.[1] Ever since, agriculturalists have been diminishing native biodiversity in order to repopulate landscapes with utilitarian or desirable species. Size, sweetness, oiliness, fiber length, ease of cultivation, hardiness and vigor, self-pollination, yield, taste, nutrition, perishability, healing and recreational properties, color: these were many of the lures for early agriculturalists as they developed place-based cropping systems. Throughout the millennia, agricultural domestication has largely been a dance of coevolution, with humankind playing a leading role as artificial selector and steward, among a full cast of essential and cooperative participants (including birds, insects, fellow mammals, grasses, pulses, food and fiber plants, and natural systems).

Many reaches we tend to imagine as wilderness—self-regulating and self-sufficient natural areas—may in fact have never been as completely free of human influence as we might think. First American societies were intensively managing some, but certainly not all, areas of the native landscape, using fire, for example, as a primary tool in maintaining open and vital grasslands. Yet through the conquest of the native landscape, the continental domination of European agriculture, and the rise of the global-industrial economy, never have the distances between farming and wildness been so vast or the human impacts on biodiversity so damaging. As Michael Pollan states solemnly in *The Botany of Desire: A Plant's-Eye View of the World*: "Even the dream of such a space has become hard to sustain in a time of global warming, ozone holes, and technologies that allow us to modify life at the genetic level—one of the wild's last redoubts. Partly by default, partly by design, all of nature is now in the process of being domesticated—of coming, or finding itself, under the (somewhat leaky) roof of civilization. Indeed, even the wild now depends on civilization for its survival."[2] This is a chilling realization and a far remove from Henry David Thoreau's edict that "in wildness is the preservation of the world."

At one time, thousands of plants were used for human food and agriculture. Today, no more than 120 plants provide 90 percent of plant-supplied human food, oil, and fiber needs; a mere dozen account for 80 percent of the modern world's annual tonnage of all crops.[3] In the 500-year period starting with Columbus's first voyage to the New World, colonization and world trade have transformed the biology and cultures of the earth at dizzying speeds. It is hard to imagine that tomatoes were not a native element of Italian cuisine, that pre-Colombian Mexican food had no cheese, that Thai food's spicy chiles were adopted from Central America, or that potatoes were strictly South American and coffee East African. In the United States, however, 98 percent of the food production can be attributed to non-native species such as wheat, corn, and cattle.[4] According to Peter Vitousek at Stanford University, 40 percent of the earth's solar energy is directed toward food and fiber production for humans; up to 60 percent of the world's freshwater resources are currently diverted for agriculture. With the rise of global corporate agribusiness over the past 60 years, the family farm has become a vanishing way of life in the United States and elsewhere, and farming is no longer even officially recognized as an occupation by the Census Bureau. As farms that combined row crops and livestock gave way to specialized factory-oriented monocultures at war with pests, diseases, and weeds, ever larger machinery necessitated ever larger areas to operate in. Fencerow-to-fencerow conversion of hedgerows, shelterbelts, wetlands, and wildways increased the distance between agriculture and the natural world. Mechanical systems engineered to pump deeper and deeper groundwater disrupted basic hydrological functions in most farming regions. Corporate consolidation of farmland led to an ever increasing amount of rented acreage, on which landscape improvements became a low priority. Today, even the small farmer who is conscientious enough to manage farmland responsibly is continually squeezed by the pressure to produce more output for less money. Overgrazing, overplanting, overplowing, chemical-intensive regimens, extensive monocultures, and other forms of land misuse are all symptomatic of efforts to make up for low prices by increasing production. Forced to compete in a globally-oriented food and fiber system, farmers have often had to forsake goals such as wildlife preservation and long-term landscape conservation (as well as health care and other basic needs) in favor of short-term economic survival.

All the while, the correlation between our shopping lists and the Endangered Species List has been growing at an alarming rate. Farming and ranching activities now involve roughly two-thirds of the U.S. land base in the Lower 48 states and are primary contributors to the imperiling of threatened species and ecosystems. Habitat destruction and fragmentation, the displacement of native species and the introduction of exotic species, pollution of terrestrial and aquatic ecosystems, soil erosion, the persecution of predators, the release of genetically modified organisms, and the overexploitation of nonrenewable resources for food production and distribution are among the many ecologically devastating consequences of modern agriculture. In *America's Private Land: A Geography of Hope* published in 1996, for example, the U.S. Department of Agriculture reported that farming activities contributed to 46 percent of species listed as threatened or endangered, and ranching activities to 26 percent.[5]

Modern agriculture's ecological footprint is drawn into particularly sharp focus by the issue of water development. Nearly two-thirds of the freshwater from lakes, rivers, streams, and aquifers supply irrigation to about one-fifth of the agricultural land worldwide.[6] While the scarcity of freshwater is predicted to become the most important factor limiting agricultural production in the future,[7] the technology to use that water remains tragically inefficient. According to the Wild Farm Alliance, U.S. irrigation systems waste 50 percent of the volume they use.[8] Globally, irrigation systems are only 40 percent efficient.[9] While these irrigated lands reap 35-40 percent of the global harvest,[10] they impart a heavy burden on ecosystems, overdrafting groundwater at rates exponentially greater than the speed of natural replenishment, contaminating riparian systems with sediment and toxic chemicals, causing soil salinization in arid climates, and dewatering entire lakes, rivers, and freshwater systems. At last count, about

Farming Against the Wild

(Photos, page 11). Top left, corn and soybean monocultures blanket nearly 45 percent of U.S. farmland–upward of 130 million acres. According to agricultural expert Richard Manning, corn accounts for 57 percent of all herbicides and 45 percent of all insecticides, while soybeans contribute 19 percent of herbicides applied to U.S. crops. Together, corn and soybeans are the leading contributors to soil erosion and the leading source of groundwater pollution with both pesticides and nitrates. The majority of corn and soybeans are only indirectly used for human consumption, going primarily to livestock feed, corn sweeteners, and processing oils. Top right, hay is the third largest U.S. crop followed by wheat. While not as chemical-intensive as most commodity crops, it consumes vast quantities of freshwater, particularly in arid areas. Bottom left, cotton is a dominant force in U.S. agriculture, particularly in arid states like Texas and California, which also have large dairy industries. Cottonseed, up to 65 percent of the crop's output by weight, is a key ingredient in confinement dairy feedlot rations.

(Photos, page 13). Top left, windblown soil in a California Central Valley farming region. Top center, in many industrial farming areas, riparian systems–used by more than 70 percent of all species at least one time in their life cycles–have been stripped of native vegetation and converted to mere irrigation channels. Top right and bottom center, industrial agriculture in the United States uses nearly 50 percent of all freshwater supplies, yet irrigation systems are highly inefficient. Bottom left, manure lagoons from Confinement Animal Feeding Operations (CAFOs) represent one of the most damaging and heinous violators of local ecosystems. Bottom right, salinization of soils is a frequent side effect of the long-term irrigation of arid soils.

(Photos, page 15). Top row. CAFOs are on the rise, even as recalls of contaminated meats escalate. Confinement poultry facilities function more as factories than farms and are dependent upon anitbiotics to thwart disease. Top right, according to one source, there are more hogs than human residents in North Carolina. Some spend their entire lives in cages, a practice now being outlawed in certain states. Bottom row, over the past century and a half, a war against predators, such as coyotes, wolves, bears, and mountain lions (not to mention the native bison), has been waged in the name of making the West safe for cattle ranching. Even indirect effects of fencing can have damaging repercussions, such as this hawk ensnared on protected federal lands.

30 percent of the protected species and the species proposed for protection in the United States have been listed due to water resource development.[11] Roughly a third of freshwater fish species globally are threatened with extinction.[12] The miraculous salmon runs, for example, that for millennia coursed dramatically through nearly every river system on the West Coast, have been decimated in just 150 years of settlement. The pallid sturgeon is now endangered in inland North American rivers due to lack of spawning sites and is joined by the Yaqui chub, the Topeka shiner, and numerous others. Writing in *The Farm as Natural Habitat* (Island Press, 2001), Dr. Laura Jackson, reports that "28 percent of all amphibians, 34 percent of fishes, 65 percent of crayfishes, and 73 percent of freshwater mussels are ranked extinct, imperiled, or rare by the Natural Heritage Network of the Nature Conservancy."[13] It comes as no surprise then that clashes over water rights between farmers, environmentalists, Indian tribes, and urban dwellers have already hit the boiling point, exemplified by conflicts such as in the Klamath Basin in southern Oregon and Northern California and the Skagit Basin in northwestern Washington. In September 2002, for example, an estimated 30,000 salmon died on the lower Klamath River, a catastrophic die-off that many people attribute to the diversion of water from the fishery to irrigated farmland. This century is sure to experience only more such escalation.

The dominating role of livestock and feedlot farming on the U.S. agricultural landscape cannot be overestimated. More than 70 percent of the national farm income is animal based. Of 1.2 billion total acres in agriculture, upward of 600 million acres of private lands (including tribal lands) and at least 250 million acres of public lands are used for grazing. Of the nearly 350 million acres of harvested crops, the majority of the top three crops— corn, soybeans, and hay—are largely dedicated to feeding and fattening livestock. And an estimated 13 percent of the ocean's fish harvests are diverted annually to cattle rations.[14] Midwestern prairie systems that hold the vast potential to support free-ranging livestock (and native game set amid unbroken grasslands, wetlands, savannas, and forests) have been converted into an ocean of corn and soybeans. More than a thousand miles away in the Gulf of Mexico, as a result of industrial corn and soybean production and concentrated animal feedlot operations (CAFOs), excess nutrients draining through the Mississippi River have generated a 8,500 square mile dead zone of hypoxia, almost completely depleted of marine life.[15] Still, much of the 130 million acres of corn and soybeans produced and consumed each year in the United States remains largely invisible, as it is heavily processed or fed to animals before it reaches supermarket shelves and tables. For beef cattle, which evolved as grass eaters, the heavy corn diet wreaks havoc on their digestive systems, necessitating increasing use of antibiotics to stave off illness and infections.[16] While growing feed and hay to sustain animals through given periods is age old wisdom, confining as many as 100,000 animals in a CAFO where they never see the light of day, raises ethical questions on existential levels. According to Robert F. Kennedy, Jr., "North Carolina's hogs currently outnumber its citizens and produce more fecal waste than all the people in California, New York, and Washington combined."[17] Cattle production in the arid West is ecologically problematic as well. Though long established across the western landscape, cows, particularly at commercial levels, are largely unsuited for dry and fragile terrain, damaging creekbeds, harming soils, altering habitats, and consuming vast quantities of irrigated supplemental hay and feed. While a number of contemporary initiatives to reform ranching impacts on arid lands are genuinely attempting to enhance biodiversity (some of which are included in this book), the long-term ecological compatibility of cattle ranching in many arid regions remains in question.

In spite of this skewed land use system and other urgent ecological challenges, with the proper incentives, assistance, and resources, farmers can and should be supported to manage their lands more sustainably, and profitably, while protecting wildland values. A love of the land, a managerial presence in rural and remote areas, years of experience, and a concern for native plants and animals are all common elements among farming communities. Practices such as pasture-based meat production, diversifying land use (growing vegetables, melons, fruits, and herbs as well as field crops and animals, particularly for local markets), establishing wildlife corridors along river systems, and protecting critical natural areas on and adjacent to farms and ranches, have already shown great environmental and economic promise. As this book will demonstrate, models and examples of landowners, land trust organizations, government cost-share and incentive programs, third party ecolabels, wildlife monitoring groups, nonprofits, and others working to achieve a compatible balance between farming and ranching activities and the protection of the natural world have emerged throughout the country in the past few decades.

A Classic Concept with a New Vision

Farming with the wild is not a novel concept. Nineteenth- and twentieth-century American literature is replete with prophetic philosophical works that attempted to

reconcile and redirect a civilization bent on the isolation or elimination of wildness from the broader culture. Henry David Thoreau's *On Walden Pond*, John Muir's *Mountains of California*, Aldo Leopold's *A Sand County Almanac*, Rachel Carson's *Silent Spring*, and Wendell Berry's *The Unsettling of America*, spring readily to mind among the hundreds of works of extraordinary vision and insight. Within the sustainable agriculture movement itself, the idea that farms must be managed as natural systems gained considerable currency throughout the 20th century under a variety of names. The organic pioneer Sir Albert Howard insisted upon "farming in Nature's image" after years of studying traditional agriculture in India. Rudolf Steiner reenvisioned the farm as a "biodynamic" organism with its own self-sustaining animal-based fertilizers and cyclical patterns of planting, crop rotation, and holistic management. U.S. Department of Agriculture programs of the 1930s were proactive and as concerned about sustainable agriculture as many present-day nongovernmental efforts. J. I. Rodale popularized healthful eating and growing of organic foods and his son Robert advanced the practices and theories behind regenerative, organic agriculture. Aldo Leopold was and remains perhaps the country's, if not the world's, most eloquent advocate for the marriage of agriculture and conservation through a new "land ethic." Geneticist Wes Jackson's "perennial polyculture"—an attempt to breed harvestable prairies that would be self-sufficient in fertilizer, weed, and pest control—derived its design inspiration from the tallgrass prairie ecosystem. Today a number of terms and their movements describe the move away from monoculture toward polyculture, from an emphasis on annuals to geographically appropriate perennial cropping systems: agroecology, regenerative agriculture, natural systems agriculture, grass farming, succession farming, permaculture, eco-agriculture, and farming with the wild.

Since the 1970s, organic farmers have been at the forefront of pioneering research in managing the farm as a natural system, demonstrating that nearly all crops can be grown without chemical inputs and successfully marketed on a variety of scales. Through the establishment of local marketing efforts and massive public education campaigns, the organic movement placed food and fiber production front and center as a major public issue, and succeeded in linking a farmer and a face with the fruits and vegetables at the nation's tables. With growth rates of 20 percent per year throughout the 1990s, organics has also become the fastest growing sector of the food industry. Willingly or unwillingly, the organic movement has been assimilated into the national and global economy, and at the turn of the 21st century, a proverbial Berlin Wall has begun to crumble. By 2008, the global organic industry is predicted to reach $80 billion with European Union governments dictating ambitious targets of the amount of arable land they want converted to organic production: Germany, 20 percent; Belgium, the Netherlands, and Wales, 10 percent each.[18] Despite the value of these successes, however, the emphasis of the organic movement has not been on managing farms at the watershed or ecosystem level in ways that complement and enhance the values and services provided by other landscape units such as large, strictly protected and interconnected ecological reserves. Such direct on-farm services of healthy ecosystems include pollination, biological insect and rodent control, nutrient cycling, the regulation of hydrological processes, erosion control, weed suppression, and detoxification of chemicals. Instead, the organic agriculture movement has understandably focused its decades-long struggle on important issues less directly linked to biodiversity loss—keeping the family farmer on the land, developing nontoxic production practices, and building markets for organic products. Under threat from development, the consolidation of processors and farmland, decreasing farmgate prices, international competition, and corporate domination, survival is at stake. With the mainstreaming of the organic movement, even the futures of small-scale farmers growing for local and niche markets now hang in the balance.

At the same time, spurred by critically plummeting wildlife populations in industrial farming areas, the U.S. Department of Agriculture resumed the allocation of Farm Bill resources for conservation in farm areas in the mid to late 1980s. What started as a series of pilot programs (the Conservation Reserve Program, Wetlands Reserve Program, Wildlife Habitat Incentive Program, and others) has over nearly two decades resulted in the protection and/or restoration of tens of millions of acres of wetlands, bottomland forests, and grasslands nationwide. While spending on conservation programs remains marginal compared to the subsidies that prop up the mass production of only a handful of commodity crops, thanks to significant pressure from conservationists and environmentalists, as much as $2 billion could be spent on significant programs in private lands in the coming decade. These efforts will help to expand the amount of wetlands under restoration and protection, fund a broad-scale grasslands conservation program, target key habitats for imperiled species in agricultural areas, and reward farmers for practices such as cover cropping and diversification. There is still much to be learned, however, to make these conservation programs more ecologically and agriculturally effective.

Adding to this picture of the Lower 48 states, contemporary large-scale wilderness recovery initiatives have set forth a bold and urgent vision for the restoration of functional ecosystems over North America in the 21st century. According to the country's

leading conservation biologists, our protected wilderness areas and national parks have become increasingly isolated through surrounding resource extraction and various forms of development. Many are unable to sustain viable populations of the species they harbor, resulting in genetic isolation, inbreeding, and ultimately extirpation. As experts including Reed Noss, Michael Soulé, and Dave Foreman argue, connecting those fragmented wilderness areas through networks of corridors and mixed-use buffer zones is urgently needed to expand habitat areas for wide-ranging species and to reverse the country's (and the world's) stemming biodiversity crisis.

The dire situation of biodiversity loss and proposals to restore native diversity across broad areas from Alaska to Central America have set the conservation and agricultural communities on a collision course. With such a large percentage of the United States' landbase in private hands and presently in agriculture—and much of that the most productive lands and habitat, which were settled long before the ethic of conservation took hold—a key to the North American wilderness recovery lies in working with farming and ranching regions. As one example, the Richmond, Vermont-based Wildlands Project, has been drafting strategies and creating maps to recover wilderness on a massive scale throughout North America—with an emphasis on ecosystem processes, the need for recovery of all species, and the role of top carnivores to maintain ecosystem integrity. The Wildlands Project has been looking to other organizations, such as the Wild Farm Alliance, for ideas on establishing and maintaining high standards for wildlife-friendly agricultural activities in compatible-use areas.

In their unpublished essay "Tame and Wild: Organic Agriculture and Wildness," North Dakota wheat farmer Fred Kirschenmann and his co-author David Gould argue for an ever closer merger between conservation biology and agriculture:

> We cannot have healthy "organic" farms within degraded landscapes. Quite apart from the problem of "drift"–whether chemical or genetic–there is the fact that the biodiversity necessary to produce the ecosystem services on which our organic farms depend can only be restored and maintained at the ecosystem level. It is the coevolution of a diverse array of species interacting with each other that gives nature its dynamic resilience–something Stuart Kauffman calls "interacting dancing fitness landscapes."[19]

With this evolved thinking, a new vision for a more functionally integrated agriculture is emerging. Such a vision begins with farms that gracefully meld into landscapes supporting a wide–if possible, full–range of native species. Arable lands would be maintained in agriculture but would favor cropping systems that mimic the surrounding landscape, while marginally productive lands would be restored to native habitat. Every farm, while still functioning as its own healthy ecosystem, would in some way act as a corridor connecting it to a larger, ultimately wilder landscape–through clear and free-flowing watersheds, through woodlots and forests, grasslands, hedgerows, or wetlands, eventually into roadless areas beyond human intervention. Society would do its part to actively encourage and support community-oriented farmers who grow a mix of crops native to or adapted to their different regions, and who are rewarded for not farming at the expense of native pollinators, carnivores, fish, or any other members of wild Nature. Ultimately, entire regions could be recognized or certified by their "wild" aspects. Such a vision, however, will require new ways of looking at agriculture's place on the landscape. Fortunately, a number of pioneering groups and individuals have already been "farming with the wild" for a decade or more, and these models can help establish the basis for a nationwide, regionally oriented movement.

Emerging Models and Wild Farm Pioneers

Building alliances between historical adversaries will no doubt require tearing down decades-old walls and stereotypes: environmentalists, on the one hand, often lumped with wealthy urbanites and bureaucrats who dispatch regulations from distant power centers, and farmers and ranchers, on the other, frequently perceived as narrow-minded and steeped in a sense of entitlement. What may in fact help to bring both camps together in alliances is a sense of unity in common goals and common foes. Common goals would include maintaining arable farmland within healthy rural communities, keeping rural lands open and free from subdivision and development, restoring native habitat on private and public lands, and creating a more natural urban-rural interface. Common foes might include land-exploiting absentee agribusiness corporations, massive concentrated animal feedlot operations, and global versus regional food systems. In a recent essay on the subject, the Kentucky farmer and author Wendell Berry wrote:

> I am a conservationist and a farmer, a wilderness advocate and an agrarian. I am in favor of the world's wildness, not only because I

like it, but also because I think it is necessary to the world's life and to our own. For the same reason, I want to preserve the natural health and integrity of the world's economic landscapes, which is to say that I want the world's farmers, ranchers, and foresters to live in stable, locally adapted, resource-preserving communities, and I want them to thrive. One thing that means is that I have spent my life on two losing sides. As long as I have been conscious, the great causes of agrarianism and conservation, despite local victories, have suffered an accumulation of losses, some of them probably irreparable—while the third side, that of the land-exploiting corporations, has appeared to grow ever-richer. I say "appeared" because I think their wealth is illusory.[20]

Fortunately, throughout the country, rural communities are launching their own initiatives at the same time they battle the forces of urban development, consolidation in food processing, the globalization of commodity production, rock-bottom farmgate prices and escalating costs, the flight of an agricultural infrastructure, increasing government regulations, and a myriad of other woes. "These efforts often begin slowly, with farmers and concerned citizens meeting together, talking, sharing, walking fields and grasslands, forming management teams, seeking advice from others," says the Land Stewardship Project's Dana Jackson, who is co-author and co-editor of *The Farm as Natural Habitat*. "Later they can develop yardsticks to monitor their progress, becoming more conscious of the biological diversity in their regions, increasingly building the knowledge of how natural processes contribute to the farm and to the quality of rural life."

Our relationship with food was once, and arguably should always remain, one of our deepest connections with the biotic community, for it ultimately determines what kinds of fellow beings we are. At this crossroads early in the 21st century, we face a revolution of no small proportions in how our food and fiber will be produced and at what economic, social, and biological costs. Our society will determine, through policies and purchasing habits, through personal and communal commitments, what kinds of landscapes we support and what species remain on them. Farmers cannot be expected to shoulder the brunt of this burden. Without technical and financial assistance in the form of incentives and cost-share programs, consumer-supported ecolabels, and land trust collaborations, farming at the landscape level might remain limited to wealthy landowners and iso-lated conservation initiatives. Ultimately, success must come through collaboration and the articulation of a new vision for agriculture: consumers who support local producers because they are protecting biodiversity; skilled ecologists who can point the way toward restoration; local resource conservation districts, transportation departments, and other programs that promote and practice restoration in rural areas; financial mechanisms that ensure long-term protection of truly viable wildlife corridors.

The challenge of making agriculture more harmonious with biodiversity, particularly in the face of other social and economic factors, conjures more questions than ready answers. How wild is wild enough? Which species are benefiting and which species are losing from our management decisions? At whose expense should these efforts be made? What is the appropriate balance between agriculture and native biodiversity? Can we make a large-scale shift away from industrial feedlots and toward a more sustainable grass-fed meat economy, including migratory bison populations in appropriate areas and a mosaic of domesticated livestock husbandry in areas where the conditions of local ecosystems and access to markets are suitable? Can a new conservation ethic muster the political, economic, and cultural forces necessary to accomplish a vision of farming with the wild? After decades of working in relative isolation, conservationists, farmers, and sustainable farming activists are beginning to view agricultural areas as critical terrain in the effort to restore large and healthfully functioning ecosystems throughout the continent. New dialogs, new collaborations, new programs indicate that such changes are indeed reshaping life down on the farm. We can only hope that time is on the wild's side.

The Organization of This Book

The following chapters consist primarily of on-the-ground case studies that have been organized into a number of different categories. The individual chapters can be viewed as pieces of the puzzle of an emerging conservation ethic, although some stories could easily have been included in a number of chapters. The Sky Islands and Sacramento Valley chapters document regional conservation efforts. The subsequent chapters explain broader concepts and initiatives. The final chapter attempts to draw together many of the ideas and approaches in a practical format. When viewed as a whole, we hope that these stories begin to formulate a more comprehensive vision of core principles, strategies, pioneering organizations, requirements, and questions about the farming with the wild movement.

SOME GENERAL TRENDS AND OBSERVATIONS

The following list was compiled to offer general guidelines and observations about the farming with the wild movement. Rather than attempting to establish a rigid template that landowners could follow to design a wild farm, per se, included below are general principles that can help to frame the broader concept of establishing agricultural systems that are compatible with healthy ecosystems. This may mean rethinking old boundaries, striving to make new connections, and even rethinking some of the very foundations of agriculture and its place in the ecological community. Every farm, and every farming region, will find its own solutions.

1. *Farming with the wild is dependent upon place.*
A wild farm exhibits a sense of beauty and uniqueness of place. On arable lands, farm systems attempt to mimic the surrounding natural systems, such as pasture operations in grasslands and forest-type cropping in forested areas. Marginally productive lands are restored to the wild, with an emphasis on native habitat.

2. *Attempts are made to limit long-term negative impacts or tendencies.*
Through place-adapted strategies, measures are taken to limit soil erosion, protect native habitat, and avoid depletion of local resources through excessive watering, overgrazing, or the use of off-farm synthetic inputs. Farm and ranch operations revolve around cycles of activity and rest, with working areas that are frequently rotated and allowed to recover.

3. *The presence of wildlife on the farm is encouraged.*
At their best, farms and ranches function as buffers, corridors, and even key habitat for certain species. By limiting productive areas only to what is necessary, by respecting seasonal nesting and brooding cycles, by optimizing wild habitat, agricultural operations can accommodate resident and migratory wildlife. Outside citizen monitoring groups can provide essential assistance and skills in mapping, observing, and documenting on-farm biodiversity.

4. *Farms should be viewed within the broader context of adjoining lands and ultimately connected to the larger landscape.*
Farms working in isolation may not be enough to restore fully functioning ecosystems. Connecting habitat patches and corridors within farming regions is an essential goal.

5. *Agricultural operations should be viewed within the context of pre-settlement conditions.*
Developing place-appropriate agricultural systems that work with rather than against Nature requires an understanding of native species and local ecosystem processes prior to European settlement and agriculture. Baseline studies, remnants and fragments of native habitat, and other specific linkages can provide invaluable inputs for restoring wild habitats in farming areas.

6. *Farming with the wild moves away from an eradication ethic.*
Rather than attempting to eliminate undesirable species in order to conduct agriculture, landowners work in partnership with native species. Nonlethal controls are favored to prevent predator losses. Native habitat corridors are established to reduce weed pressures or attract pollinators and beneficial insects. Other disturbance regimes, such as flooding or fire, are sometimes incorporated into the agricultural operation.

7. *Farming with the wild begins with conservation-minded communities.*
The most effective and impressive examples of farming with the wild have begun with communities talking together in search of common solutions to common problems. Inclusive meetings, farm tours, and other gatherings lead to the formation of management teams, the establishment of best practices and science-based monitoring procedures, and the commitment to a better quality of life.

8. *Farming with the wild represents a leading-edge consciousness.*
Farming with the wild requires extreme dedication, courage, and altruism. Embracing rather than vilifying endangered species and relinquishing a sense of historical agricultural entitlement represent acts of true leadership in society that require both an open heart and an open mind.

9. *Farming with the wild is not static, but a continual work in progress.*
Restoring wild habitats requires an ongoing interplay between the landscape, farm, and the local community. The reestablishment of native plantings requires an active farming approach at least in the short term, to be adapted and evolved as time passes. A wild farm is engaged in a continual effort to develop ever more profound ways to become "naturalized."

10. *Farming with the wild requires an interdisciplinary approach.*
Successes at the farming region level will require the collaboration between sustainable agriculture practitioners, conservation biologists, restorationists, and others. Research and on-the-ground models are urgently needed to explore the values and possibilities for integrating wild habitats in production areas.

11. *Consumers and citizens have key roles to play in determining the food system.*
Our food choices reflect our values and directly impact our visions and expectations for agriculture and the land. Everyday purchases can be used to bring land stewardship issues to the home, restaurant, workplace, and conference center. This can include supporting producers for protecting biodiversity as well as actively avoiding products that threaten native species or habitat. Voting power, particularly toward influencing the outcome of Farm Bill conservation and agricultural subsidy policies, has a critical bearing on private land use in the United States.

12. *We have the resources to leave a legacy of conservation-based agriculture.*
There are many viable alternatives to the present model of industrial monoculture which dominates world food and fiber production at increasing costs to the natural world. While it will not be easy in any way, and this occurs at a time when many farmers, ranchers, and others are struggling to survive economically in rural communities, we still have the chance to devote the resources and establish the systems necessary to develop an agriculture that is compatible with wild Nature. Our future, and the future of biodiversity, depends on our ability to fundamentally change the way we perceive agriculture and its place in the ecological community.

"None of us would want to see the entire world reduced to someone's notion of a garden, but neither would we want to see a world where no humans tended reverently to their surroundings."

—Andreas Suchantke[21]

THE SKY ISLANDS

The Sky Islands comprise a region that seemingly defies borders, a landscape that encompasses temperate and subtropical mountain forests, deserts and grasslands, where parrots live among bears, where jaguars and wolves exist on a razor's edge, and where conservationists along with a few leading ranchers embrace the presence of such endangered species. The term Sky Islands derives from the striking phenomenon of 40 separate mountain ranges, rising from an oceanic plain of deserts, grasslands, and shrublands. Beginning in the north, in the temperate forested Rocky Mountain highlands of central Arizona and New Mexico, the exotically named, solitary fault-block ranges of the Sky Islands—the Chiricahua, the Animas, the Peloncillos, Dos Cabezas, and dozens more—are dispersed across the Sonoran and Chihuahuan Deserts, span the New Mexico-Arizona-Mexico border, and finally terminate in the foothills of the Sierra Madre. Known by scientists as a megadiversity hot spot, the region hosts over four thousand plant species, and a diversity of reptiles and mammals among the world's greatest. The region is along a major flyway for migratory pollinators and birds, with more than half of all breeding birds in North America represented.[1] It's also the locus of one of North America's most comprehensive wildlands recovery movements.

Early in his career as a forester, Aldo Leopold spent many years working in and exploring the Sky Islands, an experience that provided both subject and inspiration for some of his most powerful essays. In 1937 he wrote: "To my mind these live oak-dotted hills fat with side oats grama, these pine-clad mesas spangled with flowers, these lazy trout streams burbling under great sycamore and cottonwoods, come near to being the cream of creation."[2] Although more than 550,000 acres of the greater Sky Islands region is under various forms of public protection,[3] its grasslands, woodlands, streams, and river valleys have suffered severe fragmentation. In the more than half a century since Leopold penned that declaration, logging, livestock grazing, and intensive development have severely impacted this spectacular country.

Since the early 1990s, reconnecting and "rewilding" the region's ecosystems through a broad-based network of conservation-minded people has been the mission of the Tucson, Arizona-based Sky Island Alliance. The Alliance is a lead organization in the Sky Islands Wildlands Network, whose members' long-term goal is to restore the full range of native species and ecological processes to this vast region. The 220-page Sky Islands Wildlands Network Conservation Plan calls for maximizing protected areas—parks, wilderness areas, roadless cores, and so on—to be linked together and surrounded by "compatible use" areas. The result would be a mosaic of wilderness and appropriately used landscapes, with federally protected core areas connected through a patchwork of ownership conditions—state, county, or privately held lands.

The Sky Islands Wildlands Network's reserve design has been guided by The Wildlands Project, which supports several similar wildlands network efforts throughout North America, and by the principles of leading conservation biologists like Michael Soulé, Reed Noss, John Terborgh, and Rurik List. (Soulé and Noss have both served as science directors for The Wildlands Project.) Simply stated, the Network's

Thunderhead above the Animas Valley, part of the magnificent Gray Ranch. The grasslands of the Gray Ranch frequently burn through lightning-ignited wildfire and are where a leading conservation initiative known as "grassbanking" originated.

mandate for wilderness is predicated on "the three C's": core reserves (large, untrammeled wilderness areas that provide secure foraging, seasonal movement, and other needs); carnivores (far-ranging top predators, such as bears, wolves, jaguars, and mountain lions that are essential to ecosystem integrity); and connectivity (healthy buffer zones and corridors that allow for fluidity of habitat and safe passage between the core reserves). In order to continually refine and inform local and regional plans, a large force of volunteer scientists regularly gathers data on wildlife movement patterns and habitat health. To the extent that these and other efforts succeed, the Sky Islands could eventually provide a critical link in a chain of wilderness and compatible use areas from the Canadian Rockies to the Sierra Madre Occidental Biological Corridor in Central Mexico.

Among the region's many vulnerable and critical habitats in need of protection are its grasslands. Both grassland basins that span the lower-elevation desert scrub and upland valleys that bridge mountain woodlands of evergreen oak or juniper host an abundance of open-country wildlife that matches their expansiveness. Mexican hognose snake, scaled quail, Chihuahuan pronghorn, bannertail kangaroo rat, badger, and collared peccary are just a few of the area's many characteristic and unusual species. Now missing from the landscape are healthy populations of historic top-down predators such as the Mexican wolf, grizzly bear, and jaguar, as well as keystone grassland species like the black-tailed prairie dog, black-footed ferret, and aplomado falcon. A legacy of poor grazing practices, combined with decades of fire suppression, has caused an ecological shift from arid prairies to desertlike conditions in many areas. The once sealike grasslands are increasingly dominated by "survivalist" shrub species, such as mesquite, creosote bush, tarbush, acacia, and snakeweed.[4] On top of that, human population pressures have brought agriculture, urbanization, and development infrastructures that further threaten the elimination of the region's remaining grasslands.

While livestock grazing on public lands in the arid Southwest continues to be hotly contested (and surely many grazing leases could and should be permanently put to rest through such programs as the Voluntary Retirement Option or other open space buyouts), one of the region's current strategies for conservation is to work with private landowners, many of them ranchers and farmers. According to Dave Foreman, co-author of *The Big Outside* and co-founder of both the Wildlands Project and *Wild Earth* journal, "If we look at the whole landscape and try to identify what's important for certain wide-ranging species that require wild landscapes, and particularly if we explore how we can link the Gila

Wilderness area south to the Sierra Madre in Mexico, we see that we have to deal with private lands. Some might prefer to see no cattle at all on the lands," Foreman explains, "but I believe in Traven's law: 'This is the real world, *muchacho*, and you are in it.' And while we might like to believe in Disney's first law, 'Wishing will make it so,' sometimes that's not how things work." Fortunately, explains Foreman, the Sky Islands region, perhaps more than anywhere else in the United States, is home to an extraordinary number of highly conservation-minded people who own very large pieces of property.

For example, members of the Malpai Borderlands Group, although not officially associated with the Sky Islands Wildlands Network, have reintroduced fire to the grassland ecosystems of the Sky Islands and have been instrumental in the recovery and protection of many endangered species, from black-tailed prairie dogs and Mexican wolves to Chiricahua leopard frogs. With over 20 participating ranches, the Malpai Borderlands region—which intersects the southeastern corner of Arizona, the bootheel of southwestern New Mexico, and the adjacent area of Mexico—could one day comprise a one million-acre, predator friendly core that would provide key habitat for large, top-down predators such as bears, wolves, mountain lions, and jaguars. Farther north, the Sky Island Alliance and other groups have been working to protect the highly threatened Dragoon Mountain region by linking privately held lands with National Forest lands and cultural heritage centers such as the Cochise Stronghold. There, Jerry and Marjorie Dixon, owners of the Dragoon Mountain Ranch, have been collaborating with corridor studies and have donated a 1,000-acre conservation easement to the effort.

Numerous organizations and community groups are working throughout the region to promote conservation and agriculture, some in cooperation with the Alliance and others independent of it. Dr. Gary Paul Nabhan, director of the Center for Sustainable Environments at Northern Arizona University in Flagstaff, is now combining decades of pollinator-corridor research with new studies that look at both pollinator and top predator habitat. In addition, Nabhan's long-term efforts to save the seeds, breeds, and techniques of native farmers in the Sky Islands region through Native Seed Search (see page 124) is ongoing.

The Tucson-based Sonoran Institute has for years been actively working to build communities of conservationists throughout the West who can achieve consensus around regional plans. According to Roseann Hanson, the Institute's program director for Southeast

The orange-shaded region of this map shows the vast region that the Sky Islands Wildlands Network encompasses. Already, 10.2 million acres have been studied within the U.S. planning boundary (green areas), of which 5 percent are in private lands. Planning studies are underway to create planning boundaries in Mexico as well. This bi-national effort could create one of the most critical cross-border wildlife corridors in the world.

Arizona and a former executive director of the Sky Island Alliance, the key to successful conservation lies in helping people to understand the connections between healthy landscapes, vibrant economies, and livable communities. In the Sonoita Valley, for example, community organizing resulted in federal protection of 130,000 acres of grasslands. Other communities are now poised to launch their own local conservation initiatives. "Five years ago, I would have thought that community consensus was an isolated phenomenon," says Hanson, "but that's no longer true. Many communities in the Sky Islands region now have the social capital to do this work. By social capital I mean the people, the motivation, the time, and commitment to invest in a long-term conservation vision." Among the Sonoran Institute's top priority areas are the Missing Link (55,000 acres of state-owned open space that could connect Saguaro National Park with Las Cienegas National Conservation Area) and two agricultural regions, the Santa Cruz Valley and Altar Valley.

In addition to reconnecting a fragmented landscape, however, the Sky Islands region faces the challenge of uniting conservation communities that often work in isolation, sometimes even at odds with one another. Ranchers are often reluctant to join ranks with urban environmentalists. People advocating federal lands protection often don't collaborate with

wolf recovery devotees. Local communities are sometimes more comfortable developing their own plans than signing on to an established organization's platform. Ranching advocates often point to the fact that progressive landowners are greatly improving grazing practices and at the same time are protecting land and valuable habitat against inevitable subdivisions and sprawl. At the same time, many activists argue that even progressive ranchers refuse to acknowledge the true impacts of cattle and point out the disproportionate amount of abuse that vast arid landscapes suffer from commercial-scale livestock and feed farming operations in order to produce such a small amount of the country's meat supply. These issues are extremely complex and will take many years to work through in the pursuit of ecologically viable and socially acceptable solutions. Perhaps such competition in pursuit of healing the many wounds of the land is inevitable. It could even be argued that it is desirable. Certainly leadership is needed to advocate that there is never "too much" land saved in the effort to ensure true wilderness protection.

One of the latest developments in the Sky Islands bioregional movement involves collaborations between U.S. trained biologists and ranchers in remote northern Mexico to establish a jaguar corridor extending from the Malpais to the Yaqui/Bavispe River. According to longtime southwestern resident and roaming activist Peter Warshall, the initiative, named the Northern Jaguar Project, includes a coalition of groups and a new generation of Mexican biologists, such as large cat specialist Carlos Lopez, who have been trained in the United States and who are returning home to work. By bringing leading concepts of conservation biology and environmental activism to their native territory, they are participating in a unique bi-national educational effort. The project will attempt to purchase ranches that feature prime jaguar habitat and secure conservation easements on others. Rather than compensating landowners for specific losses, the Northern Jaguar Project intends to enter into long-term arrangements with ranchers in which cowboys will also serve as rangers, monitoring for signs of jaguars (*tigres*) and reporting their findings back to researchers. Jaguars have been sighted and photographed in the United States as recently as December 2001, making the protection of its northern range a critical priority.

The Sky Islands region is slowly developing a critical mass of concerned communities and could some day represent one of the true success stories in the nascent "rewilding" movement. The many chapters of that story are as remarkable as the landscape itself and offer inspiration, hope, and guidance. Some of them are told here.

THE RANCH OF 20,000 GABIONS

In the pools that stagger and step down the elevation changes of the Turkey Creek watershed on the El Coronado Ranch, there is far more water and green vegetation than one might expect in an area that receives only 15 to 20 inches of annual rainfall. Squinting in the hot July sun, you might even be tempted to call it lush. Jho Austin, our guide and the owner of El Coronado, has spent the morning showing us some of the more than 20,000 dry-stacked stone gabions he and his crew have installed throughout the watershed over the past two decades to slow water flow, prevent erosive downcutting, and restore riparian habitat. These gabions are loose rock structures, assembled by hand and with pry bars, using surrounding stones and boulders to create small check dams between one and three feet high across a creek channel.

"When we first came here twenty years ago and were riding around, Valer, my wife, turned to me and asked, 'Josiah, what do these cattle eat, rocks?'" says Austin. "So, you know, it's sort of hard remembering back to what the ranch looked like 20 years ago. But I remember it was a lot dryer, there was a lot more exposed soil, and a lot of the washes and arroyos didn't have much vegetation on them."

Today, thick-stemmed bunches of deer grass line the banks of Turkey and Rock Creeks and their tributaries. A canopy of alligator juniper and scrub oak shades the gurgling water. In some knee-deep, algae-thick pools, fingerling Yaqui chub, an endangered fish reintroduced to the watershed by the Austins, can be seen darting. Sonoran mud turtles are abundant. Across the steep rock-strewn, gray-brown hillside, native grasses, wild flowers, junipers, oaks, and other high desert flora—and a few dozen cattle with the El Coronado brand—draw an enviable livelihood from the meager rainfall.

The massive effort of establishing 20,000 gabions on El Coronado Ranch is the Austins' direct response to decades of soil compaction and erosion through logging, overgrazing by livestock, and human alteration of the water cycle. Not too long ago, water ceased to permeate the soil and "hydrologically disappear" into vegetation on these foothills of the western Chiricahua Mountains. "We can receive 5 percent of our annual rainfall in a single one-inch rain storm," says Austin. "And for that reason, any way that you can slow down the water flow, not necessarily dam or impound it, but hold it in the soil and promote vegetation, that plant growth in turn acts as a sponge that helps hold the water all the way up into the banks."

We walk watercourses carpeted with vibrant grasses, tributaries that Austin reports were once dry nine months of the year and now hold water for ten months. Cattle are not excluded from the riparian areas during pasture rotations on El Coronado. "I don't exclude cattle from our riparian zones, but I don't keep them there for very long either. The cattle won't be in there for more than a week at a time, or three weeks a year." Thunder from the summer monsoon booms in the distance, and the southern sky fills with ominous charcoal-gray clouds. "People have asked me, 'What are you going to do when these creeks fill in?' I want the vegetation to take over. Hopefully, we can restore what was here once before."

Coexisting with Native Species

While it is undeniable that human activity has been responsible for the erosion and hydrology problems, Jho Austin is convinced that human presence—particularly agriculture that involves pro-active restoration and resting—can still be part of the land's salvation. "One of the ways to save open space is through agriculture. And the agriculture that I'm interested in is ranching. For ranching to be sustainable, and I mean sustainable two or three generations down the road, my cattle have to coexist with other species—both endangered and nonendangered species. In this case it means that my cattle need to coexist with the Yaqui chubs. They need to coexist with bats. They, the cattle and the Yaqui chubs and Yaqui catfish and long-finned dace [another native freshwater fish], have to all prosper if we are to consider this a successful ranch. And I think that we can do that."

From the economic perspective, explains Austin, a former Manhattan financier, ranching in the arid West is not always highly profitable. A well-run ranch returns 1 to 2 percent on an investment, while the market pays at least 3 percent. But through the years, he has learned numerous practices to make the cow-calf operation more sustainable. Careful rotation regimens help maintain plentiful foraging pastures. He also maintains that it is better to have fewer healthier cows than a lot of undernourished ones. Development and subdivision, the higher value short-term land use, he argues, would probably be worse for native species. "I think that the worst thing that could happen to this ranch—and the worst thing that could happen to the Sonoran turtle and the fish—would be to divide this ranch up into ten 40-acre lots. When we bought this ranch there was another buyer, a developer who was going to divide it, and there is no question in my mind that if it was developed there would be no native fish on this ranch."

The Sonoran mud turtle (*Kinosternon sonoriense*) is yet another rare but not endangered resident of the El Coronado. The only aquatic species of turtle in the Southwest, *K. sonoriense* became isolated when Lake Cochese dried up some 10,000 years ago, and was then banished to the creeks and streams of the Chiricahua Mountains. Biologist Justin Congdon has spent more than ten summers at El Coronado in an extensive study of the Sonoran mud turtle. According to Congdon, who holds up a turtle shell for us to examine, *K. sonoriense* grows from a hatchling the size of a quarter to an adult length of 6 inches and a weight of 700 grams, and will live an average of 35 to 40 years. In the year 2000, an estimated 1,000 turtles were living in and around the stock tanks and secondary tributaries of the El Coronado. The ranch has dedicated a building specifically to turtle study, complete with an X-ray radiography machine (to examine for the presence of eggs) and a shell-notching station (a means of identification). Ironically, the presence of stock tanks—holding tanks, gullies, or small dams that provide water for cattle—may unintentionally benefit the unique animals. "There are probably more Sonoran mud turtles here than there were before Europeans and ranching," says Congdon. "They probably didn't like the streams they were relegated to, but that's all they had, and when we got stock tanks, they moved over from the streams to the cattle tanks."

Such a marriage of ecology and economics has not been without confrontation, however. In the late 1990s, ranching on federal lands in the arid southwest was under attack, and questions were raised about the need to exclude cattle from riparian areas within grazing allotments in the Gila Basin in order to protect endangered species such as the Yaqui chub. The Tucson-based Center for Biological Diversity filed a suit against the U.S. Forest Service seeking compliance with regulations on protecting species on federal lands within the El Coronado National Forest. The Austins hold a permit on one of 80 grazing allotments involved in the suit and inadvertently got caught in a crossfire that involved a federal agency that wasn't abiding by Section 7 requirements of the Endangered Species Act. Because they had been pro-actively restoring habitat expressly for the Yaqui chub, the Austins decided to fight the suit. While they won on one initial issue, the decision was later appealed and reversed by a higher court. On the day of our visit, Austin is rueful about being on the front lines of endangered species reintroduction efforts. "You can get a lot more done with a carrot than a big stick," he says. "Right now people see the Endangered Species Act as a stick. I'm proud of the endangered species on my land. We have to start providing incentives to people who have endangered species." The bottom line, he insists, is that all things are connected. "The loss of one species is usually an indicator of an ecosystem out of balance and a larger domino effect to come, to which cattle will also ultimately fall victim."

Lessons from the Gabions

The Rattlesnake Fire of 1999 provided new insight into and broadened the context of the Austins' extensive gabion project. The wildfire scorched a substantial portion of El Coronado's grazing allotment, where more than 80 percent of the Austins' gabions have been established. Following that radical conflagration, the creeks flowed thick and gray-brown with ash, debris, and silt for many rainy seasons. Streams with extensive gabions, however, fared far better. The reduced water flows allowed for the high sediment loads to precipitate. Runoff more effectively infiltrated the water table. Not long after, deer grass, sedges, and other vegetation rebounded. The lesson, according to Austin, is that gabions are just an intermediate step toward the real goal, the return of vegetation and pre-disturbance conditions.

"There's a lot of money put aside for fire suppression," explains Jho Austin, "but to my knowledge little attention is being paid to the erosion problem after a fire—which is far more serious. A fire is a natural occurrence, and, yes, you want to contain it, but you definitely want to put some of this funding into the restoration after the fire. That doesn't just mean overhead planting of seed. It means actively cutting down some of the trees that are burned and arranging them across the hill so that they form barriers that prevent the soil from washing away. Maybe in some areas it requires creating rock gabions. Doing active restoration after a fire would prevent a lot of this really serious erosion." Low-cost gabions alone could someday serve as a model to revive stream flow and restore vegetation, and could bring back native fish to many watersheds throughout the oak dotted hills and juniper shaded creeks of this arid region.

The Tale of Turkey Creek

Top left, Jho Austin, owner of the El Coronado Ranch, pauses by a tributary of Turkey Creek that previously remained dry for nine months per year. Thanks to the installation of gabions and the return of vegetation, the creek now has running water ten months out of the year.

The photo second from top left, was taken following the Rattlesnake Fire and documents how the muddy runoff from an untreated hillside (foreground) commingles with the cleaner waters of Turkey Creek, which have benefited from the gabions and successive vegetation. Austin feels the results demonstrate the need for erosion and sedimentation prevention after wildfires.

On the El Coronado, the construction of simple rock gabions has been one of the primary techniques used to revive watershed health. (See photos, top center.) The stones are assembled with good old-fashioned muscle power and crow bars. While the check dams slow water flow and help recharge the groundwater, the ultimate goal, insists Austin, is the restoration of vegetation and a more ideal stream canopy. Along with reviving the watershed, the Austins have also become active in the reintroduction of native fish species.

Top, far right, the thick-billed parrot is just one of the Sky Islands' many unique species whose range sometimes reaches as far north as the El Coronado Ranch.

Bottom left. Biologist Justin Congdon has spent more than a decade studying the behavior of the rare aquatic Sonoran mud turtle, a welcome resident on the El Coronado Ranch. The ranch is equipped with a laboratory, including an X-ray machine, that helps to examine the reproductive health of the species. In this case, an X-ray photo shows a female bearing three eggs.

GRASSBANKING IN THE BADLANDS

With Arizona's grimy border town of Douglas and Bisbee's outrageous mile-deep open-pit Queen Copper Mine behind us, we drive to southwestern New Mexico's Bootheel and the Gray Ranch, a beacon in the 1990s conservation agriculture movement. In this New Mexico-Arizona-Mexico borderlands region traditionally referred to as the Malpais, or "badlands," ranches held in families for generations typically span tens of thousands of acres (both public and private). The Gray is perhaps the most magnificent of those stretches, straddling the northern edge of the Sierra Madre and the southernmost rim of the Rocky Mountains with the Chihuahuan Desert in between. Since the late 1970s, ecologists had been scheming to save the 320,000-acre (500 square mile) property, with its own mountain range (the Animas), unfragmented grasslands, 6 different ecozones, and nearly 20 endangered and threatened species.[5] The Nature Conservancy (TNC) purchased the property in 1990 as part of its Last Great Places Campaign, a kind of philanthropic triage to save ecological jewels from development. Then, in a controversial reversal just three years later, rather than creating a nature preserve, TNC sold the ranch to a foundation started by the rancher, cowboy poet, and Anheiser Busch heir Drummond Hadley, his mother, Jacqueline, and his son, Seth. Even before buying the ranch, Drum Hadley had joined the Malpai [their spelling] Borderlands Group and conceived the idea of converting the Animas Valley's nearly 70 square miles of grazing lands into a ranching and conservation commons through a radical concept called the "grassbank." But that is getting ahead of the story.

We spend a long July afternoon zigzagging the rugged roads through a few of the Gray's ecozones with Ben Brown, the ranch manager and a lifelong wildlife biologist. It is surprisingly cool for the desert summer, with enormous illuminated clouds advancing northeast from Mexico and a strong breeze pressing down the oceanic expanses of buffalo-grass and blue grama. Brown, who devised the initial reserve design of the Gray Ranch for the Nature Conservancy, expresses his deep knowledge of the area's natural history and archeology in a nonstop monologue, identifying plants by both their common and Latin names. Large populations of bison and ungulates, he surmises, have been absent from these once luxuriant grasslands for at least 8,000 years. Instead, over the eons the primary natural process that held back the incessant advances of mesquite, cholla, ocotillo, turpentine bush, and desert scrub was lightning-ignited wildfire.

Brown drives us through dune fields studded with western and alligator juniper, Emory and Toumey oaks, and Dr. Seuss-like yuccas, up and over a pass into black clay soil grasslands, eventually crossing the Continental Divide where a small herd of mule deer graze amid the cholla cactus. We pass a site on the Gray where black-tailed prairie dogs, an essential part of the grasslands ecosystem, have been reintroduced to historic sites with some success. (Across the Mexico border is North America's largest surviving prairie dog colony.) Around sunset we stop in a wash called Deer Creek that had been burned earlier that summer. Already the vegetation is resprouting through the ash and charred shrub remains. Later that evening, we sit outside talking with the Gray Ranch fire manager, Sam Smith, watching summer lightning sidewinding spectacularly across the ink-black sky, watching a parade of headlights crawling along the border, discussing the ins and outs of managing fires that rage for 15 miles at a time and that save taxpayer dollars as well as restore health to the Sky Island desert grasslands. (In 2002, 30,000 acres burned in lightning ignited fires within the greater Bootheel fire management area, reactivating the grassland restoration process.)

Putting out fires (both literal and figurative) had become a hot topic about the time that regional ranchers controlling some 1 million acres began meeting on the front porch of Warner and Wendy Glenn's Malpai Ranch and formed the now famous Malpai Borderlands Group (MPG). Decades of state and federal fire suppression and overgrazing by livestock had caused critical invasions of brush and woody plant species into what had been luxuriant grasslands.[6] But that was not all that was ready to blow. "In the early 90s there was a lot of anti-ranching activism," remembers Brown, "'Cattle Free by 93' and all that stuff—get the cattle off of public lands. Drum [who owned a ranch in the Peloncillos but not yet the Gray] had thought that environmentalists and ranchers probably had more in common than they realized. As they started talking, they did find that they had a lot of things in common. They both liked open spaces, natural communities, unfragmented and undeveloped landscapes, and they disliked the vegetation conversion going on due to overgrazing and the lack of fire. After a couple of years, they came up with the Malpai Agenda, which basically said 'We don't know what we want, but it should be led by good science, it should be led by the private sector, and it should be local in its scope and focus.'"

By 1993, the members had fashioned a color-coded "fire map" of the million-acre Malpai Borderlands area, complete with owner names, boundary lines, and contact numbers. "If the property was coded green, the rancher wanted to let it burn," explains Brown. "If it was yellow, he wanted to be consulted. If it was red, he wanted it put out right away." Following some significant scientific research and lobbying, and consultation with the Forest Service, this early prototype of what is now the Bootheel Fire Management Plan eventually cut through the tangle of interagency red tape and turned out to be both economically and ecologically effective. Fire suppression costs were reduced, and the evolutionary process of wildfire was reintroduced into the ecosystem. With that experience under their belts, the Malpai Borderlands Group officially organized as a 501 (c) (3) nonprofit with a 13-member board–and the ability to hold easements.

Around this time, the Hadley family had formed the Animas Foundation (which paid a cool $13 million for the Nature Conservancy's easement-laden Gray Ranch) with an extraordinary vision–using the ranch's miles and miles of open habitat to serve as an unusual kind of natural bank account for ranchers, wildlife, and natural ecological processes in the area. "When Drum bought the ranch, he was impressed by how people responded to it," explains Brown, "and he thought it might be possible to leverage conservation beyond the Gray by using the Gray as a commons. Back in 1993, several local ranchers were being put out of business by the drought," Brown continues. "They were looking at selling out herds they'd built up in some cases over 25 years. Drum came up with the idea of trading them grass for land-use easements that would prevent the subdivision of their private lands." Six ranchers took him up on it. Seth Hadley, who returned to work on the ranch after graduating from business school, remembers that the idea of the grassbank had been kicking around the family home for years. "When I was growing up, my dad always talked about how resting land was like having money in the bank. Twenty-five years later, he was able to turn that concept into a tool that could help ranchers protect their properties."

The Malpai Borderlands Group began using conservation easements for two primary purposes. Development rights were purchased to protect open space in the long term. In addition, short-term easements provided an essential tool for the grassbanking bartering system, which essentially worked this way. A rancher's land was appraised both for its value as rangeland and for its potential value for subdivision. The difference between those two established a "forage-use value" that determined the size of a rancher's grazing allotment on the Gray. In the early years of the program, some grasslands were restored under the fire management plan. By moving to the better pastures of the Gray, most cattle gained weight immediately. Weaning weights increased; so did calf output. In times of drought, the grassbank helped some ranchers stay afloat. In at least one case, with the credit he held in the grassbank, a rancher ran more cattle than he could on his home ranch. (For this reason, however, some leading critics of the grazing industry fear that the grassbanking concept could lead to increased livestock concentrations.) At the end of their three- to five-year agreements, most participants brought their cattle home to rested and rejuvenated ranches because millions and millions of grasses that would otherwise have been consumed by grazing cattle had been free to go to seed and germinate. (While the development easements through the grassbank program are perpetual, there are no grazing restrictions on management of the newly restored rangelands.)

According to Seth Hadley, nearly a decade after its inception, the Malpai Borderlands Group is stronger than ever, reaching from the Animas in the east to the Perilla Mountains in the west. "Most people thought it would last five years at most," says Hadley, "but we have focused on community-based conservation helping ranchers to stay on the land and offering tools to protect their properties. The purchase of development rights through conservation easements does require additional funding to address development pressure in the area. Fortunately, the philanthropic community has supported our work."

As for the grassbank, the concept has spread almost like wildfire throughout the West. Some spin-offs were commendable, such as the project in the New Mexico's Carson National Forest, in which the MPG participated. There were other instances, however, where subdivisions were started and called grassbanks. In order to preserve its integrity–which is to protect land against future subdivision and to preserve and restore the forage base–a new organization, Grassbanking, Inc., is being formed. The intention is to create a structure that will license and monitor the establishment of grassbanking programs throughout the West. "If in the past too much money has been extracted from the land, now much money must be reinvested through the grassbank to help the grasslands regenerate," wrote Drummond Hadley in a 1998 article for *Orion Afield*. "The meat-buying public may soon be willing to purchase beef that is not only organically raised, but that has been raised on grassbank lands whose land-use easements ensure that more and more rangelands will forever be open and undeveloped."[7]

Living with Fire

Top left, shows the sunset on the Peloncillo Mountains on the western edge of the Gray Ranch. The stunning grasslands and unique ecozones of the Gray Ranch earned it priority status in the Nature Conservancy's "Last Great Places" campaign, an attempt in the late 1980s to identify and save critical landscapes, primarily in the United States. After originally purchasing the 500 square mile property, TNC later sold it to the Animas Foundation, which attempts to balance its value as both wildlands and working rangelands.

Wildfires, a part of the natural evolution of grassland ecosystems across North America, are once again burning in the Sky Islands. Decades of fire suppression and improper grazing have had a devastating impact on ranches throughout the Southwest. In the early 1990s, members of the Malpai Borderlands Group began working to allow wildfires to burn on certain parts of their contiguous properties. After many years of scientific studies and close inter-agency collaboration, summer wildfires are beginning to be seen as a natural process of the grassland ecosystem. In 2002, nearly 45 square miles of grasslands burned in the region, coinciding with the timing of summer monsoon rains. The area is significant because of the size of the fire management area (more than 1 million acres), the presence of houses and roads, and an ongoing 50-year study.

Bottom left, biologist Ben Brown, career conservationist and one of the leading managers on the Gray Ranch.

Bottom far right, a jaguar captured on film by rancher Warner Glenn in 1996 in the United States. Another jaguar was photographed by a trip-camera south of Tucson in 2001. A jaguar corridor project is now underway spanning Mexico and the southern United States.

IN SEARCH OF RANCHING'S RADICAL CENTER

Jim Winder represents a new generation of rancher in the arid Southwest: an economist by training who embraces the scarcity values of endangered species on his land; a cattle producer who incorporates green development projects into the income generating matrix of his operation; a businessman who appreciates the input of environmentalists. But perhaps what really distinguishes Winder from many of his fellow New Mexico ranchers is his favorable stance on the Mexican wolf reintroduction. "We're catching hell from radical environmentalists and from ranchers too, so we know we're doing something right. My mailbox catches hell, too," he says.

The week before we traveled to the parched canyon terrain of Jim Winder's Lake Valley Ranch in the southwestern corner of the state, a transient had passed through, causing quite a stir. The wanderer was M578, a radio-collared male Mexican wolf previously released in eastern Arizona and fit enough to be roaming a vast territory. Rather than reaching for their rifles, however, Winder's ranch hands managed to squeeze off a few shots with a camera before M578 scurried off. In that summer of 2001, Winder had signed a memorandum of understanding (MOU) with the organization Defenders of Wildlife, agreeing to allow wolves to colonize his 50,000-acre property should they so choose and swearing off lethal predator control except in the case of unruly individuals. The ranch also takes a predator friendly stance against the more common pumas and coyotes. In return, Defenders promised compensation for any animal losses from predation. The agreement was part of the Wolf Country Beef initiative, an ecolabel that has quickly earned popular support among the general public, though it has had trouble cracking into the shelf-competitive grocery business.

"Thanks to the conservation biologists, we're beginning to more fully understand the concept of connectivity," says the lanky middle-aged Winder. He's dressed in jeans and a canvas shirt, and wears a baseball cap with the insignia of the New Mexico-based organization Quivira Coalition, which he helped establish and which claims the "radical center" in the debate on the future of ranching in the arid West. "We know, for example, that wolves have to travel widely and that our isolated parks do not provide enough territory for healthy gene pools. But how do you make it work? You have this huge human influence everywhere. We can't just move everyone out of the Rockies between Mexico and Canada. There have to be these core wilderness areas connected by mixed-use areas."

Achieving such connectivity on private landscapes requires economic solutions, particularly in a mature industry like ranching. "The wolf presents itself as a cost to these ranchers, and the economics of ranching are basically slow starvation," says Winder. "Talking to a rancher about wolf recovery is like taking a drowning man and pouring a cup of water on his head. Environmentalists won't get ranchers off the land but bankers will," he quips. "My great dream is to live long enough to see the time when healing the land is more economical than mining the resources here."

According to Winder the economist, ranching today requires optimizing opportunity costs on your land. In addition to grazing operations, the whole range of land-management options must be analyzed: commodity values (cattle ranching); conservation values (wetlands, grasslands, native species restoration, for example); and recreation values (hunting, guest ranching, and birding). "You have to look at the farm as a matrix and overlay complex layers to make the operation profitable, blending a mix of products and services," he says professorially. On the cattle side of the business, Winder employs many of the new ranching principles promoted by the Quivira Coalition. These include deferred grazing, controlled grazing, pulsed grazing that provide recovery periods for the land. The usual practice is intensive—many cows on the land for short periods of time, two days or so.

In addition to cow-calf and cattle stocking ventures, Winder's Lake Valley Ranch has diversified into a number of side businesses. Some twenty parcels were subdivided into 50- and 150-acre lots and sold as part of what he terms a protective development. Owners can develop a building envelope of 1 to 5 acres, but the parcels must remain natural and open. Winder retains grazing rights on those lands, while homeowners share a recreational conservation easement on the rest of the ranch. "It's kind of like a vaccination for the land. You do a little green development on a small portion and then place the rest off-limits to future development. Consider it an injection of a controlled virus to make you immune to the whole disease. It's difficult, I'll be honest with you, and I don't think you'll see a lot of people doing it. For a rancher to do a development is out of the norm and for a developer to do something green is out of the norm, but I think you'll see some more of it and it seems to work pretty well. The idea is to share the land and understand its carrying capacity and do the minimum amount of development. One way to do that is by finding ways to place the most value on what's not developed."

Randall Gray, a career conservation biologist for the Natural Resources Conservation Service (NRCS), was among the 20 conservation-minded owners who bought parcels on the Winder property; he built a rammed-earth house sheltered from other home-owners in a small valley. "Jim Winder is trying to make conservation pay, and I am supportive of living in a community where carnivore and native species reintroductions are valued," says Gray. While "green development" has allowed Winder to pay for the ranch, the conservation easement prevents him from ever doing any more development on the rest of the ranch. "That lowers the opportunity costs that you're facing in ranching and makes ranching relatively more profitable," Winder explains.

We walk to Winder's favorite part of the ranch, down a steep sandstone path that descends into the canyon dissected by Berrenda Creek. Even with the seasonal monsoons a month late, the creek is filled with shallow, sparkling pools, cool, flowing water, and lots of life: leeches, tiny fish, bugs. Where not long ago the arroyo was usually dry and barren, cottonwoods, willows, ash trees, and deer grass now grow lush along the banks. "We use a tool called marginal reaction," he explains, regressing into economics jargon, "to determine where we invest our time and money. We want to do the best thing for the land and want the biggest bang for the buck–the biggest marginal reaction. And until you get your riparian areas just spiffy, it's hard to go out on these other spots. You get enormous returns by restoring riparian zones." In addition to the revival of Berrenda Creek, Winder is also working with the NRCS to restore a seasonal wetland on the property.

Winder has also benefited from his proximity to another of the region's progressive land-holders, Turner Enterprises' Ladder Ranch, with whom he collaborated on the reintroduction of the black-tailed prairie dog and the Rio Grande chub. Placing Winder's work in the broader scheme of the Sky Islands recovery effort, Dave Foreman says, "fortunately, many of the private landowners in the Sky Islands region are concerned about the overall landscape and biodiversity. Jim Winder is the reality on the ground, and I think that he is the future of the livestock industry, and I say more power to him."

Heritage Ranch

Jim Winder, co-founder of the Quivira Coalition, at his Lake Valley Ranch in southwestern New Mexico.

Upper right, a rammed earth house built as one of 20 parcels that are part of a "green" development within the ranch. Lower left is a Mexican wolf, protected on the property through a Memorandum of Understanding with Defenders of Wildlife. Below right, a riparian restoration project has aided in the reintroduction of the Rio Grande chub and Rio Grande sucker.

ALONG THE POLLINATOR TRAIL

On a sunny July morning not far from the U.S.-Mexico border, Gary Paul Nabhan and his graduate research assistant Laura Williams are inspecting rows of flowering crops at the Tubac U-Pick Vegetable Farm like detectives dusting for fingerprints. They're cataloging the presence of native bees and other pollinators in among the squashes, peppers, beans, and tomatoes, and on the margins of the farm's five acres of cultivated vegetable plots. Throughout the morning exclamations carom from opposite sides of the field and its wild edges. "Xenaglossa!" calls Williams excitedly at the sight of a sweat bee. Other identifications include *turgida* (a ground-nesting bee), *melissodes* (a digger bee), *halictus* (another sweat bee), and *megachili* (a leaf-cutter bee).

This historic farming area in the Santa Cruz River flood plain, 40 miles south of Tucson, bordered on three sides by Sky Island ranges, represents a critical connecting throughway for native flora and fauna. For decades, chemical-intensive, groundwater-irrigated cotton and hay operations predominated. But that industrial farming regime collapsed with the energy crisis of the 1970s and has slowly been replaced by smaller farms that integrate row crops and livestock grazing—a scale and balance between agriculture and wildland habitat that Nabhan believes resembles what settlement may have been like two centuries ago. At Tubac Farm, the river is banked by a gallery of cottonwoods, willows, and mesquite. Beyond the farmed flood plain rises a desert scrub range of mesquite, ocotillo, and upland plants, stretching toward the serrated silhouette of the Tumacacoris. Nestled within these wild borders, Tubac Farm has the sense of a multi-tiered mosaic. Two large (1- to 2-acre) market garden plots are separated by a shelterbelt of mesquite scrub and other natives. Cattle and horses graze lazily in the shade of large trees framing two large pastures, seeking shelter from the midmorning desert sun.

According to Nabhan, director of the Center for Sustainable Environments at Northern Arizona University in Flagstaff, 1,200 species of native bees can be found within a 50-mile radius of Tucson. The region also hosts 25 species of bats and nectar-feeding birds, including hummingbirds, warblers, two species of nectarivorous Mexican migratory bats, and a miscellany of omnivorous birds that transport pollen when feeding on flowers. Welcome to Pollinator Eden—or at least what should be Pollinator Eden.

"This may be the richest native bee real estate anywhere in the world," says Nabhan, an acclaimed ethnobotanist and co-author with his colleague Stephen Buchmann of the seminal 1996 book, *The Forgotten Pollinators*. Several distinct life zones stretch out around Tucson, from 10,000-foot peaks down to 1,000-foot desert scrub, and these provide diverse habitats, each with a seasonal pulse of bees. This is also one of the few deserts in the world blessed with a bimodal rainfall pattern, in which alternating wet seasons accommodate completely different bee faunas. Winter rains bring on blooms from late February through early April, to be followed by the monsoon rains that generate a summer flowering stage. The prolific diversity of pollen and nectar rewards for pollinators has been drastically altered, however. The conversion of millions of acres of desert and scrubthorn habitat to pastures of exotic grasses and industrial monocultures has left pollinator and nectarivore flyways frayed and fragmented. The adverse impacts on ecosystem health and on farming are inestimable.

Nabhan was drawn to working with farmers in the Santa Cruz River region following a dramatic decline of honeybees that posed a great threat to pollinator-dependent agriculture. (The European honeybee now pollinates four out of every five crops grown by U.S. farmers, contributing significantly to the more than $10 billion annual fruit and seed output in North America.)[8] The first fall-off came with the appearance of parasitic mites in the mid-1980s, followed by the arrival of Africanized honeybees five years later. The valley's native bees had also suffered heavy declines due to the loss of riparian and wild habitat, coupled with heavy use of pesticides on cotton.

By 1996, Mark Larkin, the owner of Tubac Farm, was collaborating with ecologists in a project to restore water flow to the Santa Cruz River with influxes of treated sewage effluent. He kept his livestock out of riparian areas during critical times, and native vegetation quickly rebounded. Then, with Larkin's participation, Nabhan and his research team initiated an active management plan to monitor and attract wild pollinators. Bee boxes made of drilled-out 4x4's were set out, and nests of yucca stalk were fastened to fence posts to attract colonizing carpenter bees. Straw stems were buried vertically on field edges to increase habitat for stem nesters. Nectar-rich wild and non-native flowers were planted on field margins. Larkin also stopped plowing out the buffalo gourds—the rambly wild relatives of squashes that attract native squash and gourd bees.

Within three years, Tubac Farm was once again a "stepping stone" on the pollinator flyway, providing precious nectar refueling plants along the migratory insect trail between tropical Mexico and the temperate and boreal regions of the United States and Canada. During that time, Nabhan's researchers documented over 25 vertebrate pollinator species and some 230 insect pollinators in or adjacent to the fields. "While the artificial nesting techniques were effective, they weren't nearly as important as Mark's habitat restoration efforts," explains Nabhan, who published the findings in 2000 in a technical paper for the Arizona-Sonora Desert Museum as well as in the winter 2001 issue of *Conservation Biology in Practice*.[9] The most effective actions were: the restoration of river habitat as the result of using treated sewage effluent to increase stream flows; the maintenance of hedgerows and shelterbelts adjacent to the farm; minimized use of toxins; and the recovery of the mesquite woodlands through rotational grazing practices, which brought back numerous native flood plain tree species.

"When we first started, the edges were there but probably not as robust," Mark Larkin remembers. He is a no-nonsense worker of the land: strong, limber, with close-cropped thick brown hair, and an infectious love of his farm. "This had been a small cotton and grain farm that used a lot of both herbicides and pesticides. We don't use any synthetic pesticides here. The only herbicides we do use are spot applications of Roundup. These edges were also continuously grazed. In areas where they didn't have cotton, there were almost no fences, so the animals would just eat stuff down to the ground. In an area where there were 2 distinct pastures, I created 18 different paddocks. So I can put more animals on and pack them in, but keep them in for shorter periods of time and achieve regrowth."

Maintaining wild edges has, according to Larkin, required little extra effort other than sound range management techniques. "You do have to pro-actively keep the edges from encroaching on your fields—cultivate, plow, and rotate pastures. If you didn't have the wild edges, you'd be better able to control weed growth and pests in your fields." But he adds, the benefits of the wild edges outweigh the downsides. "They provide habitat to beneficial insects and for predators and prey too. So I don't have the coyotes eating my melons as much. Hopefully they're out there eating rabbits!"

He lists key advantages such as soil erosion protection, wind blockage, and shade—especially important when you're in the livestock business. "As you can tell, standing out here right now, you see how those animals are packed in. Shade in the summer and weather protection in the winter is a big deal. Aesthetically, I like the fact that it breaks the vista a little bit. Plus I like to go hunting in the fall."

Nabhan, dressed more like an Amish farmer than a desert mystic, seems at once time traveler, botanical warrior, preservationist, and activist. From the narrow starting point of considering a local pollinator, he can stir imaginings of continental proportions in a single run-on sentence. One feels the connection between bee, wild gourd, domesticated squash, reestablished native hedgerow, and large carnivore corridor. His narrative sweeps from Michoacan to central Arizona and beyond, with connected nectar trail corridors not just for nearly invisible native insects or large carnivores but also for the wild plants that are the overlooked and undervalued ancestors of modern crops—plants that may hold precious clues to 21st-century ecological agriculture through their localized biological secrets and assets. The formative stages of such work are already under way. A collaborative effort with the Sky Island Alliance, Northern Arizona University, and the Sonoran Institute's Working Landscapes Program intends to restore flood plain corridors in the San Pedro River area that would accommodate use by bees, butterflies, and mountain lions. It also becomes easy to understand how one small, diversified farm fits into the vast 9-million acre landscape mosaic of the Sky Islands Wildlands Network. "Our goal is to see enough healthy agriculture and healthy wildlands along these corridors from the tequila fields of Jalisco up through central Arizona."

Mark Larkin is cultivating a field of pumpkins with his team of draft horses. Nabhan looks on at the scene admiringly, then shifts his gaze toward the ridgeline of the Tumacacori Mountains. "Behind us we still find wild cotton, wild tobacco, wild beans, wild grapes, and wild gourds. In this very setting, we see the uplands of the watershed that produces the water these riverine systems depend upon. That's also where you find the wild relatives of crops that give us the genetic resistance to pests and diseases and drought adaptations that our modern cultivated crops need. Historically, there was a tremendously rich relationship between the mountain wilderness areas and the flood plain agricultural plots. We need to reestablish that dialog and have our agricultural producers turn outward and seek the messages, the genes, and the strategies that are still conserved in the mountain wilderness areas around here."

Corridors for Pollinators

Top left, ethnobotanist and pollinator expert Gary Nabhan in a shelterbelt that transects Tubac Farm, south of Tucson.

Top center, Tubac Farm owner Mark Larkin preparing a field with his horse-drawn cultivator.

Top, far right, Laura Williams combing the field of vegetables for native bees and other pollinators. Tubac Farm has been the site of a long-term research project studying the decline of native bees in the region. Despite numerous attempts to attract pollinators with artificial habitats (such as the nest lashed to a fence post bottom center), researchers have determined that the return of streamflow to the adjacent Santa Cruz River and the subsequent return of riparian vegetation have been most significant. According to Nabhan, 1,200 species of bees live within a 50-mile radius of the farm.

Bottom left, Navajo sheep and a century plant (third from left) are just two crops adapted to the southwestern ecosystem on Gary Nabhan's farm outside Flagstaff.

Bottom right, insects photographed during a morning visit to Tubac Farm.

THE TURNER BIODIVERSITY LEGACY

Bouncing over the rocky roads of Turner Enterprises' 156,000-acre Ladder Ranch is a bit like being in a boxing match without ever getting in a punch. Narrow roads climb and snake through sometimes radical elevation changes, bucking and bouncing the stoutest of off-road vehicles, churning the insides and whiplashing white-knuckled passengers. To describe this southwestern New Mexico hill country as remote and rugged is both cliché and understatement. To experience this southern extremity of the Great Plains is to imbibe a landscape of sweeping grasslands studded with shady junipers and ringed by distant purple, hazy peaks, of rare box canyons lined with lush riparian woodlands. And always in the background hangs the aura and anticipation of large carnivores. Though we're not lucky enough to sight them on our short trip, it is easy to visualize black bears feasting on the crimson prickly pears or a mountain lion striding across a canyon ledge.

In late July of 2001, Tom Waddell, a career conservationist and the manager of another nearby Turner property—the 358,000-acre Armendaris at the northern tip of the Chihuahuan Desert—gave us a two-day bucking-bronco jeep tour of both these ranches. Waddell is a voluble talker whose life as a wildlife biologist was fundamentally shaped by the epic environmental struggles waged throughout the 1980s against the eventual placement of an observatory on Mt. Graham. That first day at the Armendaris, Waddell drove us from early morning till sunset, showing us a reestablished black-tailed prairie dog town, reintroduced desert bighorn sheep, and even a flow field of what he identified as petrified dinosaur excrement.

On the following day, the scene at our first stop on the Ladder Ranch harks back at least a few centuries, if indeed such a scene ever existed. In a bowl-like grassland valley, we come upon a herd of a few hundred grazing bison. Without much interest, they observe us observing them chewing and strolling and carrying on with the clanlike behavior of their species, as we obediently keep our distance. According to the Ladder Ranch manager, Steve Dobrott, a wildlife biologist who took over when Turner Enterprises bought the property in 1992, bison probably didn't spend a lot of time in these grasslands in historic times—though perhaps in prehistoric times. But bison raising is one of the two primary money-earning operations established on most ranches owned by Turner Enterprises; the other is game and trophy hunting. With nearly 30,000 bison on different ranches across the country, Turner Enterprises accounts for 8 percent of the United States' buffalo herds and is poised to distribute buffalo meat through a restaurant chain called Ted's Montana Grill and through supermarkets. Today, robust native elk populations join the introduced bison as the primary herbivores on the ranch.

"Not only are bison a wildlife species that Mr. Turner is interested in propagating on all his properties, I see the bison as a management tool," says Dobrott, a sun-weathered, fit man, wearing wire-rimmed glasses, a faded denim shirt, and jeans. "The bison are strictly grass eaters that go quickly for water then leave, which means that other resources such as the riparian corridors are not affected as they would normally be by cattle. So just by selecting this particular species to graze on the lands and to profit by them provides a tool that is probably more natural for this environment and allows for it to grow in other ways."

In addition to bison, Dobrott and the Ladder Ranch staff oversee an aggressive wildlife and habitat management program, some of which involves hunting. "These days, the ranching industry has to develop as diverse an array of economic activities as possible," says Dobrott. "And we do utilize our wildlife resources here to provide additional income to the ranch. We sell permits and lead guided hunts, and the wildlife program provides opportunity for income even though it's not the main goal." Between the two ranches, commercial hunting opportunities are currently offered for bison, mule deer, elk, oryx, and mountain lions.

These seemingly divergent goals—restoring native diversity and creating profitable ranching operations—continue to draw fire from various sides. Writing for *Outside Magazine*, Jack Hitt surmised: "If the work of colonial and industrial settling deflated once-thriving ecosystems in all these places, then the Turners seek nothing less than to reinstate the bustling climax landscapes that naturally thrived there. And in those redeemed ecosystems, to seize on what opportunities lurk for the entrepreneur. It's a view of nature guaranteed to thrill and piss off everyone from Greenpeace to the beef industry."[10]

Despite what might seem to some to be an overly zealous interest in the introduction and proliferation of bison and quail species in areas that may fall outside their historic ranges, the media magnate Ted Turner and his son Beau are extremely committed to restoring "pre-Anglo" biodiversity to their properties across the country. The conservation biologists they have hired have been empowered with the means and authority to enhance or restore native biodiversity on their ranches. And the Ladder is already unique among lands in the Southwest, having the highly endangered Chiricahua leopard frog, as well as peregrine falcons, elk, mule deer, white-tailed and Cous white-tailed deer, black bear, mountain lion, javelina, pronghorn antelope, Mearn's or montezuma quail, Gambel's quail, scaled quail, and neotropical song birds, including orioles and tanagers. Add to this a species reintroduction program that includes black-tailed prairie dogs, the Rio Grande chub, the Mexican wolf, and future collaboration on the California condor and aplomado falcon. The program has had a spillover effect to neighboring landowners, including Jim Winder's Lake Valley Ranch and the Animas Foundation's Gray Ranch. Freed from bureaucratic gridlock and energized by both ready resources and a willing and committed management, the staff is influencing federal and state agencies as well. "We have the ability to consider the best techniques possible or to invent new techniques," says Dobrott.

Wildlands Project co-founder Dave Foreman sees the species restoration programs on private lands throughout the Sky Islands region as a very positive development. "In this way we have some healthy competition going on between private landowners and the federal government. Some of the things that the Austins or Hadleys or Turners or Winders are doing, restoring riparian areas, reintroducing natural fire, restoring endangered species, I think are going to surpass federal efforts on federal lands. Private landowners in some ways have a greater range of motion and can be more experimental, and I think that they're coming up with some good techniques that can then be applied elsewhere. So a little competition in who can do best on healing the wounds on the land is a really good thing."

At one point in the journey, Tom Waddell stops on a mesa and walks out to a cliff's edge to get a good perspective. He pulls out a beat-up pair of field glasses and fixes on a scene across the valley. At the foot of the hills opposite is a series of five sprawling pens built into the natural contours. Mexican wolf families are being raised there for eventual release by the federal government in the wilds nearby, mostly in the Gila National Forest. About the wolf reintroduction Waddell says, "Cattle people say it's not going well. The wolf people say it's on schedule." It is hard to fathom that such a small, remote, pen, could harbor so much potential life and controversy. The fact that wolf reintroductions have occurred in Arizona and New Mexico as well as the Northern Rockies is significant; if populations were reestablished in the nearby Colorado Plateau region (which many experts argue is the most suitable habitat for such an initiative), it would complete the most sweeping recovery of a species in modern history.

The Turners believe they are providing an example in how to live with endangered species and how the total ranch environment can contribute to the biodiversity of the state and the country. "We try to set an example for other large landowners to show that you can manage a viable bison operation and manage for wildlife species and be better off for it," says Dobrott.

"Most good ranchers who have been in the business for a long time are conservationists in their own right," Dobrott continues. "They have to conserve their resources in order to have a sustainable operation. We may have taken just one or two steps further. Our philosophy is that if we can provide habitats and take that into consideration with our management, then we're not only creating a sustainable operation with bison, but we're also providing for the future of native species, including those that need to be reintroduced. I hope that my time here on the ranch will result in some great strides in wildlife conservation."

With its vision of restoring the frayed fragments of once staggeringly complex ecosystems, the Turner biodiversity legacy may one day be seen on a par with those philanthropists who worked to create some of our first designated wilderness areas or who have preserved successive generations of great works of art. Developing the necessary skills to revive unraveling landscapes and reinhabit them with species in decline is certainly one of our most important and neglected fields. Compounding the problem is the controversial nature of intensively managing landscapes with restoration goals in mind. Searching the sun-soaked grasslands to the Gila Mountains beyond, however, one can only hope that the foundations of future models lie here. And that these large blocks of land will not remain isolated fragments but rather become sections of a landscape that can somehow be rehabilitated and reconnected into a continental web of life.

Aspiring to Pre-Anglo Conditions

Bison are primary residents on Turner Enterprises' western ranches, which now hold an estimated 8 percent of the country's reintroduced buffalo population. The photo third from bottom left shows a bison's fur shedding.

Ranch managers Steve Dobrott top row, fourth from left, and Tom Waddell, top row center, oversee two Turner Enterprise ranches that collectively total over 500,000 acres.

Native species restoration is a key component of ranch management on the Ladder and the Armendaris ranches. Mexican wolves are being bred in captivity on the Ladder for potential future release (top center). Black-tailed prairie dogs have been introduced on both ranches, (bottom center). Home to pronghorn antelope (bottom left), elk (center right), and Texas hornback lizards (bottom center), the Ladder is a breathtaking property with some exceptionally healthy riparian areas (two photos in center row).

THE SACRAMENTO VALLEY

The Sacramento Valley, the predominantly agricultural area of northern California that lies between the Sierra Nevada and the Coast Range, is slowly becoming one of the focal points of the farming with the wild movement. Ecologically, the valley is of tremendous importance, as its post-harvest wetlands provide the annual overwintering habitats for more than 10 million waterfowl. In a region where 95 percent of wetlands have been altered, where once miraculous salmon runs have been all but extinguished, and where major rivers have been relegated to straitjacketed irrigation ditches, it is heartening to see that ecological triage and restoration projects are under way. The clash between agriculture and conservation in one of the world's most rapidly urbanizing areas has often been simplified to the divisive issue of water allocations, but there are emerging examples of regional farmers and environmentalists finding common ground as well. "After all, this is our home, and we don't want to live in scorched earth," says longtime conservation farmer Sally Shanks. In the early 1990s, the late Marc Reisner, author of *Cadillac Desert* and water rights entrepreneur, helped convince Sacramento Valley rice growers to stop burning crop residues and allow flooding in winter fields to support waterfowl and native fish. In the intensive farming and ranching district of Yolo County, farmer and former veterinarian John Anderson set off a groundswell by "bringing farm edges back to life" that is spreading, hedgerow by hedgerow and pond by pond, as a viable and essential model for the rest of the state. The wildlife-friendly practices of some of Anderson's nearby colleagues, such as the Rominger Family Farm and Sierra Orchards farm, demonstrate the power of positive example. The Nature Conservancy of California, in cooperation with many other groups and agencies, has been working for decades to change the course of river destruction. Two such waterways embedded in the heart of northern California industrial agriculture—the Sacramento and Cosumnes—provide different models in bringing riparian systems back to life. The Cosumnes provides a groundbreaking example of what can happen when flooding and fire are given a free hand in ecosystem revival. The Sacramento, the only California river with four genetically distinct chinook salmon runs, represents a bold experiment in controlled restoration within intensive riverside farming operations.

Throughout the Sacramento and Central Valleys, irrigation ditches are often kept bare by costly discing and herbicide spraying regimes. Native vegetation, properly restored, provides valuable habitat, filters runoff, and creates aesthetically pleasing farm edges.

THE REVOLUTION AT HEDGEROW FARMS

In an industrial farming region best known for crops like rice, canning tomatoes, and walnuts, Hedgerow Farms has an unusual specialty: wildlife habitat. Since 1976, John and Marsha Anderson have slowly been reassembling vestiges of oak savanna, forested stream banks, and wetlands that evoke a sense of a more idyllic time and place. Today, one-fifth of their 500 contiguous acres of Sacramento Valley farmland property has been given over to native vegetation. Drainage ditches, which are scraped bare on most surrounding properties, here are lush with native grasses, forbs, wildflowers, and shrubs. Roadsides have been recreated as "prairie corridors," densely planted with purple needle grass. Where the Union School Slough meanders through the farm—connecting the Coast Range with the Sacramento River—stands of cottonwood, oak, and willow now grow thick and tall, harboring more than 100 migratory and resident wetland, riparian, grassland, and shrubland bird species. Between fields of native grass seed crops, sold for large-scale restoration efforts throughout Northern California, are hedgerows of shrubs like toyon, coffeeberry, western redbud, California lilac, and elderberry that harbor wildlife and offer year-round pollen sources to beneficial insects.

On a hot day in May, Anderson, a sinewy, suntanned man of medium build now in his mid-fifties, is dressed in loose clothing to fight the searing Sacramento Valley sun. "We've essentially taken areas that were previously 'clean farmed' and put them back into corridors of native vegetation," he explains. "Once that happens, the wildlife come back immediately."

Full-time farming came late to Anderson. For more than two decades, he worked as a research veterinarian at the Primate Center of the University of California at Davis. He and his wife, Marsha, who have been married for over 30 years, bought Hedgerow Farms in 1974. The opportunity to take an early retirement in 1993 allowed Anderson to pursue his vision of combining conservation and agriculture.

Like many of his neighbors, Anderson began with clean farming to keep weeds at bay. It didn't take long, however, before the veterinarian became acutely aware of the impacts of "clean farming" on wildlife. In the late 1970s he began experimenting with hedgerows, using mainly non-native plants recommended by the Natural Resources Conservation Service. An avid hunter and outdoorsman, he had always been attracted to the study of natural systems. Inspired in part by hedgerows he had seen in England, he began studying intact ecosystems and farming native seeds for habitat restoration projects.

"I understand the urge toward clean farming. If farm edges are left alone, unruly and costly weed problems will develop," says Anderson. "But clean farming should mean weed-free, not vegetation-free. When revegetated with native species that are given a healthy chance at survival, weeds are controlled by natural systems in farm edges. A balanced, self-sustaining native grassland eventually out-competes any weedy invasion. And the excellent, year-round wildlife habitat these vegetated corridors provide has no negative impact on farming practices."

Such restoration projects are not hassle- or investment-free, however. They require irrigation and weed control in the first two to four years before they become firmly established. "The trick is to learn how to install these plantings right the first time, then to control weeds until the native cover is established," says Anderson. In order to foster the natives and root out the alien weeds, he and his employees have memorized *The Grower's Weed Identification Handbook*. In addition to the natural weed control that develops, these native corridors harbor large quantities of a diversity of insects that provide pollination, pest control, and food for many bird species. Nesting boxes attract other useful species, including barn owls, wood ducks, tree swallows, flycatchers, bluebirds, and bats.

An important part of the work at Hedgerow Farms has involved going beyond on-farm efforts, to work with neighbors as well. In particular, Anderson has had a long history of collaboration with Rominger Brothers' Farm (see pages 48-49), who lease part of his land for commercial row crops. The Rominger family, which has been farming in the area for three generations, taught him a great deal about farming and have also participated in his restoration mission. Perhaps most significant has been the demonstration of the side-by-side compatibility of the Romingers' large-scale no-till and organic row crop operations with Anderson's restored wildlands and row crop farming.

As we walk and talk, Anderson alternately identifies dozens of bird species that fly above us, then drops to all fours to assess the reproductive success of tiny plugs of native grasses in a meadow he's trying to reestablish. He rattles off a list of species that have been attracted to the farm through habitat creation, then adds, "How often do you see snakes in ag land? Snakes don't get along with discs and plows. Reptiles have really come back in a big way on this farm because they have permanent places to live underground. We now see garter snakes, king snakes, gopher snakes, yellow-bellied racers, and somewhat to the dread of some of my neighbors, Pacific rattlesnakes."

At one point he takes us to a small knoll at the low end of one of his fields, the site of a well-established tailwater pond, one of seven scattered throughout the 500-acre property. Ringed by bunch grasses, sedges and rushes, and taller trees, the small pond is about 20 yards in diameter, shimmering like a mini-oasis amid the arid landscape. "Every farm that is furrow irrigated and leveled drains to a corner," explains Anderson, "and that drainage picks up chemical residues and sediment as it moves down the system." Creating half-acre wetland habitats that filter irrigation water before returning it to the canal system, he explains, is just one example of what farmers should be doing to promote conservation. It's a simple, yet powerful tool that should and could be used throughout much of both the Sacramento and the even larger Central Valleys.

"Many of us in farming recognize that agriculture is the number one producer of non-point-source pollution in this country. If we can start running our water through vegetated systems, not only riparian systems but also wetlands, this will enable farmers to comply with the Clean Water Act," says Anderson, "not to mention aiding all the wetland-associated species that will find these ponds and start reproducing in them. The nighttime choruses of tree frogs emanating from these ponds in the spring, and the myriads of dragonflies over the vegetated canals in the summer are just two of the many experiences we are able to enjoy as a result."

A small crew of laborers is hoeing in a field of thigh-high needle grass that waves purplish blond in the hot sun. Just as weeds are the bane of the row crop and pastureland farmer, aggressive exotic species are one of the critical challenges Anderson faces as both a native seed producer and a restoration ecologist. It is imperative that he produce seed crops free of weeds and unwanted species, or else annual grasses like zorro fescue, ripgut brome, and annual rye grass will overwhelm a new planting in a grassland restoration project. In order to rid edges and fields of weeds in the short term, Hedgerow Farms employs a number of carefully timed strategies: mowing, fire, grazing, hoeing, and herbicides.

"Typically we let the early germinating rains bring up the first flush of weeds. We then drill the seed in and wait seven to ten days. This is followed by a low rate of herbicides on those germinated weed seeds to reduce competition so that the slower growing native seedlings have a chance. I wish we didn't have to use herbicides," Anderson laments, "but without them in the early phases of establishment, we usually lose the battle against weeds. We really depend on herbicides to get systems going, but only for the first or second year. Our workers are trained rigorously in weed identification, and use plastic cones and other devices to ensure selective applications only on unwanted plants. Flamers and burners are an alternative to chemicals, and Hedgerow Farms employs them whenever possible. But for these, timing is critical in order to be effective. You can also fallow ground for several years," says Anderson.

The seed-sorting facility at Hedgerow Farms is a functional-looking metal building edged with native plants and surrounded by tractors, discs, and other large farm machinery. Inside the warehouse is a multi-tiered Rube Goldberg-like contraption with screens, blowers, and chutes used to clean, sort, and bag seeds for restoration plantings. While this is one of the farm's primary money-making ventures, the restoration seed market remains small and fairly competitive. Anderson admits that marketing has not been a top priority. There are still a few racks loaded with unsold sacks of last year's crops. Yet he holds out hope that the market for farming edges and intercropping in orchards and vineyards with native plants will take off, along with projects in parks and golf courses, and along roadsides and irrigation ditches. The largest potential market for the seed is watershed and grassland restoration, where millions of acres of degraded rangeland dominated by exotics could be restored to native perennial systems—although this would have to be subsidized. This is a vision, not just for the Sacramento Valley, but for the entire country; yet it must be accomplished on a local basis, with care taken to use plants native to each separate region.

Having redirected his career from veterinary medicine to the production of habitat, Anderson knows firsthand about the amount of time and expertise that restoration work requires. "I certainly don't expect farmers to give up portions of their fields the way we've done here. And farmers can't be expected to do this type of work. They just don't have the time. But I do foresee a day when roadsides, irrigation canals, tailwater ponds, hedgerows, and shelterbelts can be managed for biodiversity. We can create jobs, provide habitat, clean up our water, and reverse the wildlife-unfriendly forms of monoculture we've been promoting throughout the country for the past half century." Anderson views partnerships with local conservation groups, land trusts, and local transportation departments, and a leading role by Resource Conservation Districts (RCDs), as essential. He served as an RCD director in Yolo County for 10 years, helping to stimulate interest in and activity with the district throughout the area. "The Resource Conservation Districts are the key to making this work. That's what they're supposed to be doing."

Because of Anderson's passion, scientific bent, and abundant energy, Yolo County has become a focal point for conservation agriculture projects. His activities outside Hedgerow Farms have perhaps been even more important for the region than the exemplary work within his own farm boundaries. As a board member of the National Audubon Society, Anderson inspired a collaborative program between Audubon California and the Yolo County RCD to win a $636,000 grant from the CalFed Program, a coalition of state and federal agencies working to resolve water conflicts. In part these funds were used to hire Jeanne Wirka and Judy Boshoven as restoration ecologist and watershed coordinator, respectively. As described in the January-February 2001 issue of *Audubon Magazine,* "Wirka and Boshoven have spent much of the past two years bouncing over rutted roads to meet with landowners on stream banks, in pastures knee-deep in invasive yellow star thistle, in farmhouse kitchens, and in community centers."[1] The partnerships they created have built fences to

exclude cattle from streams, dug ponds to trap sediment and filter runoff from fields, and planted native shrubs and trees along sloughs and creeks. Yet the progress can be ploddingly slow, as if the effort will only be done one square yard at a time. "A couple of native grass plugs won't change the world overnight," says Wirka. "People might."[2]

When not managing his own farm, Anderson leads grassland restoration workshops throughout the state. Though he bemoans the lack of qualified restoration practitioners at the present time, he does believe a few simple rules can be applied for those who want to take the initiative. "Copy what's local. That is, identify ecosystems that are intact in your area and begin to mimic them. In a riparian zone, study the understory, not just the trees." Much of what Anderson has gleaned from two decades in the restoration game can be found in the newly revised edition of *Bring Farm Edges Back to Life!,* published by the Yolo County Resource Conservation District and directly suitable for projects throughout Northern California.

We watch a marsh hawk swoop and glide as it hunts along the side of Union School Slough. It's one of ten hawk and three owl species on the property. "Protecting remaining natural habitats must certainly be a priority, but farmland is one of our resources that we must also protect for the future," Anderson believes. "Even though industrial agriculture throughout the country is now dominated by monocultural clean farm systems, it is still land that has the potential to support corridors of native biodiversity. While it may take a few generations to change this landscape, we must also remember to keep that land in agriculture. Once it is lost to development, it is gone forever."

Bringing Farm Edges Back to Life

Native seed farmers John and Marsha Anderson of Hedgerow Farms in a mature stand of purple needle grass, *Nassella pulchra*.

A hummingbird inspects the blooms of an evening primrose, a native whose seed serves as an important food item for finches, sparrows, and other birds.

An aerial view shows how physical landscape features determine habitat areas within the 500 acres of Hedgerow Farms. At least one-fifth of this row crop farm has been returned to native habitat, including ponds, wetlands, roadside grasslands, and field borders. The result has been a spectacular return of species to this and adjoining properties, whose owners have also taken restoration seriously.

An accomplished photographer, John Anderson captured a Pacific rattlesnake extending its forked purple tongue.

TOWARD A WILDER FAMILY FARM

Even before we shut the pickup door to explore some of Rominger Brothers' Farm's 2,500 acres of noncontiguous fields (of which two-thirds is rented ground), Charlie Rominger begins rattling off a list of authors and books that have influenced his thinking about farm stewardship–primary among them, Aldo Leopold. He hands me a stack of books and pamphlets he has prepared for me to peruse as we drive. "I've been very impressed by Alan Savory's ideas," he says, echoing what many other farmers have told me. "Just his simple question addressing your land management practices–Is biodiversity increasing or decreasing?"

As we drive between different fields and chores, he explains a number of the efforts he, his brother Bruce, and his parents have undertaken in pursuit of better stewardship and increased production. His father is Richard Rominger, a former Assistant Secretary of Agriculture during the Clinton administration. For many years, the Romingers have implemented no-till planting regimens, rotating cotton, safflower, wheat, and corn. Their no-till system also includes a livestock element. Each fall, a neighbor's goat herd is used to clean crop residues and control weeds in fields for two to three months following harvest. They carefully schedule mowing and minimal cultivation so as not to disturb nesting and brooding cycles. For 15 years, certified organic production has also been part of their cropping plans, including processing tomatoes, sunflowers, safflower, and various types of beans.

With John and Marsha Anderson as both neighbors and landowners of fields they lease, the Romingers long ago caught the hedgerow and habitat restoration bug. Tailwater ponds were installed at the lower ends of fields to trap silt and filter irrigation and runoff. Hedgerows and wind breaks were planted along roadsides and field borders. Charlie offers his quick take on the costs and benefits of hedgerows. "The expenses include taking ground out of production and the hard costs of planting and maintenance. And hedgerows can harbor undesirable plants and animals. On the plus side, however, wind protection makes crops grow better. Rather than a sterile habitat, you have the values of wildlife. And then there are the quantifiable values of providing year-round insectary habitat." To cite an example, he recounts how plantings of California buckwheat

(*Eriogonum faciculatum*) harbored populations of syrphid flies that preyed upon the Russian wheat aphid, preventing a potentially costly infestation. "Even if our goal was just to make our farm more productive and economically viable, these practices would work. But the things we're doing to increase production are also benefiting wildlife. And we couldn't be doing this by sticking with the conventional approach."

We meet Charlie's brother and partner Bruce at a tomato field, where he is in the middle of repairing an irrigation system. At the crest of a rise above the field we come upon a 15-acre hill pond that was constructed with financial assistance from the Conservation Reserve Program and the U.S. Fish and Wildlife Service's Partners for Wildlife Program. It is just one of a dozen ponds the Romingers have constructed since the mid-1980s, surrounded by native trees and grasses, and supported by various USDA programs. The grasslands are knee-deep and dip down to a basin where a large pond sits, rimmed by cattails and a stand of self-seeded willows. It doesn't take long to find a clutch of duck eggs nesting in the long grass.

"Many farmers are realizing that you don't have to bang heads with Mother Nature," Charlie says. "In fact, you can make it work for you, though that's not the reason we're doing it. By trying to make farm operations more closely mimic how Nature works around here, we can save money, work more efficiently, and create a real legacy."

It's not one single thing the Rominger brothers have done to make their farm wilder, says Charlie, but all of their efforts in combination. The no-till provides winter foraging habitat and reduces erosion. The hedgerows attract large quantities of beneficial insects. The hill ponds and tailwater ponds link the foothills to the low fields through similar habitat. All of these efforts connected with what the Andersons and others are doing generates a larger edge effect. "I remember Leopold wrote that you can attract a covey of quail when you provide the four habitat types they need: water, brush, grassland, and trees," says Rominger. "Doing anything is certainly preferable to doing nothing. But all are better in combination."

Committed to Habitat

Charlie and Bruce Rominger pose in front of their dramatic 15-acre hill pond, installed in the early 1990s. The willows in the far upper right appeared naturally soon after the wetland was established. The restoration is supported by federal programs in order to provide critical nesting habitat for waterfowl. In low water years, the wetland can provide late-season irrigation supplies in addition to its year-round habitat values. This is just one of a dozen ponds and wetlands the Rominger family has created on their Yolo County, California farm.

The photo at bottom left shows a shelterbelt that provides a wild edge beside a field of certified organic processing tomatoes. While land has been taken out of production and must be maintained to create the shelterbelt, the Romingers insist that wind protection, beneficial insect habitat, and wildlife and aesthetic values more than compensate.

BATS AGAINST BUGS

At one point in the middle of a balmy June morning, Mark Kiser finds himself behind the controls of a pruning tower, a mobile minicrane used to hoist workers up into a 30-foot orchard canopy. Shortly before Mark's maiden voyage, Sierra Orchards owner Craig McNamara gave him a brief demonstration of how to operate the machine, then disappeared in search of a posthole digger. Suspended 15 feet off the ground in the hydraulic platform, Kiser struggles to guide the lurching machine to a proper perch at the side of the barn, just below the roof.

Mark and his wife, Selena Kiser, emissaries from the Austin, Texas-based organization Bat Conservation International (BCI), are on a trip to install bat houses on ten select organic farms throughout California. This research project in the summer of 2001 is sponsored by the Santa Cruz, California-based Organic Farming Research Foundation and organized by the University of California Cooperative Extension farm advisor Rachel Freeman Long, an ardent proponent of innovative biological pest control strategies.

Despite bats' reputation (mostly undeserved) for blood sucking, hair tangling, and rabies transmission, BCI and the Kisers believe that farmers and ranchers should welcome native bats as permanent residents. These flying mammals devour unfathomable quantities of insects on their nightly flights, and a number of bat species are effective crop pollinators as well. Earlier that morning, Mark, head of BCI's North American Bat House Research Project, had explained: "A mouse-eared bat, or *myotis*, eats 600 to 1,200 mosquito-sized insects in an hour and can also consume crop pests such as cucumber beetles, codling moths, leaf hoppers, and cotton boll worms. For that reason, we've been installing houses on organic farms as a means of nonchemical pest control." In California during the summer months, a bat's diet can consist of up to 80 percent moths. And that's why Craig McNamara was an eager participant in the study, for codling moths are one of the primary pests in the walnut trees he grows organically.

Bats provide a cost-free first line of defense against many agricultural pests—even without eating them. Researchers have shown that many insects can detect bat echo-location calls and will avoid areas where bats are present. In one Canadian study, broadcasting bat calls over a test plot of corn appeared to reduce crop damage by 50 percent.[3] According to BCI literature, a Georgia pecan grower who was losing 30 percent of his crop to hickory shuckworms and other pests, used boxes to attract a bat colony within just two years and eliminated his crop damage.[4] And an Oregon organic farmer reportedly overcame a serious corn earworm problem by attracting just 600 little brown bats.[5]

Up in the tower, Mark wrestles a rectangular bat box into place against the barn siding, holding it still with one hand while drilling with the other. As part of the research project, each of the three boxes attached to the barn has a different color and design, in an attempt to understand how differences in temperature, ventilation, and texture attract bats to a man-made structure. There is a light-colored one, a dark model, and an experimental house made of a gray synthetic insulation board. All have open bottoms with three slats inside creating narrow chutes. The houses chosen for the study have been made by Marvin Mayberry of Mayberry Centre Bat Homes in Daingerfield, Texas, one of the country's leading research and manufacturing organizations. A house as small as 24 by 24 inches and 12 inches deep can attract nursery colonies of as many as 500 to 800 bats. The different colored exteriors can accommodate the bats' needs for solar heating throughout the year. The best sites for boxes are between 12 and 20 feet off the ground and at least 20 feet from trees. It is also important to erect three or more houses in the same location.

On the ground, Selena takes exact notes of the placement of each house, documenting their distance from water, their solar orientation, and the closest obstacles in their flight path. "Internal temperatures are very important, and those needs vary by season and by region," Selena explains. "Roosting sites need warmth. Morning sun helps the young bats grow more quickly." In addition, a good bat house is reasonably close to water (less than a quarter mile), wide and tall, well sealed, and made water-tight with caulk or glue, ventilated in both front and back, and protected from predators such as snakes, owls, raccoons, and possums.

Before leaving, the Kisers and three volunteers also complete a pole-mounted installation with a box on either side. A few months later, Mark Kiser reports that guano was found beneath all three barn-mounted boxes and one pole-mounted house at Sierra Orchards. Half of the farms in this California study had attracted bats within a few months of installation, though the Kisers feel that number would have been higher if they were installed by February rather than in early summer.

According to Rachel Freeman Long, California has 26 native species of bats, of which at least half are threatened. As traditional habitats such as caves and large hollow trees have been disturbed or destroyed, remaining species have become increasingly dependent upon man-made structures. In fact, a number of widespread and common species rely on man-made structures for their roost sites, and it's not uncommon to find bats under bridges, in old abandoned mines and buildings, or in barns.

Long, who has been working not only with bat house introduction but also with insectary hedgerows and other initiatives, describes the ultimate goal of this project. "Colonies are what you want rather than just small populations of individuals," she explains. "There are some well-known orchards where bat colonies play a significant role in pest control." About the rabies mystique, Long says that most cases involve an animal that has been bitten. "There are some basic rules that you can apply to protect your family from rabies," she says. "Don't ever pick up a dead or injured bat. Locate the houses away from your home and places where children play. And the most important action you can take to protect your family is to vaccinate your dogs and cats."

Bat Conservation International was started in 1982 by photographer and activist Merlin Tuttle to help conserve bats and their habitats worldwide, relying on partnerships with other organizations and agencies. The goal of BCI's North American Bat House Research Project is to develop a network of bat houses and restore native colonies across the country. Reestablishing healthy populations of native insect-eating bats in farm communities can only be beneficial for U.S. agriculture. Consider Bracken Cave, north of San Antonio, Texas, site of the country's largest bat colony, where 20 million bats consume some 200 tons of insects per night.

Housing Development

Research weighs strongly in favor of the use of native bats as beneficial residents in agricultural communities.

Mark Kiser of the Austin, Texas-based Bat Conservation International erects both barn- and pole-mounted houses to attract bats. Varying designs, colors, materials, and locations are part of the study.

Selena Kiser steadies the pole while Mark Kiser, Rachel Long, and a volunteer ready cement.

CHANGING COURSE: THE NATURE CONSERVANCY AND A TALE OF TWO RIVERS

In a state where rivers have been dammed, diverted, and dried up in pursuit of agriculture and urbanization, the Cosumnes River stands out as a diamond in the rough. It is one of only two remaining undammed rivers in California, with remnant valley oak forest and invaluable Pacific Flyway real estate. In the early 1980s, The Nature Conservancy of California (TNCC) and other agencies committed themselves to preserving the river's habitat in this region southwest of Sacramento, the state's rapidly sprawling capital. Not a moment too soon, active restoration efforts were initiated along the flood plains of the lower Cosumnes River: pond construction and replanting of oaks, both of which were successful. But the Cosumnes River Preserve's biggest boon came by accident.

In winter 1985, the Cosumnes breached a levee and flooded a farm field, depositing sand, sediment, and debris, and leaving a 15-acre area uneconomical to reclaim for farming. To many people's amazement, fast-growing native willows and cottonwoods sprouted almost immediately. Within a few years, an "accidental forest" appeared, with 15- to 20-foot-high cottonwoods, Oregon ash, and willow thickets. A dozen years later, the cottonwoods had grown to over 40 feet tall. Deer, beaver, waterfowl, otter, and raptors were foraging and settling down in the accidental forest. Valley oaks poked through the forest understory and edges. According to scientists from the Point Reyes Bird Observatory, migratory songbirds were enjoying nesting success rates on the Cosumnes far higher than at other monitoring sites in the Central Valley.

Farming in the Flood Plain

With the restoration of natural flood processes (and later, as we shall see, of fire), and the integration of farming and ranching activities in buffer areas, the Cosumnes River Preserve became a Nature Conservancy flagship project. Adjacent to the riparian zone, farm partner Allen Garcia adapted 1,000 acres of organic rice cultivation to the area's cold nighttime conditions. Farther out beyond the flood plain, livestock grazing operations continued. TNCC and its allies–the U.S. Bureau of Land Management, the California Department of Fish and Game, Ducks Unlimited, Sacramento County, the California Department of Water Resources, and others–worked to unify the preserve through land acquisition and conservation easements. By the year 2000, the Cosumnes Preserve encompassed more than 40,000 acres, with only a few high priority properties remaining unprotected.

Flooding continued to shape TNCC's science-based management of the preserve. Intentional levee breaches were used to actively broaden and reforest the floodplain. But the floodwaters of January 1997 convinced Conservancy staff, Garcia, and other farm neighbors that they could and should go levee-less. Rather than repairing damaged levees, resources were directed at designing a farm infrastructure that could be both floodable and floodproof: raising pumps, elevating and graveling access roads to limit flood damage, constructing berms to separate farmed areas from the floodway. Over time, Garcia's organic rice farming operation became optimized for wildlife, particularly waterfowl. "Improving wildlife habitat is simple, you just add water," Garcia told an audience at the November 2000 California Small Farm Conference in Santa Rosa. In order to farm the flood plain, he explained, his highly capitalized operation included laser-leveling and aerial planting, as well as less technological intensive management techniques such as cover cropping and summer flooding for weed control.

As the riparian habitat improved and fragmentation diminished, native Sacramento Delta fish such as the splittail minnow and juvenile Chinook salmon returned to the Cosumnes flood plain. Tens of thousands of waterfowl were making annual winter migrations on the preserve. The lessons of the levee breaches and the accidental forest soon became models for the state in terms of "nonstructural flood control" and earned a victory for natural-process flooding as a preferred habitat restoration technique. The next step was to restore fire to the upland grasslands and savannas of the preserve and adjacent areas, where controlled burns have now been conducted for several years.

By 2001, only a few key properties remained to be acquired, including a 10,000-acre neck of land just southeast of the Preserve called Staten Island, cut off by the north and south forks of the Mokelumne River. Then, in a controversial move in November of that year, The Nature Conservancy used a $35-million government grant to purchase—not an endangered ecosystem—but a nationally acclaimed "wildlife friendly" farming operation that occupies the whole of the Delta's Staten Island.

The Staten Island Waterfowl Feedlot

As we approach Staten Island from the south, a sign reads: "Walnut Grove, Elevation 0." The 30-foot-high levee road separates the Sacramento River from the orchards, vineyards, and town of Walnut Grove like a medieval city wall. Without flood control, none of these below river-level activities would be here—this trip would be by boat. Instead, we drive across the bridge that fords the north fork of the Mokelumne and stop at the grain elevator on Staten Island.

The way Sally Shanks tells it, the 9,200-acre M&T Staten Ranch she and her husband, Jim, have been managing for almost 50 years is a feedlot for overwintering waterfowl. The Shankses' management system, developed over those 50 years, is nothing less than a well-choreographed dance between intensive farming and waterfowl habitat cultivation. Blocks of conventionally grown wheat, (non-genetically modified) corn, and tomatoes are rotated, planted, and harvested to accommodate early fall flooding and wetland habitat, early spring planting, and late spring-early summer nesting habitat. While the corn harvest is getting underway in early September, a slow transformation from crops to wetlands unfolds. The already harvested, stubble-strewn wheat fields are gradually submerged, and the first winged arrivals drop by the thousands to the standing water and uncultivated levee banks. By winter's end, 5,000 acres or more will be under various depths of water. Up to 20,000 greater and lesser sandhill cranes, as well as hundreds of thousands of waterfowl and shorebirds, will feast on crop residues and bug blooms in the M&T's flooded fields.

Incorporating a wildlife ethic into daily decisions on the M&T hasn't come cheaply. Jim Shanks estimates the costs for pumping and creating waterfowl habitat at $40 per acre, ranging between $150,000 and $200,000 annually. "In order for us to play this game, we have to hustle our rear ends and get some farming done in the time of year where we're supposed to make some money," says Sally Shanks. The grain elevator allows them to harvest and process 50 loads of corn per day, a vertical operation that pays off in terms of both timing and quality. And with 9,000 acres, they can spread out crops and habitat over a large area. "We are always thinking two years in advance about our cropping patterns.

But it's not as if we've changed our practices to holistic or 'outcome-based management' or whatever the current buzzword is. My husband came here in 1952. We have been doing winter flooding since the 1960s when we started planting winter wheat. As others needed to make more money and maximize economic values, we have stayed the same."

Driving along the levee separating the river and the fields, Sally Shanks takes the time to show off some innovative habitat improvements they have employed to protect levee banks. While the typical management response after a flood crisis has been to hardscape the levee's entire 30-foot (river-side) slope with boulders, she and her husband developed preventive vegetated solutions that provide habitat, cost less, and prevent scouring. She points out how a long pyramid-shaped pile of bowling ball sized rocks—a "rock prism"—was deposited at the base of the bank. Some soil was then brought in to backfill the gap between the rock prism and the bank, with vegetation planted to stabilize the system. As water levels rose and fell, sediment was increasingly deposited and the vegetation sprang back immediately. Years of jumping through regulatory hoops were involved in what Sally Shanks sees as a logical, valuable, economical model. "All irrigation ditches throughout the state should be treated as habitat," she says defiantly. At a second stop we come across a crescent-shaped beach, now filled in with a thick bend of alders, their leafless limbs glowing coppery in the winter light. The way Shanks describes it, eight years ago when the rock prism was installed, there was just a beach with no vegetation, which summer water skiers used as a jump. The M&T deposited a few old logs and stumps between the bank and the rock prism, which immediately established some pools. Alder branches were pushed down into the bank. Those took root and restored shaded riverine habitat. "This section of the river wants to heal, it wants to come back, and we just have to give it a little nudge and get out of the way," says Shanks. "We do this on our schedule while we're waiting to farm. We do what we can, where we can, when we're not busy farming."

Buying the Farm as Habitat

TNCC's purchase of Staten Island stoked fires of criticism from all sides. Beyond the large sum of money paid to the real estate company that owned the profitable agricultural operation, the Sierra Club and other conservationists were concerned that scarce conservation money was going to a working farm rather than an endangered ecosystem. Public advocates objected that any money made from the farm would go to the Conservancy and not public coffers, even though public money funded the deal. Local residents questioned the effect on tax revenues if the farm would be taken out of production altogether. The fact was, though, that TNCC and the agencies who funded it purchased Staten Island specifically because it provided habitat value and because it offered a floodable area during infrequent flood events, such as the mighty storms in early January of 2000. And they made sure the Shankses would stay on to pass their management skills down to future farmers.

"We bought an economically sustainable operation that had already been maximized for wildlife habitat–at least on bottomland," explained Keith Whitener, a fish ecologist for The Nature Conservancy. "The farming regimen that they have developed over four decades has created phenomenal wildlife habitat. The crop residues remaining in the nonburned and nondisked fields provide far more food than simple brooding ponds or wetlands could. We bought it precisely because it was great for the ecosystem and don't plan to make any major management changes. It's hard to understand why there is so much suspicion around the project."

"If 95 percent of the wetlands in the Central Valley have been lost, then you've got to put these birds in here like they are a feedlot," says Sally Shanks. "They need more than pickleweed and tules. You've got to pour the food to them. That's why it's so important that we lead them around: Here's your roost, here's your food. But we can't dictate what the neighbors are doing. And the market is driving farmers toward vineyards, orchards, golf courses, and tract homes. If we put 1,000 acres into vineyard, that food would plummet. If we don't get more efficient in how we manage every little corner, the losers will be the birds." Shanks's last point cuts like a knife into the heart of the issue, one that stays with us as we head back along the levee. The Sacramento and San Joaquin Valleys have lost so much natural habitat that farms must function as massive bird feeders along the Pacific Flyway, even though they may lack in the full range of species, from predators to fish to rodents or reptiles. We are continually reminded by conservation biologists that while such efforts are invaluable and mandatory, they are rarely large enough. Perhaps for TNCC, the purchase of Staten Island will serve as an anchor in the Delta that can be built upon long into the future.

Reclaiming the Sacramento

Compared with the somewhat free-wheeling Cosumnes, the Sacramento River exists in a virtual straitjacket–by virtue of the upstream Shasta Dam and the systems of levees, banks, and irrigation canals along its course. Gone is the majestic meandering advance, the self-willed processes of flood and retreat. Of the mixed hardwood forest that crowded its oxbowed banks and broad floodplains, just 2 percent remains.[6] These forest banked floodplains–home to federally listed endangered species like the Valley long-horned elderberry beetle and the yellow-billed cuckoo and to migrants such as chinook salmon and Swainson's hawks–were gradually cleared for farming, and in most recent decades for walnut, almond, and prune orchards. Even with the river's constricted state, however, farming on the Sacramento's margins has proven a dubious endeavor. In February 2000, Hamilton City orchardist Jim Pavia told Glen Martin, an environmental reporter for the *San Francisco Chronicle* that "Undeniably, the best soil is there, but it's a real headache. We had a flood in 1995 that took away 30 percent of our trees on that ground." At one time, beavers were gnawing through an acre of Pavia's trees in a day. He sold 460 acres of riverside land he had once cleared to the California Wildlife Conservation Board and is now participating in replanting the forest. "Sooner or later," he said, "that river will make a believer of you."[7] By the early 1990s, congressionally mandated plans were underway to protect some of the Sacramento's sacred terrain, including a 100-mile stretch between Red Bluff and Colusa, encompassing some 34,000 acres of "interriver" zone, the flood plain on either bank within which the river channel used to naturally shift and meander. Essential to the project would be the creation of "meander belts"–pockets of undeveloped or restored land where the river could wander at will, dissipating water and energy during floods. Throughout the hot summers, additional moderated releases from reservoirs by the Bureau of Reclamation would help establish riverside reforestation. The U.S. Bureau of Land Management, CalFed, The Nature Conservancy, the David and Lucille Packard Foundation, and other state, federal, and nonprofit agencies and organizations began participating in the acquisition of habitat along the river corridor, making it the largest river restoration project ever undertaken in the country's largest agricultural state.

Interriver Zone, Tehama County, December 2001

TNCC's entry into Sacramento River riparian habitat conservation in 1994 coincided with a general shift in the organization's land management philosophy. "We realized that it was no longer enough to save land as part of a vast collection. In order to manage land well, you have to worry about the ecological processes in the landscapes which they are part of," explains Dawit Zeleke, a Tehama County citrus grower and Sacramento River Project Director for TNCC. "The primary ecological process in this area is flooding. That got us involved for the long term here."

Life in the Flood Plain

The 40,000-acre-plus Cosumnes River Preserve is one of The Nature Conservancy of California's premier restoration projects. Located in one of the most rapidly urbanizing areas of California, its agricultural and wildlands provide key corridors and habitats for wildlife. With the restoration of natural processes of flooding, and more recently fire, species such as migratory waterfowl and native fish have rebounded. According to the Point Reyes Bird Observatory, the Preserve enjoys higher nesting successes than at any other monitoring site in California's Central Valley.

Restored native forests and preserved grasslands provide habitat for numerous bird species, such as flycatchers (top left), flickers (center left), shrikes (bottom center), and California quail (bottom left).

Agriculture in compatible use zones is a key part of TNCC's management of the Cosumnes River Preserve. The photo at the bottom right shows a flock of greater sandhill cranes alighting in a recently harvested rice field. Rice is grown organically in the flood plain, while still providing habitat values. The Cosumnes Preserve also leases grazing lands within the region.

TNCC's engagement grew as the U.S. Fish and Wildlife Service (USFWS) bought land to add to the effort. USFWS soon found that it had acquired not just remnants of pristine riparian forests, but a considerable amount of agricultural land, which it was unprepared to manage. By 2000, a consortium of conservation agencies, of which TNCC was a member, had acquired 20,000 acres in the area. According to Zeleke, TNCC made USFWS an offer. "Why not let us manage those properties? We will restore them, then return them back to you." According to the subsequent Cooperative Land Management Agreements, TNCC can lease out any viable, already planted agricultural land–but with no further replanting after the orchards are played out, which averages 10 years or less. Leasehold earnings are then used to fund habitat restoration. Ultimately, the land management responsibility returns to USFWS. "Our leases also put restrictions on chemicals that would harm fish and birds," explains Zeleke. "So the farmers we're working with are already the cutting edge commercial farmers, practicing biological IPM [integrated pest management]."

On a bone-chilling December morning we tour one such property with Zeleke, TNCC biologists Phil Stevens and Daryl Peterson, and Tanya Meyer of Hedgerow Farms. Previously the flood plain farm had been planted in more than 1,000 acres of almonds; the trees had long since succumbed to improper variety selection, root diseases, spotty gravel deposits, and other problems. At one point along the dirt road that divided farm boundaries, we stop at the convergence of three different fields: an orchard belonging to one of the world's largest walnut producers, in full production; a 4-year-old reforested plot; and a two-year-old restoration planting. In the recently planted field, one could see TNCC's novel horticultural approach. Rather than using asymmetrical patterns to mimic a natural forest, TNCC planted this future riparian woodland in rows, orchard style (see photo, p. 57, bottom right). Valley oak, sycamore, cottonwood, coyote brush, wild rose, elderberry, ash, and arroyo willow were growing at various heights, between knee- and waist-high, on a standard linear drip irrigation system. Nearly all of the plant material had been collected within 2 miles of the site and grown out at nearby Chico State University.

"In this way, you have fast growing structure shooting up in the short-term, providing immediate habitat benefits, with the slow-growing valley oaks requiring much longer time to mature," says Stevens. "Laying out the restoration plantings in orderly rows results in a huge financial savings. It's easier to get supplemental irrigation to the plants while they're establishing, and as Nature takes over, it soon becomes forestlike." On the adjacent plot, planted two years earlier, willows, elderberries, and other plants now reached well over-

head. Once the irrigation had been cut off, some plants had died out, others had been recruited, and the whole was starting to resemble a more natural woodland. TNCC restorationists are now aggressively growing out and planting plugs of mugwort, goldenrod, Santa Barbara sedge, and purple needlegrass as understory crops to keep out exotics.

We stop for lunch at the Jewett Creek Farm, a recent TNCC acquisition that includes an aging walnut orchard, a wetland slough, and a riparian forest along the Sacramento. While marginal lands have been easier to purchase for retiring, bringing in larger properties like this one help prevent ranchette subdivision and habitat fragmentation. Still, there are fears that habitat restoration will have a negative and incompatible effect on farming in the area. "A number of people are really concerned with how restoration activities will affect their farms," says Zeleke. In order to reach out to the community, the organization is producing a Good Neighbor Management Toolkit to encourage dialog and share basic information (see *www.tnccalifornia.org*).

"At present it would cost $90 million to buy out the rest of the key farmlands in the inter-river zone, so in the short term, it's critical to figure out how to make agriculture and wildlands protection compatible," says Phil Stevens. "And a lot of the issues we're facing as part of our restoration, such as restricted chemical use and flooding, are already the same issues farmers are facing. So this has ended up creating a good working relationship." Zeleke believes orchards are one of the best crops for mixed conservation along the river. New walnut varieties, such as Chandler and Hartley, are somewhat resistant to flooding and pests, though they, like almonds, are scraped to bare ground for harvest. Prunes can be grown with a permanent native cover crop understory.

Accordingly, the TNCC team has recently sharpened their priorities, removing hardscaped and bouldered areas in order to increase river meander, restoring row crop operations to native forest in order to decrease nitrogen leaching, and encouraging orchard operations as the chief agricultural activity in the interriver zone. The important thing to remember, says Zeleke, is that restoration is a work in progress rather than a short-term project. "Our question is not whether we can restore the Delta to pre-settlement conditions, but how can we restore wetlands and preserve farms at the same time. It's our obligation to create lasting, durable programs that involve local people, local communities, and local economies as well. California is urbanizing at staggering rates. Someone has to take these risks, and I feel The Nature Conservancy of California is up to the challenge."

Farming for Wildlife

A rock prism revegetated with alders on the water side of the levee at M&T Staten Island Ranch. The photo at top center shows the typical boulder hardscape on levee banks. Other photos on the left show a ditch border between fields, winter flooded corn stubble, and lifelong wildlife farmers, Jim and Sally Shanks (bottom row, center).

The Interriver Zone

Walnut orchards are common in the flood plain of the Sacramento River, whose pre-settlement jungle-like riparian forests were home to species such as the now-endangered yellow-billed cuckoo. Center right, restoration team members Peterson, Stevens, Zeleke, and Meyer. The photo at bottom right details how former orchard grids are being used to restore native riparian forests. After three years, irrigation beomes unnecessary.

BUILDING A MATRIX OF FARMLAND HABITAT

There is probably no more significant legislation shaping U.S. environmental policy on private lands than what is generally referred to as the Farm Bill. The passage of the Farm Security and Rural Investment Act of 2002 allocated $170 billion (of which a record $40 billion has been slated for a broad umbrella of "conservation" programs) through 2007, exceeding the combined budgets of the Environmental Protection Agency and the Department of the Interior.[1] With such staggering amounts of citizen tax dollars at stake, today's multiyear Farm Bill essentially determines the health and diversity of rural landscapes, the socioeconomic makeup of life in farming communities, and ultimately, what and how we eat, and who profits from it. For that reason, sustainable agriculture advocates, environmentalists, and other concerned citizens have been attempting to raise the bar on conservation standards funded by this legislation, as it gets revised every five or six years.

Since the 1950s, United States farm policy has narrowly focused agricultural land use on sponsoring the overproduction of a handful of crops (corn, wheat, cotton, rice, sorghum, oats, barley, and later soybeans and oilseed crops), as well as large-scale livestock production. Heralded by politicians as being "good for our family farmers," economists have consistently demonstrated that these subsidies and bailouts (begun as a temporary measure in 1933) have in fact hastened the demise of rural communities. Supporting a commodity-based landscape has increased the specialization and capital intensity of agriculture, spurred overproduction, depressed crop prices, raised land

Intact wetland in the Red Chute Bayou region, northwestern Louisiana.
Previously drained wetlands are being slowly reconverted to bottomland hardwood forests across the southeastern United States. While it is important
to drastically rethink the management of marginal agricultural lands, maintaining natural habitat is essential on productive lands as well.

prices, and sponsored farm consolidation.[2] In the name of generating "cheap food for the masses," the lion's share of the benefits has increasingly fallen to the country's largest agribusinesses while surplus commodities are provided at rock bottom prices to traders, distributors, and particularly the feedlot industry.

Farmers dependent on the commodity payments system remain locked in a no-win situation. They desperately need to diversify to make healthy economic and environmental changes to their operations. But because payments are tied to "base acreages" and historical yields, their primary incentive is to continue feeding the commodity surplus pipeline. Doing the right thing for the land, such as shifting from corn and soybean rotations to perennial grass-fed grazing operations, means taking a penalty in the form of lost subsidies—a risk that could ultimately lead to foreclosure.

Conservationists have historically had at least one seat at the farm policy pork festival, however. As far back as the 1930s, conservation programs were established to attempt to compensate for the continual erosion, water contamination, habitat degradation, and other forms of subsidized land abuse generated by farm policies. Popular legend has it that in 1933 Hugh Hammond Bennett strategically timed his congressional request for the establishment of a nationally funded soil conservation program to coincide with a mudstorm. As the story goes, it was the height of the Dust Bowl, and the combination of airborne eroded soil particles and precipitation produced a dramatic and irrefutably brown downpour. Congress could hardly disagree that our beloved country was blowing away before their very eyes, and thus Bennett sired the Soil Erosion Service (SES), made part of Department of the Interior. By 1934, the service (working in tandem with the Civilian

Conservation Corps) began offering farmers and landowners technical assistance in conservation practices, resource management, financial planning, and other endeavors. The SES became the Soil Conservation Service (SCS) a few years later and was transferred to the U.S. Department of Agriculture; in 1996 its name was changed to the Natural Resources Conservation Service (NRCS).

Under the direction of H. H. Bennett and influenced by such visionaries as Aldo Leopold, the early years of the SCS generated sweeping changes in land stewardship that began to reverse the catastrophic soil losses of the Great Depression. Looking back on the shortcomings of those efforts in *A Sand County Almanac*, Leopold argued for a new land use ethic based on conservation rather than economics. "There has been visible progress in such practices as strip-cropping, pasture rotation, and soil liming, but none in fencing woodlots against grazing, and none in excluding plow and cow from steep slopes. The farmers, in short, have selected those remedial practices which were profitable anyhow and ignored those which were profitable to the community, but not clearly profitable to themselves."[3] Further, in the post-World War II years, the emphasis on conservation faded, as the United States mobilized to feed the world.

With the advent of Green Revolution technologies, the move toward commodity monocrop agriculture, and ultimately the Get Big or Get Out policies of Earl Butz's reign as Secretary of Agriculture in the 1960s, conservation programs all but vanished. Instead, the agency aided farmers with massive projects to control flood waters, to drain wetlands, to clear forests, woodlots, and hedgerows, and to turn lands once considered marginal into semi-productive fields. According to the NRCS conservation biologist Randy Gray, who started his career with the Soil Conservation Service in 1977, countrywide wetland losses to agriculture and development throughout the 1950s to 1970s were reaching 400,000 to 500,000 acres per year, primarily in the Mississippi bottomland forests. "At one time we thought draining wetlands, clean farming, and promoting flood control meant more agriculture and was best for society," explains Gray. "But the environmental movement of the 1970s changed all that."

On the heels of a disastrous drought cycle and collapsing commodity prices, significant reforms were manifested in the Farm Bill of 1985. Dollars were made available to enroll up to 37 million acres in the Conservation Reserve Program (CRP). That same Farm Bill included the "Swamp Buster" and "Sod Buster" provisions, which withdrew all federal subsidy payments to farmers who drained wetlands or plowed protected grasslands. Critics, among them the global grain conglomerates, predicted that the protection of such acreages would result in massive shortfalls. Throughout a decade and a half of conservation programs, however, just the opposite has occurred—surpluses persist, and global commodity prices have fallen to record low levels. And more farmers are interested in enrolling acres in conservation than there are programs to assist them.

Following the overwhelming success of the CRP program, the 1990 Farm Bill added funding for 1.1 million acres in the Wetlands Reserve Program, the majority of which have gone into permanent easements. Gray, who was charged with implementing the program, remembers colleagues cautioning him, "'Randy, no one will sign up for a program of permanent easements.' But it was an unanticipated success. They lined up at the door immediately." The 1996 "Freedom to Farm" Bill introduced new pilot initiatives such as the Wildlife Habitat Incentive Program (WHIP) and the Environmental Quality Incentive Program (EQIP). According to a *New York Times* article by Elizabeth Becker (June 18, 2001), farmers and ranchers applied for $3.7 billion in payments to set aside an additional 68 million acres, but the programs had run out of money. In 2002, the cap was raised on the Wetlands Reserve Program by 1.3 million more acres. And an additional incentive program, the Grassland Reserve Program (GRP), was established to protect up to 2 million acres of native grasslands from development. WHIP was renewed and greatly expanded by the 2002 Farm Bill as well, receiving at least a twentyfold increase in funding, which should allow the program to become focused and operational. "Our challenge now," says Gray, "is to develop a backlog of good applicants in every part of the country who want to do anything from prairie restoration to preserving habitats for threatened or listed species such as bears or gnatcatchers." Yet another hurdle remains: whether the current adminstration and Congress will follow through on the allocation of funds for genuine conservation programs. As this book goes to press in early 2003, numerous efforts are being made to strip or limit allocations for already agreed on conservation programs from the 2002 Farm Bill.

The passage of the 1996 Farm Bill made it clear even to the environmental community that agricultural policies such as these cost-share programs—if properly administered—could be powerful agents in the struggle against biodiversity loss. "With nearly three-fourths of all land privately owned in this country," says Gray, "it is imperative that the conservation community work with private landowners—including farmers and ranchers—who took the best lands when they were available." Gray sees these major federal and state programs, which bring billions of dollars per year to the table, as offering the possibility of establishing a broad matrix for habitat connectivity across the country. Priorities could be set to purchase and preserve remaining habitat, such as grasslands and wetlands, as well as to restore large continuous blocks of marginal farmland and rangeland throughout the country. These efforts could then be enhanced and augmented by programs at the local and regional levels and by buffering the more rigidly protected areas of public lands. Within such a matrix, it is highly conceivable that cross-pollination of numerous ideas, programs, and practices could materialize. Creating ecologically functional buffer zones within farming areas as part of continental wilderness recovery initiatives proposed by the Wildlands Project and other conservation organizations springs readily to mind. Greatly expanded wildlife and pollinator corridors could help reconnect fragmented habitats and simultaneously provide benefits to agriculture. The restoration of grasslands and forests may provide opportunities for hunting and fishing, recreation, and wildcrafting (the gathering and cultivation of native plant products). Experimentation with perennial polyculture (the crossing of annual grains with native perennials) and diverse cropping systems that mimic the structure of native ecosystems could potentially provide food and fiber while helping to heal wounds on private agricultural lands.

Although two decades of conservation programs have had an overwhelmingly positive effect on wildlife, habitat reserve programs are far from perfect, and many salient questions remain. One issue involves whether the stewardship requirements of long-term easements are mandating enough habitat protection and restrictions on land use. In addition, more "conservative" legislators prefer short-term contracts to permanent easements or buy-out programs, thereby limiting long-term protection and raising the question of wise tax dollar spending. Another concern is whether simply planting CRP lands to grass, rather than actively managing them through fire, grazing, mowing, or native plant restoration, constitutes a best practice. Many would like to see CRP lands harvested for fiber and biomass fuel

production—but what would be the impact on reestablishing wildlife populations? Then there are those loopholes in the CRP program that have actually initiated the loss of native habitat. For example, according to Richard Manning, author of *Grassland*, Montana farmers with remnant virgin prairie simply idled wheat land by planting it to grass, received the CRP subsidies, then plowed up the native grassland to plant more wheat.[4]

George Boody, the executive director of the Minnesota-based Land Stewardship Project, believes that a 21st-century farm policy must move from one that merely induces bulging grain bins to one that rewards the multiple benefits of agricultural lands. "There are plenty of goods that don't appear on any label but that people value all the same: aesthetic landscapes, songbird and waterfowl habitat, carbon capture, and community jobs. A public good can also take the form of removing or avoiding the public 'bads' currently created by industrialized agriculture: contaminated drinking water, polluted streams, reduced wildlife populations, and increased lung disease problems produced by working conditions in livestock confinement. But how do we create incentives to provide these goods?...We need a new farm policy that clearly promotes nonmarket benefits as well as market benefits."[5]

With so much of the United States' land base at stake, we can no longer remain silent on farm policy issues. Agriculture must move from public problem to public good. To do that, as Leopold professed, we must quit perceiving land use solely as an economic problem and create solutions that "preserve the integrity, stability, and beauty of the biotic community." This, he perceived, would require a revolution of societal conscience, rather than merely the redirecting of funds from the public coffers and the provision of technical assistance. Still, we are left with the challenge and the possibilities of leveraging government policy to initiate agroecological restoration at the national level. The habitat legacy of recent Farm Bills, while still far from Leopold's ethic, is a move in this essential direction.

BRINGING A WATERSHED BACK TO LIFE

No book covering the vast subject of conservation and agriculture would be complete without shining a spotlight, however briefly, on Coon Valley, in west-central Wisconsin. The glaciers that carved much of that state's topography bypassed the Coulee Region on the eastern flank of the Driftless Area, but windborn glacial silt deposited a productive layer of topsoil on its ridges and valleys. Lured by favorable grain prices and cheap acreage, settlers plowed all arable land in the mid-19th century, running rows straight up and down the steep bluffs. Cows pastured in remnant woodlots and along creeks compacted soils, limiting the ability of rain to sink in. Although it was clear by the 1870s that these erosion-inducing practices were unsustainable, successive waves of English, German, and Norwegian farmers arrived, growing wheat and grains, sheep, dairy cattle, and tobacco. By the height of the Dust Bowl farm crisis, Coon Valley was a dying watershed. Its once vital trout fishery was collapsing. Gullies large enough to swallow a house were common. During increasingly frequent floods, siltation buried roads, bridges, and buildings in valley bottoms.

Enter the Soil Erosion Service (SES), predecessor to the Soil Conservation Service and today's Natural Resources Conservation Service. In 1934, the SES chose the 92,000-acre Coon Valley watershed south of La Crosse, Wisconsin, as a testing ground for a multi-disciplinary approach to work with farmers on land conservation plans. The community-based effort that unfolded took the form of kitchen table meetings, campfire gatherings, educational skits (featuring Old Man Erosion), and perhaps most important, Civilian Conservation Corps (CCC) work parties. Farmers who entered the five-year program benefited tremendously: free lime and fertilizer to stimulate played-out soil; tractor-built terraces and contour strips planted with free alfalfa seed to control erosion and establish crop-rotation regimens; fencing materials to keep livestock from grazing woodlots; farm plans that embodied what we now refer to as holistic resource management or whole farm planning—including field maps, cropping plans, budgets, and annual reports. What resulted was nothing less than a grassroots transformation of the community, earning trust among farmers, establishing new standards for conservation, and influencing the land ethics of the region for generations to come.

The SES plans prescribed land use according to each farm's soil types and slopes.

The steepest grades (40 percent or more) were designated as woodlands, to remain in trees with cattle excluded. Fields with slopes of 20 to 30 percent became managed pasture. Only slopes of less than 20 percent were to be used as croplands. Terraces were built into those between 10 and 20 percent, while more gradual slopes were planted along the contour to prevent erosion in alternating strips of hay between corn or wheat. Sometimes terraces and contour strips were used in combination. Crops were rotated on an annual basis.[6]

On a rainy October morning, we pile into a jeep with Jim Radke, the Vernon County Natural Resource's Conservation Service District Conservationist, for a tour of Coon Valley. Radke is a career conservationist, a tall, fair-haired man with the healthy vigor of a life lived outdoors. As we switchback up to the ridgetop farms above the valley, Radke takes us on a quick time travel through the natural and human history of the area. Across the steep bluffs, contour strips of alfalfa hay lay in contrast against the dried fields of corn and soybeans (only recently grown in this cold climate), all alternating with pockets of dense forest. Dairy herds graze in the drizzle. From our ridgetop vantage, we can see the lower-lying woodlots of the many small- and medium-sized farms and sense an enormous potential to increase wildlife habitat by expanding and connecting these forests. While grass-fed dairy operations would perhaps be the lowest impact agricultural activity in the area (see Art Thicke, pages 88-89), Radke notes that small grass-fed dairy farms are being replaced by large-scale no-till corn and soybean operations. At stake is the reversal of over 60 years of conservation gains.

We stop at the tidy dairy farm of Ernest and Joseph Haugen, bachelor brothers of Norwegian descent, both teenagers at the time of the Soil Erosion Service's Coon Valley project. They invite us out of the rain into a spartan kitchen that seems to have changed little since the 1930s. Soon Ernest clears the table and in a fluorescent glow spreads out the original parchmentlike farm maps, record books, and the actual contract their father signed with the Soil Erosion Service. In heavy Norwegian accents, they explain how the terraces "put in by the 'CCC' men" healed the land and changed their farming practices forever through narrower strips and more frequent rotations. "Before the Soil Erosion

Service program, we had to stuff hay bales in the gullies and sometimes we couldn't even get the crops out," remembers Ernest. He recounts the burning eyes from spreading lime across their damaged fields. But the benefits came rapidly for the Haugens and the 417 other Coon Valley farmers who agreed to the program. "The barn got full of hay afterward," Joseph says, adding, "The soil does not run away now." Within a few years, Radke explains, participating farmers enjoyed extra feed. The butterfat content in the cows' milk increased. As less steep croplands became more productive, the steeper lands were converted to pasture, and erosion diminished exponentially.

Radke drives us from the amphitheater-like contoured farms down to a bend of Coon Creek, which meanders through the valley bottom. He admits that the sweeping changes that transformed agriculture in Coon Valley haven't been 100 percent successful and that the recent loss of small dairies to the large soybean and corn operations has threatened further setbacks. But he reports enthusiastically that he and his colleagues are heavily engaged in the next step of landscape restoration. "We are now connecting the hillside farming practices to the trout streams below," Radke says. According to Warren Gebert, District Chief of the U.S. Geological Survey in Middleton, Wisconsin, studies have shown that the historical changes in Coon Valley farm practices have led directly to improvement in the fishery. Increased infiltration of ground water has resulted in streams receiving more and colder water, a boon for the native brook trout.[7] Efforts to restore wild brown and native brook trout habitat have included exclusionary fencing for cattle, the installation of lunkers (submerged tablelike platforms to create habitat), stream bank stabilization, the placement of V-shaped vortex weirs to disperse sediment, selected tree planting for increased shade, and the stocking of hatchery-bred native strains. Today the area boasts some of the most robust trout populations in the Midwest.

Writing about the watershed restoration project in the May 1935 issue of *American Forests Magazine*, Aldo Leopold (who was involved in studying wildlife populations in Coon Valley) reported, "After selecting certain demonstration areas on which to concentrate its work, the project offered to each farmer on each area the cooperation of the government in installing on his farm a reorganized system of land use, in which not only soil conservation and agriculture, but also forestry, game, fish, fur, flood control, scenery, songbirds, or any other pertinent interest were to be duly integrated." Seventy years later, the Coon Valley project seems visionary and one worth carefully examining as our farm policies move ahead.

USDA's First Watershed Restoration Project

Ernest and Joseph Haugen were teenagers in the mid-30s when the USDA's Soil Erosion Service brought conservation programs to Coon Valley, Wisconsin.

At center right, NRCS biologist Jim Radke beside a restored trout stream.

The photo at bottom right shows the desperate conditions of farms in the 1930s. Contour strips, terraces, crop rotations, and other measures were implemented as a result.

NATION'S FIRST WATERSHED PROJECT

This point is near the center of the 90,000 acre Coon Creek Watershed, the nation's first large-scale demonstration of soil and water conservation. The area was selected for this purpose by the U.S. Soil Conservation Service (then Soil Erosion Service) in October 1933. Technicians of the S.C.S. and the University of Wisconsin pooled their knowledge with experiences of local farm leaders to establish a pattern of land use now prevalent throughout the midwest. Planned practices in effect include improvement of woodlands, wildlife habitat and pastures, better rotations and fertilization, strip cropping, terracing, and gully and stream bank erosion control. The outcome is a tribute to the wisdom, courage and foresight of the farm families who adopted the modern methods of conservation farming illustrated here.

Erected 1955

THE PRAIRIE POTHOLES

The subtle landscape of the Missouri Coteau is the expanse of northern plains that feeds the Missouri River and spans parts of Iowa and Minnesota, the Dakotas, northeastern Montana, Saskatchewan, and Alberta, known also as the Prairie Potholes. Rolling hills of farm fields and grasslands are studded with countless water-filled potholes (up to 100 glacially scoured basins per square mile), as well as larger wetlands and sloughs—at least during rainy years. Those wetlands often fall within farm boundaries and serve as critical nesting and brooding habitat for tens of millions of waterfowl, to the extent that the region is sometimes characterized as "North America's duck factory."[8] Up to 70 percent of North American ducks are born in this region. Thirty miles outside Jamestown, North Dakota, in the remote Chase Lake National Wildlife Refuge, resides a nesting colony of 30,000 white pelicans. According to Mick Erickson of the U.S. Fish and Wildlife Service at the Chase Lake Prairie Project, early records state that the population was only 50 when President Theodore Roosevelt established the preserve in 1908.

Many of North Dakota's (and the region's) wetlands and native prairies have been lost over the past century and a half, as both tillable and marginal soils were converted for intensive grazing, grain, and oil-seed crop production. The land has been carved into a mosaic of multithousand-acre farms divided by loose gravel roads, punctuated by fragmented and sometimes breathtaking pockets of unaltered terrain. Contoured fields of flax, wheat, sunflowers, barley, and corn are often separated by thin windbreaks and shelterbelts and bordered by wetlands or mixed prairie. At the time of our visit in late August, hay lay harvested in great round bales, in hulking, wooly mammoth-sized piles, and in swaths of mower-cut stubble.

With approximately 95 percent of the land in private ownership and relatively large remnants of wetlands and grasslands, North Dakota farmers are essential participants in successful conservation programs. But both participation and conservation are relatively recent developments. Nearly two decades ago the North American waterfowl flyway that encompasses Canada, the United States, and Mexico was on the verge of crashing. Until the mid-1980s, farmers throughout the Prairie Pothole region frequently drained potholes to increase their grain output, plowing up nesting cover in the process. The loss of vital habitat, combined with severe drought conditions in the early 1980s, reduced the populations of ducks, pheasants, grouse, deer, and other species to record low levels. But as the costs of producing a bushel of hard red winter wheat surpassed $4, and the prices at the grain elevators hovered around $2.70, farmers survived only through loan deficiency payments.[9] The establishment of the Conservation Reserve Program (CRP) through the 1985 Farm Bill resulted in the enrollment of some 3 million acres in the state to be maintained or restored to grasslands—requiring less upkeep than cropland and providing nesting cover. (The "Swamp Buster" provision of that same Farm Bill also withdrew federal subsidies to farmers who drained wetlands, thereby protecting potholes.) Then in 1987, the U.S. Fish and Wildlife Service in North Dakota became the first state to initiate a Partners for Fish and Wildlife program. Nonprofit organizations such as Ducks Unlimited, the Nature Conservancy, the North Dakota Wetlands Trust, and others later joined these state and federal forces, providing further incentives with complementary cost-share programs (such as Grasslands for Tomorrow, Adopt-a-Pothole, and conservation easements) to protect wetland and upland habitats on private lands. Suddenly the Coteau's millions of migratory mallards, pintails, gadwalls, and teals became the latest federally subsidized crop, and farmers joined waiting lists to put their land in conservation programs.[10] The large grain conglomerates vocally criticized these conservation subsidies, arguing that American farmers would underproduce wheat and corn by putting aside so much acreage. But the opposite occurred. Today there is a worldwide glut of grain, due to technological advances and the globalization of commodity food production, and prices have fallen to 1960 levels. Nearly 20 years later, conservation has become an economically competitive use on rural lands. Rather than working on a first-come-first-serve basis, subsidy programs are now trying to raise environmental standards for participation, focusing on erosion prevention, pristine grassland protection, carbon sequestration (the capture and storage of carbon dioxide in living plants), and habitat connectivity.

On a bright, breezy August afternoon that deceptively transforms North Dakota with the feel of a vernal paradise, we talk with Don Hoffman, owner of the 2,500-acre Hanging H Ranch, in Medina, North Dakota. "We wanted to increase our herd without harming

Vital Breeding Grounds

The North American Waterfowl Management Plan was enacted in the mid-1980s in response to plummeting populations of migratory birds across the continent. Between the 1970s and early 1990s, northern pintails had declined by more than 60 percent, blue-winged teal by 31 percent, lark buntings by 55 percent, and grasshopper sparrows by 70 percent.[11] Because of the significance of its breeding habitat, the Prairie Pothole region that spans five U.S. states and three Canadian provinces was targeted with the highest priority status. According to the U.S. Fish and Wildlife Service, 177 species of birds reproduce and raise their young in the wetland complexes known as the Prairie Potholes (49 neotropical songbirds, 47 resident songbirds, 36 waterbirds, 20 species of waterfowl, 17 raptors, and 8 upland game birds).

A pothole can be as small as a fifth of an acre or as large as 500 acres. Periods of drought and abundant rainfall make up the natural cycle of the Prairie Pothole region. Protecting potholes throughout both wet and dry cycles is critical for wildlife of all types. Large tracts of grasslands and wetlands are necessary to maintain a healthy balance between predators and ground-nesting birds.

In order to restore and conserve habitat, the Chase Lake Prairie Project now encompasses portions of 11 counties and more than 5.5 million acres. Over 1,000 owners, such as Don Hoffman of the Hanging H Ranch in Medina, North Dakota, pictured below left, are involved in the protection and restoration of wetland and upland grass habitats. Numerous agencies and organizations provide landowner agreements, cost-share programs, and conservation easements for wetland restorations and creations, grazing systems, grass seedings, island creations, and nesting structures.

the grass," Hoffman tells us. "Some of our land needed rest, and we needed more pasture. I got hold of some brochures and became interested in the CRP program because I could see how it could become very beneficial to me and the waterfowl too." The U.S. Fish and Wildlife Service came out to the Hanging H and evaluated the land to determine stocking rates and carrying capacities of pastures. They established a fencing calendar that set up a rotational grazing system, providing for rest and nesting cover. The paddocks were laid out in a roughly north-south direction so the herds could be easily moved from pasture to pasture. A previously drained wetland was restored and marginal croplands were reseeded to grass. Cost-share options supported the program. "They provided the materials, we put in the sweat, and we were very glad to do that," says Hoffman, who started farming in the late 1950s and won a 1993 Conservation Achievement Award for stewardship. Hoffman's son, Kendall, and daughter-in-law, Patty, had earlier enrolled their nearby 450-acre farm in a conservation program that has included perpetual grassland and wetland easements, restored potholes, rotational grazing systems, and native prairie restoration. Although sadly Kendall died in 2000, the combination of conservation subsidies and a seasonal hunting and lodging operation have allowed Patty and her young family to stay on the farm.

"The game, the birds, and the wildlife have always been an intricate part of this land," says Don Hoffman. "In past years, it's been mistreated. At one time, our wild birds, our grouse, our pheasants, our deer were almost extinct here. Gradually, the younger generation has come along and looked at things differently. They loved to hunt, loved to see the pheasant crow early in the morning, this sort of thing, and took the time to show us that this is part of us. We were too busy making a living. They could see it and we couldn't. They came out and said, 'Hey guys, give us a little time. We can work this out. You can continue your work, nobody's going to hurt that. Let us come along and help you out, and we'll have a win-win situation.' It's a fun thing."

"It wasn't that long ago in North Dakota," remembers Mick Erickson, "that people thought that farming and wildlife couldn't coexist." Today the Chase Lake Prairie Project may be the state's most impressive landscape-scale project. In the headquarters, Erickson shows us a giant map studded with pins that outline the project's sweep from the South Dakota border across central North Dakota to the northwest, encompassing portions of 11 counties and over 5.5 million acres and involving the participation of over 1,000 landowners. The color-coded pins represent agreements with landowners.

Ongoing projects include wetland restorations and creations, grazing systems, grass seedings, island creations, and nesting structures. Intermingled among these private land agreements are lands owned in fee-title and perpetual wetland and grassland easement contracts by the U.S. Fish and Wildlife Service.

While the map demonstrates an area still immensely fragmented, Erickson believes real strides toward wildlands connectivity are being made in some areas. "Habitat fragmentation is a big—if not the biggest—concern to wildlife agencies and organizations, wildlife managers, and people who love the outdoors. Obviously, we'd like to see all ecosystems healthy and capable of supporting all the necessary habitat components that migratory and resident wildlife species rely on to live," Erickson continues. "We are fortunate in North Dakota. While it is true that this state has lost over 50 percent of our original wetlands and 65 percent of our native prairie grasslands, we still feel fortunate. Many other midwestern states have lost 60 to 90 percent of their wetlands and 50 to 90 percent of their native prairie grasslands. Canada currently doesn't have very strong environmental protection programs. We still have some areas with intact native prairie grassland. But in some areas, much of this native prairie has been plowed and converted to cropland and hayland. Connecting these remaining tracts is the struggle. That's why it is absolutely vital that programs like the USDA's Conservation Reserve Program, the USFWS Partners for Fish and Wildlife Program, and large landscape projects such as the Chase Lake Prairie Project exist. These programs provide a means to restore millions of acres of marginal land to grassland cover, restore thousands of wetland basins, improve existing native prairie grasslands, and connect these lands with state and federal public lands."[12] In Stutsman County, where we are visiting, 18 percent of farmland is registered in the Conservation Reserve Program.

The conservation agreement process starts when a farmer voluntarily comes in with farm maps. As Erickson describes it, "We explain all the projects that are available. We try to provide the landowner with options to gain better income, allow for more efficiency, lower input costs, and simultaneously improve the land for wildlife. Grazing systems are a good example. A grazing system emphasizes rotating cattle within a pasture so that portions of the pasture are grazed while the remainder receives rest and the grass plants are allowed to grow taller, reseed themselves, and establish a better root zone. If they get into a 15-year plan, they will realize better weight gain, better land health. The cost-share allows for improvements many farmers can't do on their own, such as native seeding in marginal lands, boundary fencing, and water development. All of a sudden he gains extra pasture, can make more money running cattle or buffalo, and reduces stress on his pasture. It's better for the soil, better for the grass, promotes better breeding conditions and weight gain. And it also brings back the robins, sharp-tailed grouse, and pheasants."

Erickson walks us to some experimental burn areas, where the prairie hills are blackened to stubble in all directions as part of an effort to combat leafy spurge. Spring burnings, combined with the release of spurge beetles as beneficial insects, are proving effective in controlling this noxious weed.

On this particular visit, however, water was the highest concern on everyone's minds. The Coteau region had been experiencing an extremely wet cycle, which is usually followed by bone dry times of drought. One can only hope that the profound changes that have taken place here over the last fifteen years will provide a buffer against extremes in weather. It is clear that something very important has been established here, and that the Prairie Potholes and the wildlife they support are much better off for these efforts.

Protecting Potholes, Pelicans, and Prairies

The photos in the upper right and at center show a colony of white pelicans at the Chase Lake National Wildlife Refuge. Documents show that at the time of its establishment by Theodore Roosevelt in 1908, the population at the refuge was only 50. Today there are an estimated 30,000.

Mick Erickson of the U.S. Fish and Wildlife Service at the Chase Lake Prairie Project poses in front of a recently burned grassland, an effort to control a noxious weed called leafy spurge. Spring burnings, combined with the release of spurge beetles, are part of a chemical-free, biological weed control program in the region. After just two years, the combination of carefully-timed burning and beneficial insect releases has produced outstanding results in waterfowl production areas.

Native birds in North America's grasslands have suffered steeper, more consistent, and more widespread declines over the past 25 years than have birds in other habitat types.

RESTORING THE BOTTOMLANDS

Approaching our morning's first destination–the USDA Natural Resources Conservation Service (NRCS) district office in southwestern Arkansas–we pass a large brown placard on the interstate that reads: Hope, Arkansas, Birthplace of William Jefferson Clinton, 42nd President of the United States. It seems a fitting marker. Federal Farm Bill programs funded during the Clinton administration were responsible for permanently restoring hundreds of thousands of acres of marginal farming lands to wetlands and bottomland hardwood forests in Arkansas, Louisiana, their neighboring states, and the rest of the country.

At the humble brick headquarters of the NRCS Hope Technical Service Center, we meet our amiable guides for the day, Jody Pagan, the State Wetlands Coordinator, and Randy Childress, an agricultural engineer. Crammed into Childress's office, which is densely packed with files, maps, and engineering drawings, we immediately launch into a discussion of the Red River Basin Project of the Wetlands Reserve Program (WRP). The Red River originates in eastern Colorado, winds across Oklahoma, then spans five counties in western Arkansas before flowing into the Chappalaya in central Louisiana. Since the 1940s, however, most of the basin's associated wetlands have been compromised by agricultural activities, in particular the great soybean rush of the 1970s. Randy Childress sums it up: "We levied, drained, and farmed the stew out of it." Only about 10 percent of wetland habitat remains, and the riverine systems that depend on the rising and falling flows of seasonal flooding are no longer hydrologically functional. Gone are the bottomland hardwood species such as native pecan, green ash, overcup oak, willow oak, hackberry, Nuttall oak, and cypress. Wintering and permanent habitat for neotropical migratory songbirds, waterfowl, and shorebirds has all but disappeared. Among threatened or endangered species in the Red River Basin are nine freshwater mussels, bald eagle, least tern, peregrine falcon, and American alligator.

Changing economic conditions, however, have brought a significant shift in land use throughout the region. Even with an average rainfall of 52 inches, there is limited potential for groundwater irrigation to bring crops through late summer and fall dry spells. As commodity prices fell to record lows, marginal croplands were converted to pasture, but even livestock grazing became uneconomical. By the mid-1990s, wetlands restoration through the USDA's WRP program emerged as a competitive option for landowners. In the Red River Basin alone, 22,000 acres had been brought into the WRP by 2001, 15,000 acres of which had been restored from agricultural use, and 7,000 that were undisturbed lands. "Eighty-five percent of those are in perpetual easements, otherwise they are 30-year easements," says the earnest Pagan, speaking with an easy drawl. When prioritizing projects for funding, he emphasizes both the potential for broader habitat connectivity and the opportunity for permanent protection. Full agricultural land values are paid for perpetual easements, with most land costing $500 per acre or less. (The state has a $700 per acre cap.) The focus is on establishing habitat for migratory songbirds, waterfowl, and shorebirds, the three target groups of the congressionally mandated program. "In a state approaching 90 percent loss of wetlands, this is probably Arkansas' most ecologically significant complex because of the habitat potential," says Pagan.

"During my seven years of working in the state," he continues, "I've heard landowners say again and again that we never should have cleared this, it's just too wet, we can't make a crop off of it. That's telling me the best purpose of that land is wetlands." Throughout Arkansas, 100,000 acres were brought into the voluntary program between 1995 and 2000. Even greater acreage was brought under WRP protection in Louisiana and Mississippi during the same time period, and Arkansas already has an additional 100,000 acres on the waiting list. "I've never met a single landowner who did it solely for an economic reason, and I've been to all 236 projects in the state," says Pagan. "They do it because they love wildlife and they want to be stewards of the land. The thing that humbles me is the amount of need out there."

Ironically, it was the Soil Conservation Service, predecessor to the Natural Resources Conservation Service, that helped landowners drain and replumb the Red River Basin in previous decades. "Sixty years ago the big push was agriculture, and as the technical arm of the USDA, the SCS was there to assist to the farmer in clearing the land fencerow to fencerow to feed America and the world. That seemed to make sense to those people at the time," says Childress. "But now I do as much wetland restoration work as I do agricultural work, and for the next generation it might go toward a greener side. We don't necessarily feed the world anymore. We have to take care of what we have."

Thinking Like a Wetland

We climb into our vehicles and head south to Texarkana. The first stop is Clear Lake Hunting Properties, and father and son owners Paul Hardy Senior and Junior cordially greet us in syrupy Texas accents. The Hardys' 2,000-acre property is an integral part of the Red River Basin Project. Just a year and three months ago, we are told, it was a flat-bottom corn, wheat, and cotton operation. But that's hard to fathom now. We look out into what seems to be fairly lush wetland habitat, with a dirt road snaking though its midsection and wooded edges framing the perimeter.

"In a riverine system, floodwaters rise and then fall," explains Pagan. "We don't have that anymore. So we built a levee and created our wetland, driven by precipitation. In 15 months, thanks to a very wet fall, we went from agriculture to wetlands. Almost like instant oats—just add water and they will come. You see the ibis today. Last week there were pintail and 400 teal here."

Pagan insists that what Aldo Leopold might have referred to as "intelligent tinkering" has been science and observation based. "Biologists have spent seven years wading through swamps learning to mimic pristine natural wetland systems," he says. He describes the emerging wetland as early successional habitat, somewhat similar to what would have been there if beavers were still manipulating the system. "We become the beavers," says Pagan, "reconstructing what we can from leveled land. It doesn't take long at all." Across what not long ago were plowed fields are the "beaver complexes"—habitat mounds, loafing and nesting areas, scooped out bowls, "micro highs and lows" that can range anywhere from five feet deep to a six-inch mudflat. By de-straightening ditches to recreate oxbows and creating asymmetrical meandering levees, the NRCS attempts to recapture pre-agricultural conditions.

"Doing this restoration looks like fun from the safety of the levee," says Pagan, "but when you're out there in the 100-degree-plus weather stomping through the chest-high brush, swallowing pollen, it's a different reality. The satisfying part of the job comes after the habitat is established." There are nine members on the NRCS team who, Pagan says, "eat, breathe, and sleep wetland restoration. We've spent our whole lives in the woods, and it means a whole lot to give back what's been taken away. The research is now ahead of us. The information and the perspiration are there. It's the money that's the difficult part."

The direct objective of the Wetlands Reserve Program in the south is to connect to the massive efforts of the Conservation Reserve Program and WRP in the north—the Prairie Pothole region—with a focus on the restoration of nesting habitat. "Our goal and our jobs are to restore the wintering habitat for the fall and spring migration of shorebirds and waterfowl. Everything is directly correlated between those two regions. Those migratory waterfowl are molting when they come in from the Prairie Pothole region and they need protein." This also becomes the nesting habitat for songbirds that winter in New Mexico and Central America and points farther south. For those reasons, Pagan gets excited about smartweed, wild millet, and other high-protein foraging crops that spring back so easily in the wetlands.

Mosquitoes swarm voraciously about us as we walk along the levee. Pagan stops at a water control structure, a simple valve-and-culvert system that allows water to pass from one side of the levee to the other. "If we just had a levee," he explains, "all the water would just be impounded. With a water control structure, we can manage different water levels for different species needs—more water for foraging, less for mudflats, maybe not doing anything, but the opportunity is there." Fire ants begin crawling up our photographer Roberto Carra's pants when we stop to take pictures. Pagan and Childress warn him to brush off his trousers—then they start identifying bird species and exclaiming like excited teenagers in the presence of celebrities. Ibis! Pintail! Yellowlegs! Did you hear that Virginia rail?! Nothing—winged, finned, scaled, vegetative, or otherwise—escapes their attention or admiration. "Avocets? Ibis? Two years ago they were unheard of. They lived on the coast and they stayed on the coast."

At one corner of the property is a wooded backwater remnant that never fell under the plow. Pagan excitedly describes the habitat complexity of this relatively small site. "From a waterbird perspective, this is a multi-use zone. It has a structural component of woody vegetation, more emergent vegetation like cattails, a foraging component like smartweed, and a canopy and scrubby component behind. There are a sheltered habitat for wood ducks, open water for wading birds, mud flats in drought cycles for shorebirds, and denser herbaceous areas that provide rail habitat. In a nutshell, you have everything we're shooting for right here."

Defending Against Eternal Subsidies

By the end of the day, it becomes obvious that dedicated restorationists like Pagan and Childress who are involved in large-scale, contiguous-acreage conservation programs are modern-day public defenders. "This is more like an obsession than a job," says Pagan. "Ten hour days are common in our department. And that doesn't include driving." The public defender analogy makes sense not only in terms of professional commitment, but from the standpoint of fiscal and ecological responsibility as well.

"It costs about $150 per acre for restoration, and we turned this whole farm into a wetland," says Pagan. "Yes, we're spending tax dollars and taking marginal crop lands out of production for something that's very critical–the waterfowl and other birds that migrate up and down these basins. But we've also been paying subsidies and disaster payments on some of these properties. In my mind, as a taxpayer, not an agency employee, we'll regain that over time because we won't be paying those payments to those landowners for marginal cropland." While it could cost a million dollars to buy a property, that same property could have been receiving up to $200,000 in payments every year. As a permanent wetland habitat, savings start to accrue after the fifth year.

"You've seen that credit card commercial?" asks Pagan. "Here's my version. Water control structure: $1,500. Levee: $2.40 per cubic yard. Restored wetland: priceless. That's the way these guys that are breaking their backs feel about it, and these landowners too."

Just Add Water

The photos across the top of the page feature a former diary farm in southwestern Arkansas restored just one year earlier by the state's extremely dedicated NRCS staff.

Natives like Pennsylvania smartweed and wild millet naturally regenerate following the restoration of wetlands. Migratory species on their way from the Prairie Pothole region to wintering habitat in the southeast typically stop in wetland areas like these in desperate need of nourishment.

Researchers spent years wading and walking through wetlands in order to learn to mimic natural contours and channel patterns. The two photos at bottom left detail how quickly vegetation appears in a reconstructed wetland.

The two photos at bottom center show the water control structures that are standard features in these bottomland restoration projects. Water levels can be managed on either side of a levee with variable flow rates.

Arkansas has a long waiting list of landowners anxious to enter parts of their properties into similar conservation projects.

REHYDRATING THE ARKLATEX

To describe the low-lying areas in northwestern Louisiana's Red Chute Bayou as a flood plain is supreme understatement. According to Rick Adams, the District Conservationist for Bossier Parish, last spring he steered a boat through four feet of water over the now dusty road that transects Flat River Farms, where our interview is taking place.

Frequent flooding in the ArkLaTex region, however, didn't keep Bossier Parish farmers from clearing and leveling land all the way to the bayous in the past 60 years. "They planted corn, soybeans, wheat, milo—anything to bring in a subsidy payment," explains Adams, "leaving little or no vegetation at the bayou's edges to filter rain and runoff." During drought cycles, farmers got away with pasturing, but flood-related disaster payments were more often the norm. In addition, as development progressed in the upper reaches of the watershed, greatly decreasing that land's capacity for infiltration, flooding in lower areas became increasingly more severe.

Ten thousand contiguous acres of the Red Chute Bayou, a massive watershed that drains into the Red River Basin, have been designated as a priority project for the Wetlands Reserve Program (WRP). As of October 2001, 4,000 of those acres had been enrolled in the program, with the goal of reestablishing as much bottomland hardwood forest habitat as possible. (Mississippi had approximately 150,000 acres enrolled in WRP by 2001, the majority along the Mississippi River floodplain, where up to 25 percent of lands are eligible for the Wetlands Reserve Program, even several miles from the river itself.)

On a foggy October morning, Adams and NRCS wildlife biologist Mike Nichols guided us through several projects in the Red Chute Bayou area. Adams recounted zigging and zagging with ribbon tape through the lowlands as they designed the ridge-and-swale topography to mimic former oxbow sloughs. Mounds for nesting cover were created, as well as lower depressions to enhance habitat for amphibians; these would dry up in summer and flood in fall and winter. Local school children erected wood duck boxes in many sites.

"You just build the habitat, then rely on Mother Nature to fill it up," says Adams. "Over time

who knows what will come in here," continues Nichols. With flooding came all kinds of native seed, such as Pennsylvania smartweed and wild millet, both excellent forage for waterfowl. Areas were reforested with Nuttall oaks, overcup oaks, cypress, and mayhalls planted on 12-foot spacing, to create a diverse stand for wildlife benefit. To control a surge of opportunistic honey locusts, bush hogs were brought in. A tremendous drought year made it difficult for the hardwood plantings to achieve the 150 seedlings-per-acre goal the NRCS was trying to achieve, but the trees have survived and grown.

"The most suitable use of this land is bottomland hardwood, even though the soils are fertile," says Adams. Those soils are great for growing things other than crops for export. "The deer in this area are massive," he notes with a hunter's gleam in his eye, owing, he says, to the calcium and phosphorous in the soil.

Everywhere in the Red Chute Bayou region, Adams and Nichols tell us, are areas that never should have been cleared, and there is a good chance that the program could extend beyond the 10,000 acres designated. Landowners are volunteering readily, so there is hope for a wide range of expansion. The more that contiguous landowners participate, the greater the wildlife benefits. And immediately adjacent to the WRP area is a 4,500-acre wildlife area established more than 30 years ago and managed by the Army Corps of Engineers. Between his program and this one, Adams sees a 14,500-acre bottomland hardwood area in the future.

At one point on our tour, we stop at a bayou by the side of the road. The surface of the pea-soup-green water is thick with tiny dots of vegetation. Wide-skirted cypress trees stand in three feet of water. It looks like perfect alligator territory. Remnant habitat types like these are an important part of the natural mosaic the WRP is intended to mimic as it reestablishes a more appropriate balance between farmland and the wild. Joining so many of his NRCS colleagues who have been interviewed for this book, Adams proudly confides: "This is one of the most worthwhile projects I have ever been involved with."

Down in the Bayou

In Bossier Parish's Red Chute Bayou region of northwestern Louisiana, nearly 4,000 acres had been entered in WRP by the fall of 2001. Connecting habitat within a region is essential to successful CRP and WRP implementation.

NRCS staff members hope this particular area will one day span nearly 15,000 contiguous acres of bottomland hardwood forest—including a tract already managed by the Army Corps of Engineers (photo, upper right).

Research has shown that placing wood duck boxes in open areas like the one at top left can be counter-productive. Wood ducks need nests in healthy forests. Boxes in marshes encourage females to compete and lay multiple clutches of eggs in the same box. According to one study published in *Audubon Magazine*, as few as 10 percent of those eggs successfully hatched.

MUCH TO DO ABOUT MUCK

In south Florida, they're known as muck farms, lowland soils that, when drained, become extraordinarily productive. These ancient soils, however, have high levels of phosphorous and are fairly short-lived as farmland. Exposure to air eventually causes the feet-thick mucky soils to oxidize and shrink. In this southeastern extremity of the United States, a few hours north of Miami, at least a half dozen multithousand-acre muck farms have been entered into the Wetlands Reserve Program (WRP) and restored to wildlife habitat. "This type of farming has externalities," explains our guide, Ken Murray, the WRP Coordinator for the State of Florida. "In order to farm these fertile soils, you have to release water every once in a while, water that has high levels of phosphorous, and that eventually means you will be creating pollution somewhere else in the river system."

Broadmoor Farms is a 12,000-acre property, with a 9,000-acre stretch of sandy uplands, used for both range and vegetable row crops, and an additional 3,000 acres of lower restored wetlands that border the St. John's River Basin. Entering the farm from the north, we pass large pastures with grazing livestock, part of Florida's thriving cow-calf industry, where young cattle are fed on grass before being shipped off to the grain belt for fattening and slaughter. The springtime scene seems almost tropical. Brahman-crossed cows are spread out across the palmetto and pine dotted range. At one point, we pass a complex of dairy barns, which, on closer inspection, are abandoned and overgrown, angled and slouching. As part of the larger conservation effort on Broadmoor Farms, the St. John's River Water Management District recently purchased a conservation easement over the uplands with the only restriction that dairy operations can no longer be conducted there.

Farther down we pass fields of recently harvested potatoes, their wind strips left intact to prevent erosion. Next is a stretch of corn, shoulder high, luminous and lush, bouncing in the soft wind. Row crop vegetable farming is completed in this part of the country before the summer solstice; dry periods are compensated for with a massive traveling lateral irrigation system. Finally, we arrive at the site we have flown 3,000 miles to inspect: a series of square-shaped fields separated by levees and backed up against a taller dam that holds back the broad and wilder wetlands of the St. John's River Basin beyond. Just a year ago, this was a muck farm corn silage operation. Taken out of production by the Wetlands

Reserve Program, the 3,000-acre site quickly reverted to brush. In the height of a drought, numerous patches of muck caught fire in summer lightning storms and burned for days. In the meantime, however, a number of water control structures were installed to regulate water levels, and on this windy April afternoon it is difficult to imagine that this was anything but a wetland. Ibises are beeping, white pelicans float like bright rafts on the almost metallic-looking water surface. Alligators of various sizes sun themselves on levee banks and mud flats, then slosh away beneath the water as we approach. A pair of wood storks, an endangered species, sail gracefully by. In one corner of the restoration project we see a series of habitat mounds, obviously fabricated, looking strangely out of place in their regularity. These hummocks, Murray tells us, are "Misso Mountains," named after the NRCS's WRP expert, Bob Misso. Essentially, the mounds were constructed by pushing together the organic soils as the levee was constructed to provide protected resting and nesting areas for birds and other wildlife.

"This is obviously enhanced habitat," admits Murray, "and it is managed specifically for wading birds." He points to the levee beyond that borders an adjacent Florida Fish and Wildlife Conservation Commission Waterfowl Management Area. "That area is managed for ducks, and the water levels and habitat are regulated accordingly. But we've lost so much that I believe we can afford a little bit of enhancement, especially if there are some functions and values that we can achieve without disrupting the restoration goals." This land, he continues, will never go back to untrammeled wilderness, particularly given Florida's heavy-handed replumbing of the state's natural hydrology.

As we drive across the levee, swarms of dragonflies zoom in and out of the open car windows. On what is now an open herbaceous marshland, a flock of pelicans rises up with a great roar of flapping white wings. In the state, Murray tells us, there is already a $60-million backlog of requests for projects, without any advertising at all for the program. The WRP and other conservation programs, he says, have given him "a new lease on life" and infused in him a sense of enthusiasm and purpose in his job that had somehow gone lacking. "My message is to just send money, we can do so much good here. Taxpayers are definitely getting their money's worth."

From Muck Farm to Marsh

In southeastern Florida, muck marshes have been farmed for their fertile organic soils. But plowing the muck causes it to oxidize and shrink and to release phosphorous, which pollutes waterways and wildlife habitat. 3,000 acres of low-lying lands on this working farm were entered in the WRP program in 2001.

These photos show wetland habitat just one year after the project was completed. Alligators, ibises, white pelicans, wood storks, bitterns, and many other species are common here. The project links to a waterfowl management area that spans 25 miles along the St. John's River.

Top center, shows the now-abandoned dairy facility. The confinement dairy operation is no longer permitted by the terms of the conservation easement. Just below that photo, a field of sweet corn gets a start in the cultivated fields of the 9,000-acre property.

Top right details a screw gate used to regulate water levels in the renovated wetlands. All photos were taken in one two-hour session.

NATURAL SYSTEMS FARMING

Nowhere is the separation between farming and the wild drawn into sharper contrast than in the midst of industrial monoculture. In a multithousand-acre field where the focus is on the maximum output of a single type of plant, the nuances and complexity of the native landscape all but disappear. The farmscape is reduced to a factory arena where soil, water, nutrients, energy, and plants are transformed into abstract means of production. It could be argued that the age of industrial monoculture has been an inevitable progression in the economic, social, and agricultural march of 20th-century Western civilization. Driven by a mechanistic worldview of Nature that developed in the 17th century, such agriculture was largely made possible by fertile soils and temporarily abundant and cheap sources of petroleum and water. When viewed strictly from the perspective of efficiency and output, its achievements are staggering: U.S. agriculture has continually generated record surpluses of food and fiber even as the farm population declined fifteen-fold since the 1940s. But as industrial agriculture continues to spread throughout the globe, a host of associated social and ecological problems have come home to roost—issues that can no longer be ignored. Environmental concerns alone include serious problems of water contamination and over-drafting, the rise in pest and disease problems resulting from overuse of agrochemicals, toxic pollution, the uncontrolled release of genetically modified plants and animals (GMOs), and cumulative impacts of agriculture and development on wildlands and wildlife. Fred Kirschenmann noted recently: "Perhaps the single greatest challenge facing us as we enter the 21st century is the need to articulate a vision for agriculture that meets the requirements of the new world in which we find ourselves."[1]

An aerial view of the Land Institute in Salina, Kansas, headquarters of a leading perennial grain research effort and the Sunshine Farm, a project to operate a farm without petroleum.

Part of that new vision, Kirschenmann suggested, requires abandoning the command-and-control management strategies that seek prescriptive or mechanistic solutions to the challenges of agriculture. Industrial problem solving may be appropriate in a factory setting (and is the discussion of many current books), but applying a factory mentality to the ever-changing dynamics of local ecosystems has failed to create long-term sustainable solutions for farming. Attempts to boost yields or to eradicate undesirable pests with "silver bullet" technologies and inputs, for example, have almost always been short-lived. While temporarily effective, they almost always generate unanticipated problems and side effects in the mid-term. The answers to these side effects are nearly always more short-term technical fixes. The way ahead, Kirschenmann and many others have argued, lies instead in understanding, designing, and managing a farm as a unique natural system. For decades U.S. farmers have been learning to use adaptive rather than control management techniques, taking advantage of inherent plant defenses, plant complexes, soil conditions, natural enemies, and other components of a farm's naturally occurring self-regulating powers and processes.[2]

Alternative frameworks to the conventional-agriculture paradigm had emerged early in the 20th century, their seeds sown far and wide by a large cast of practitioners. In his book, *Tree Crops: A Permanent Agriculture*, published in 1929, J. Russell Smith argued that in order to use the land sustainably, a farm should be adapted to the physical conditions that surround it. Put simply, "farming should fit the land." Among Smith's primary concerns was that most land, especially hilly terrain, was subject to erosion, particularly under the monocultures increasingly practiced across the United States. In order to break the catastrophic cycle of "forest-field-plow-desert" that had for centuries been the end result of bringing the agriculture of the valleys to the hills, he proposed as one practical solution a two-tiered perennial cropping system. With trees above and a pasture understory, he envisioned a flexible model that could potentially provide food for people and feed for foraging animals, and at the same time protect slopes and maintain fertility and yields. A few years later, the Dust Bowl would generate dramatic evidence of an agricultural system largely unfit for the land. Yet in the ensuing 70 years, Smith's hope for a nation of small farms that would compose a diverse patchwork of cultivated valley bottoms, hilltops, and gentle slopes, along with unplowed but productive uplands, remains marginalized. Nonetheless, his voice has been joined by many other influential works that argue for more place-adapted forms of agriculture. Among them are Sir Albert Howard's *The Soil and Health*, Paul Sears's *Deserts on the March*, Andre Voisin's *Grass Productivity*, Wes Jackson's *New Roots for Agriculture*, Miguel Altieri's *Agroecology*, P. A. Yeoman's *Water For Every Farm*, Masanobu Fukuoka's *One-Straw Revolution*, and more recently, *The Farm as Natural Habitat* by the mother and daughter team of Dana and Laura Jackson. These authors and other experts have spawned a number of terms to describe alternative approaches to agriculture, including agroecology, regenerative agriculture, grass farming, succession farming, perennial polyculture, permaculture, and ecoagriculture.

Natural systems farming, the term chosen for this chapter, is used as an umbrella category to describe agricultural approaches that are strategically integrated within their surrounding landscapes. As the term implies, this is first a systems approach, taking into account the complex and dynamic relationships that occur in the field, orchard, pasture, or grassland. Like a building designed to fit harmoniously into its environs and maximize the benefits of naturally available heating, cooling, and lighting, a natural systems farm exhibits a similar sense of belonging, taking advantage of the local ecosystem's structures and functions to the greatest extent possible.

Diversity–both agricultural and biological–becomes one of the integral foundations of natural systems farming, just as diversity is a key characteristic of successional and climax ecosystems. Polycultures (a diversity of crop types either interplanted or planted in close proximity) are typically favored over monocultures. Perennial, reduced-till, or no-till systems with high species diversity are emphasized to minimize negative impacts resulting from intensive annual cropping systems. Rather than exporting soil, overdrafting groundwater, or relying on high-input fertilizers and pest-control chemicals, natural systems practitioners work with locally occurring synergies and dynam-

ics to boost biological efficiency. Wild habitats may be incorporated to establish populations of beneficial insects and pollinators. Cover cropping and/or animals may provide on-site sources of organic matter and fertilizers. Locally adapted varieties and species can create regionally specific genetic resilience. The ideal natural systems farm attempts to live within its local means as much as possible.

According to Wes Jackson, co-founder and director of The Land Institute in Salina, Kansas, such an agricultural approach begins best by engaging in a dialogue with the local landscape. "What was here before us? What will Nature require of us here? What will Nature allow us to do here?" Each response in turn informs the next level of questioning, until a deep and thorough understanding of the local ecological mosaic is formed. How agriculture departs from that ecological mosaic, Jackson believes, should depend on the resilience of individual ecosystems, some of which are far more forgiving than others. Following this basic line of reasoning, an ideal form of land use will emerge. Tree crops might be appropriate on steep slopes, forested lands, or river bottoms; pastures or grain polycultures in grasslands where rainfall is abundant; less water-intensive systems in arid regions; marginal lands or critical habitats would be restored to wildlands.

Miguel Altieri is a Chilean native and a longtime sustainable farming researcher and professor at the University of California at Berkeley. Writing about the systems approach of the world's natural farming practitioners, Altieri explains: "The idea of agroecology is to go beyond the use of alternative practices and inputs, emphasizing complex agricultural systems in which ecological interactions and synergies between biological components provide the mechanisms for the system to sponsor their own soil fertility, productivity, and crop protection."[3] Altieri describes five practices commonly used to promote self-sustaining dynamics in agroecological farming operations:

> 1. Crop Rotations. Crop diversity that provides nutrients and breaks the life cycles of several insect pests, diseases, and weeds.
> 2. Polycultures. Complex cropping systems in which two or more crop species are planted within sufficient spatial proximity to result in competition or complementarity, thus enhancing yields.
> 3. Agroforestry Systems. An agricultural system where trees are grown together with annual crops and/or animals, resulting in enhanced complementary relations between components increasing multiple use of the agroecosystem.

4. Cover Crops. The use of pure or mixed stands of legumes or other annual plant species under fruit trees for the purpose of improving soil fertility, enhancing biological control of pests, and modifying the microclimate.

5. Animal integration. The inclusion of animals in agroecosystems aids in achieving high biomass output and optimal recycling.[4]

A further principal concept of the natural systems farm is the mimicry of local ecosystem structures in order to benefit from functional processes such as nutrient cycling, shade and wind protection, predator/prey interactions, competition, symbiosis, and successional changes.[5] To demonstrate how agriculture could be tailored to mimic its natural surroundings, during the 1980s, Jack Ewell, then a University of Florida, Gainesville, botany professor, conducted groundbreaking research in the Costa Rican rainforest. The idea was to create a jungle of domesticated crops that could serve as a model in tropical areas where nutrient loss and land exhaustion all too frequently follow clearcutting and cattle pasturing or slash-and-burn agriculture. Students substituted domesticated stand-ins for wild tropical forest species on a vine-for-vine, tree-for-tree, and shrub-for-shrub basis. Each of these plants was to be a structural analog of the native rainforest, mimicking the successional stages of rainforest regeneration after clearing: grasses and legumes first, followed by perennial shrubs and, finally, larger trees. Plantains, squash varieties, yams, and fast-growing nut, fruit, and timber trees such as Brazil nuts, peach, palm, and rosewood, were slotted into the mix of annuals, herbaceous perennials, trees, and vines that volunteer after a forest is cleared and left to regenerate. Almost always, Ewell and his colleagues found such structural substitutions yielded the same functions of sinking roots, spreading canopies, shedding leaves, and restored soil fertility as would the natural system.[6] Other on-the-ground examples of polyculture include the work of permaculture pioneers such as Bill Mollison in Australia, Tasmania, and New Zealand. In England, wheat has traditionally been drilled straight into nitrogen fixing clover, combining two of the North American prairie ecology's functional groups, a legume and a cool season grass. This experiment was recently modeled to a successful degree by writer Gene Logsdon on his Ohio pasture.[7]

As can be seen from the examples in this section, the articulation and evolution of natural systems farming can take place over a broad spectrum of standards and interpretations. In recent years, a trend toward small-scale rotational grazing systems has been on the rise in many parts of the country. Many are irrigated minimally or by rainfall only and represent an economically viable, locally adapted system for grassland areas. As southeastern Minnesota dairy farmer Art Thicke explains, since he shifted to a grass pasture dairy operation nearly two decades ago, the need for external inputs such as seed, fertilizers, and inoculations needed to sustain soil productivity and maintain animal health on his farm has nearly vanished. He and his wife, Jean, find they earn more money with a smaller herd. And perhaps most important, the farm has become a vital habitat for rapidly disappearing grassland bird species. While the cool-season grasses Thicke grows on his farm are not native, they have become locally adapted, and appear to successfully mimic much of the structure and function of the blufflands of the upper Mississippi River where he resides. The rotational pasture system allows for adequate resting periods, while the surrounding forested acreage provides benefits for wildlife, water quality, and aesthetics. On the extreme end of the natural systems spectrum, researchers at the Land Institute in Salina, Kansas, have been attempting to farm the way nature farms, by developing a grain agriculture system ideally suited to the prairie, known as "perennial polyculture." This high-concept approach is predicated upon the successful crossing of annual grains with wild perennial relatives in order eventually to produce high-yielding, "edible" prairies that can be harvested without the need for yearly tillage and planting.

Increasing the number, complexity, and interrelatedness of crop species is yet another example of natural systems farming strategies. In Virginia's Shenandoah Valley, the Salatin family has evolved a highly choreographed free-range rotational system that includes beef cattle, egg-laying hens, broiler chickens, and sheep. Each species fulfills an additional function within the natural pasture system, eliminating the need for outside sources of soil fertility and animal hygiene. Two other examples in the chapter, Kenagy Family Farms in the Willamette Valley, and Four Season Farm in Harborside, Maine, demonstrate successful commercial family farming operations thoughtfully tailored to challenging local conditions, such as seasonal flooding and cold winter temperatures.

Perhaps no occupation is more rewarding, more stressful, more demanding, or more fundamental than farming. Among the many challenges before us is the need to define and develop an agriculture that both honors the people and species involved in its practice and truly respects the land where it takes place. Natural systems farming offers an important vision for people and the land in the 21st century, one whose present examples should leave us urgently searching for more.

"If I were to draft a Latin description of *Homo sapiens*, I would begin with grass eater," says the farmer, geneticist, and natural systems agriculture pioneer Wes Jackson. "Seventy percent of humanity's calories presently derive from a single family, the grass family. Wheat is first, rice is second, and corn third, followed by a root crop, potatoes." And if you look at the top 20 crops, Jackson reasons, most of the calories that humanity depends on are directly or indirectly derived from grasses and legumes.

Historically, growing and harvesting sufficient quantities of these grasses have not posed the greatest challenge for agriculture. Instead, the real problem has been retaining the fragile erodable and sloping soils (about 85 percent of the farming landscape[8]) and the precious nutrients that disappear as a result of continuous tillage, lack of rotation and recovery, and a lengthy list of other unsustainable practices. Throughout our 10,000-year pursuit of the human granary, explains Jackson, agriculture's pull has been toward the monoculture of high-yielding annuals. Nature, in contrast, favors the polyculture of perennials. In order to continually boost the output of grain monocultures, 20th-century industrial agriculture resorted to ever-increasing subsidies of fossil fuels and mined materials; depleted ancient groundwater reservoirs; developed high-yielding, chemically-dependent hybrids; and finally, turned to genetically modified varieties to withstand ever-intensifying doses of toxic sprays. By the start of the 21st-century, the American corn crop topped 140 bushels per acre, up from 100 in 1980, and 30 in 1930. "Unfortunately, nothing fails like success," Jackson quips, "and corporations fail to acknowledge the extremely high prices we are paying for the subsidization of industrial monoculture."

Perennial Polyculture: High Concept Agriculture

Jackson is America's poet of the prairie, a recipient of both the MacArthur Fellowship and the Right Livelihood Award, and the director of the Land Institute, a research farm located in Salina, Kansas. In 1976, he left a tenured position at California State University at Sacramento and moved his family back to his boyhood state of Kansas to found an alternative school with his then-wife, Dana. The school evolved into a nonprofit research organization called the Land Institute, grew from 28 to 580 acres, and ultimately focused on a unique scientific mission–to explore whether the opposing forces of annual monocultures and perennial polycultures can be reconciled. The idea was high concept, really: a botanical fusion that would create a high-yielding, grain-producing agriculture that reflected the many functional characteristics of the surrounding native prairie ecosystem. The holy grail would be "perennial polyculture," a mix of edible grains grown in complementary arrangements that could produce a low-input, no-till, and low-maintenance food supply, with an average self-sustaining yield of 1,800 pounds per acre (the equivalent of the 1930s output of 30 bushels of wheat).

The Land Institute lies at almost the exact center of the Lower 48, at the intersection of the tallgrass and mid-grass prairies. This is grain and livestock country, part of the Great Plow-up, a sky-filled landscape shaped by fierce northern winter winds and sometimes violent summer storms, receiving nearly 30 inches of annual rainfall. Studying the remnants of never-plowed prairie in this area for clues on how to design a locally adapted farming system, researchers discovered a number of salient features. Prairie polycultures are endowed with a tremendous diversity of four functional plant groups: warm- and cool-season grasses, legumes, and sunflowers. Throughout the year, these complementary plant groupings provide fertilizers and nutrients; weed control; shade, wind, and rain protection; and resistance to pests and diseases. The prairie's synergistic plant groups actually generate topsoil (quite the opposite of a century and a half under the hegemony of the plow). "Before we expend any more of our precious topsoil, we should consider a model for the future of the 'breadbasket' that mitigates soil erosion while providing edible seeds," said the former Land Institute researcher John Piper in *Gardening for the Future of the Earth*. "The few remnants of intact prairie serve as prime examples of inherently sustainable biotic communities in which complex webs of interdependent plants, animals, and microbes garner, retain, and efficiently recycle critical nutrients."[9]

In order to mimic the polycultures they were after–ones that could be nearly self-fertilizing and that could reseed themselves without plowing–Land Institute researchers worked on a variety of levels. They began planting plots consisting of representatives from three of the prairie's four functional groups: corn, sorghum, soybeans, and sunflowers.

No cool-season grass was represented so that the seeds could be sown all at once, harvested together, then sorted with a seed cleaner. "I call it the first annual domestic prairie," says Jackson. "The driving concept is that if we mimic the structure of the prairie, then we can be granted its ecologically sustainable function." While planting in polyculture requires two additional steps over a monoculture during the seed cleaning process, it did reveal some advantages in terms of both pest protection and nutrient cycling. (More "nuanced" questions about the approach are ongoing.)

The task of developing perennial varieties from domestic annuals, however, has been and continues to be the work of decades, perhaps generations, and some question whether it will ever be possible to coax a high-yielding grain into a perennial metabolism. The research involves identifying and growing out native high-yielding seed-producing varieties—such as Eastern gama grass, Maximilian sunflower, or Illinois bundle flower—or producing crosses between domesticated annual grains and their wild perennial relatives. Such crossings have paired grain sorghum and Johnson grass, wheat and intermediate wheatgrass, rye and *Secale montanum* (perennial wild rye).[10] According to Jackson, all the major crops are in the process of being perennialized, including oats, barley, sunflower, and chick pea in addition to sorghum, wheat, and rye. Plant breeding work takes place throughout the winter, starting in the laboratory and then proceeding to both refrigerated and greenhouse conditions. Modern laboratory techniques such as embryo rescue (not related to transgenic modification) permit more advanced breeding than was possible just ten years ago, supplemented by manual field pollination. Each summer, hundreds of new annual-wild perennial crosses are grown out in the field for selection.

Throughout its quarter-century quest for perennial polyculture, the Land Institute has consistently focused on four fundamental ecological questions: (1) Can perennialism and increased seed yield go together? (2) Can a polyculture outyield a monoculture? (3) Can we manage insects, pathogens, and weeds? (4) Can the system sponsor its own nitrogen and provide the same bountiful yields? The first three challenges, according to Jackson, support the development of perennial polycultures as a viable agroecological system. "We are satisfied that perennialism and increased seed yield can go together at no cost to the plant. The subsidization of nitrogen and phosphorous, however—a critical concern in industrial monocultures—has not been nailed down. I'm afraid that we will have to have the subsidy of nitrogen from the extractive economy," says Jackson. "And I'm not talking about backyard gardening. There are small scale systems where you can supply the nitrogen. I'm talking about 400 million acres of till-ag acreage alone."

Running the Farm on Sunshine

Marty Bender, a longtime Land Institute researcher, has spearheaded a ten-year project to determine the potentials and shortcomings of running a farm exclusively on nonpollutive, renewable energy. The Sunshine Farm project began in 1995 on 220 acres: 60 tillable acres of non-erodable bottomland and 160 acres of grassland pasture. The intent was to conduct a rigorous audit of the true ecological costs of agriculture based on the extractive economy—detailing the energy, materials, and labor needed to produce crops. A quarter of the tillable acreage went to growing soybeans and sunflowers to provide the biodiesel fuel for a tractor; an additional 25 percent was required to supply nitrogen for fertilizers in the form of compost and green manure. Longhorn cattle ("as close to wild as you can get," insists Jackson) and poultry were raised for meat and eggs. Five years into the study, the results were sobering, with the pressing demands for fertilizers being a consistent Achilles heel. In a food system where 70 percent of our grain calories go into what Jackson calls the United States cow and pig welfare program, however, he believes there is some definite room for maneuvering. "Using existing farmland to produce biofuels, fertilizers, and food–rather than feed–could shake off some of our dependence on synthetic inputs," he says. "It doesn't mean that we can't continue to eat chicken, beef, and pork, though perhaps not to the same dietary excesses."

At any time in a conversation, Jackson can launch into a historical trajectory, one that can whirl through U.S. history, the ten-millennia saga of agriculture, or the geologic stages of the earth's development. Just under six feet tall, with blue eyes, Jackson waves his large hands in circular motions as he takes such temporal flights. It becomes clear that he is interested in the future of farming, the future of the soil, the future of human culture. He declares how lucky we Americans are to be the beneficiaries of such soil-producing events as the uplift of the Sierras, the Coast Range, the Rockies, and the Appalachians, and the Pleistocene glaciation that created the Great Plains. "Soil should be viewed and respected as a nonrenewable resource like petroleum. And we can do a lot better by watching the way that nature hangs on to those nutrients, by mimicking those systems to the best of our abilities."

"In the 1960s," Jackson continues, "University of California at Berkeley ecologist Dick Luten described the European settlement of America as a poor people who came to a seemingly empty land that was rich. We built our cultural, economic, educational, and political institutions around that reality, and now we've become rich people, in an increasingly poor land that's filling up." To meet the challenges of sustainable agriculture we must expand our critique far beyond the issues of organic perennial polyculture, or energy, says Jackson. "We have to figure out how to shake ourselves from this extractive economy, how to enliven community life, how to reduce our addiction to carbon emissions. Ultimately, we have to develop deep affection for places and become defenders of those places."

Matfield Green

Some years ago, I drove south and east from the Land Institute, to Chase County, a place made famous by William Least-heat Moon's book *PrairyErth*. We passed slowly pumping oil wells and road signs that proudly proclaimed that each Kansas farmer feeds 90 people. There weren't many cars on the road, not many communities, not much at all at first glance but Flint Hills prairie studded with isolated pockets of cottonwoods and that expansive Kansas sky. Our final destination was the nearly deserted town of Matfield Green, population 50, a community victimized by the "Get Big or Get Out" family-farm eradication program that began in the 1960s. A few years before, Jackson had developed a keen interest in the isolated rural town because of its potential for reviving the agrarian movement. Since the early 1990s, he had been buying properties in this depressed area: ramshackle houses for $1,000 or less, the rock-solid bank building, the abandoned public school overtaken by pigeons. At one point, things had unraveled so thoroughly that some Matfield Green residents just walked away from their houses, leaving behind appliances and possessions as a bitter testament to the rural exodus. Jackson and Land Institute interns spent countless hours there, repairing roofs and fortifying foundations, working with locals, trying to be good listeners rather than providers of heady answers. "There is a tremendous value in being in a rural place that is in decline, among people who are facing moving themselves," says Jackson. The renovated one-story brick school building has become the site for meetings, conferences, and other gatherings primarily geared toward increasing ecological literacy. It's symbolically in keeping with what the Land Institute feels is the next urgent frontier in the move toward sustainable agriculture—the generation now in elementary school, high school, and college.

The Path Ahead

When it comes to predicting the rise of perennial polyculture and, perhaps more broadly, natural systems farming, Jackson believes we are merely at the beginning. Nearly 25 years into the great experiment, he predicts at least two more decades of concerted research will be needed to achieve the lofty goals he is looking for. Sending out an untested and unproven product would only, in the long-term, cause serious damage to an already hard-fought effort. "We are where the Wright brothers were at Kitty Hawk," he is prone to say. "I don't want to trivialize agriculture by comparing it to human flight, for I really believe that our results to date and their implications are more profound for human civilization than the results the Wright brothers achieved on December 17, 1903."[11]

Perhaps, as was suggested in Janine Benyus's 1997 book, *Biomimicry: Innovation Inspired by Nature*, one of the first applications for perennial polyculture could be on Conservation Reserve Program lands. This could offer farmers income in addition to preserving soils. Domestic prairies could be hayed, harvested for human consumption, or grazed with livestock. Income could be generated and the soil healed while growing food. In that same book, John Piper suggests that perennial polyculture's most likely applications would be on the erodable and sloping soils that constitute so much of the agricultural landscape.[12] If this seems fanciful, one only has to look at the explosive growth in present-day farming systems such as organics and Biodynamics, which had their origins in the 1920s and 1930s, to understand the incubation periods of such ideas.

If one were to reproduce the Land Institute's efforts elsewhere, Jackson recommends starting with place-specific discussions. "We always start with some simple questions," says Jackson. "What was here? What will Nature require of us here? What will Nature allow us to do here? Then we find the crop analogs according to those very localized conditions." Some areas are more forgiving than others, he explains, such as the Nile Valley, where soils will be built as long as mountains and steamy jungles exist and perhaps little mimicry is necessary. In contrast, the steep southwestern slope of the Colorado Plateau requires that the vegetative structure remain or ecological capital will quickly vanish. Where agriculture departs from the native landscape, then, depends upon the resilience of the ecological mosaic. He describes this as a "Nature's Wisdom Approach," as opposed to the "Smart Resource Management Approach," which assumes technology can always be relied on to trump the limitations of ecological laws.

FARMING IN LEOPOLD'S FOOTSTEPS

Of all the places on the western North Dakota farm where Fred Kirschenmann spent his boyhood and to which he returned after his father retired, his favorite is a 400-acre stretch of native mixed-grass prairie–gentle hills that slope into two large wetland basins. At dusk in late August, formations of white pelicans and Canada geese occasionally glide over the large mirrorlike ponds. Leopard frogs as fat as chicken eggs leap over our feet as we walk to a grassy knoll for the vista. An evening wind is traveling audibly through the prairie grass, and in the distance, a neighbor's vast sunflower field glows faintly golden. Cattle graze placidly in a lowland section of the prairie. And Kirschenmann, an organic farmer, philosopher, and educator, talks about one of the most profound influences on his life, Aldo Leopold.

"I first read *A Sand County Almanac* when I was a junior in college in 1955 and was absolutely blown away by it," says Kirschenmann, a tall man, now in his sixties, with a strong angular frame shaped by decades of farm labor; he wears a baseball cap, jeans, a long-sleeved T-shirt, and thick eyeglasses. Not coincidentally, when not farming, Kirschenmann serves as the executive director of the Leopold Center for Sustainable Agriculture in Ames, Iowa, nine hours away, a post he only recently accepted. "At the core of Leopold's understanding was that all of the earth is a community. He referred to it as 'the biotic community,' and he felt that one of the major challenges facing us *Homo sapiens* was to find our place in the community rather than being controllers of the land.

"Clearly for Leopold this meant that we are simply members of this land community, and consequently, we need to have an ethical relationship with all the other creatures," continues Kirschenmann, who earned a doctorate in religion and philosophy at the University of Chicago. His voice is low and nasal, his dialog clear and fluid. "Microorganisms, vertebrates, plants, humans, all form an ecological whole. Each takes something from and gives something to the community, and that's what provides its ecological balance. And then he had this unique notion that 'the tame and the wild' are separated only in the imperfections of the human mind. So he understood that wildness and the domesticated work of humans in agriculture or other activities were all part of the same whole. You couldn't separate them. You couldn't have wilderness over there, and agriculture over here. We need

to figure out how to practice agriculture and sustain wilderness together in the same ecological neighborhood. I think we're just beginning to be able to come to terms with the depths, the profoundness, and the opportunity of that concept."

Some argue that certain contemporary interpretations of Leopold's ethic give too large a place to humanity when, in fact, the presence of wilderness untouched by man is the only hope for many shy, sensitive, and wide-ranging species. But certainly his advocacy of a much deeper and greater harmony between the wild and the domestic is sorely needed. That sense of membership in, rather than control of, the biotic community is apparent throughout the contours of Kirschenmann Family Farms. Despite encompassing more than 3,500 acres in two different locations, the fields are imbued with a gardener's touch. A thousand of those acres are in never-plowed though frequently grazed prairie. A committed organic practitioner for more than a quarter century, Kirschenmann has developed an intricate annual rotational system based upon ten cash crops and two soil-reviving legumes. Up to 500 acres of organic wheat are grown in rotation with rye, buckwheat, sunflowers, millet, flax, soybeans, lentils, barley, and oats. Alfalfa provides fodder for his animals and yellow-blossom sweet clover is plowed under as a green manure. The cash crops are combinations of cool- and dry-season, grassy and broad-leafed, shallow- and deep-rooted plants. Alternating the cash and cover crops enables him to keep weeds at manageable levels and to maintain fertility. Nitrogen is supplied through the rotations of cover crops and applications of on-farm composted livestock manure. Plantings of heavy feeders such as wheat after green manure cover crops, and light feeders like buckwheat later in the planting schedule help to efficiently meet and manage fertility requirements. As a result of these carefully evolved biological practices, no off-farm inputs have been applied to the fields since 1978.

Kirschenmann walks us to a field of millet, a sea of golden-stemmed grains dancing in the liquid light of a late summer sunset. The field is 34 acres in size and bordered on the uphill side by a windbreak of tall trees. Like this millet plot, most of the fields on the farm are 50 acres or smaller, separated by native habitat. "The leguminous plants provide excellent cover for nesting birds early in spring," Kirschenmann explains.

"Winter rye is usually up six to eight inches high by the third week in April and makes wonderful habitat." His cropping patterns are arranged so that some habitat is available on some part of the farm at all times.

"Clearly every farmer knows that wildlife can be damaging to your farm," he says. "But on balance, the wildlife also eat enormous amounts of insects. So the question is, how do we manage the system to not only provide a place for wildlife, but to create a habitat so that they're here to do those other services for us? Red-winged blackbirds love sunflowers as any farmer knows. So there's a huge campaign to get rid of the blackbirds. But my question is, if we get rid of the blackbirds what else are we getting rid of?"

To make time before the light disappears, we pile into his 25-year-old dust-coated pickup, and Kirschenmann continues his discourse. Blackbirds really only damage sunflowers about three weeks out of the year, he says, and they eat enormous quantities of grubs and other insects. Blackbirds are habitual creatures, using the same flyways all the time. Ideally, they want proximity to a slough with a few cattails, maybe some trees, and sunflowers. All day long they fly back and forth, drinking water, roosting in the trees, eating some sunflowers, roosting again, drinking more water. "So we try to not plant sunflow-

ers in their flyway or roosting areas, and there is never a blackbird in those fields. And in those fields where we know there'll be blackbirds, we try to provide an alternative source of food–and fire a shotgun, harass them, modify their behavior a little bit, so we can all enjoy this together. That's the objective, I think." He estimates crop losses from blackbirds as never greater than 5 percent, an acceptable level considering the benefits provided during the rest of the year.

Kirschenmann also raises over 100 brood cows that graze rotationally in the pastures around the farm. The cattle operation is managed with a sensitivity toward local predators, which have been persecuted in the area for decades. "The farmers and ranchers around here declared war on the coyotes in the 1920s and 1930s," he remembers, "and when I was a kid you rarely saw one. But the foxes were prolific. In fact, there was a population explosion of foxes, because the farmers never realized that coyotes and foxes were natural enemies. There was a natural limiting factor to their populations. Also coyotes feed on flickertail gophers, and once the coyotes were gone, there was a proliferation of gophers. Then the farmers had to poison the gophers. I started looking at that and saying, this does not make sense." Kirschenmann maintains a herd he describes as "just a little bit on the wild side," an Angus-based herd crossed with French Tarrentaise. This crossbreed, he

reports, exhibits excellent mothering instincts; the cows will circle around and aggressively defend a calf until it can survive on its own. At any given time there are a half dozen coyotes on the farm, and he is unaware of any calf losses to predators.

Kirschenmann's mastery of biological farming methods is matched by his understanding of agricultural economics. The difficulty of organic farming, he insists, lies not in the growing of crops, but in successful marketing and running an operation free of debt. Since 1980, his farm has not borrowed any operating capital and has slowly built an international clientele for organic grains. Meanwhile, the economics of conventional wheat farming at the close of the century turned brutal, leaving a trail of below-cost world commodity prices, consolidations, foreclosures, even suicides. Of the 63 million acres of wheat grown in the United States, less than 1 percent is organic, and with the demand for organic and nongenetically modified (GMO-free) products rising briskly throughout the world, for the moment, Kirschenmann Family Farms is thriving.

Despite the impressive strides organic farmers have made over the past three decades, however, Kirschenmann has been struck by the profound realization that isolated organic farms, even large ones like his, are not, on their own, sufficient to stem the biodiversity crisis. "The idea that organic farms are enclaves of purity–that everything within their boundaries is God-like and everything that lies outside is evil–is a patch-ecology perspective that must be reconsidered." Chemical and genetic drift are just two examples of why organic farms, no matter how innovatively managed, can't be walled off from the larger landscape. Eventually, he believes, entire regions or landscapes rather than individual farms could be certified as organic or even "wild." In an unpublished paper that he co-authored with Eugene, Oregon-based organic certifier David Gould titled, "Tame and Wild: Organic Agriculture and Wilderness," Kirschenmann posits:

> Organic agriculture must begin to reinvent itself in terms of landscape ecologies. If we are to be successful as organic farmers, long term, we cannot ignore the intricate and complex ecological processes of nature which sustain the whole local ecosystems of which our farms are a part. At the same time, we can begin to similarly restore wild areas and sustainably harvest organic products from them.

A few years ago, in an effort to deepen their commitment to regionally sustainable agriculture, Kirschenmann and his wife Carolyn Raffensperger, decided to try to cultivate

The Organic Grainary

Fred Kirschenmann grew up on this 4,000-acre North Dakota farm and returned after a career in academia. For the past 30 years, his sophisticated crop rotation system allows him to produce up to a dozen grains, oilseed crops, legumes and livestock without synthetic fertilizers, herbicides, or pesticides. His herd, crossed with French Tarrentaise cattle, exhibit protective instincts against predators. The farm includes 1,000-acre never plowed but frequently grazed prairie, now protected through a perpetual conservation easement.

a truly local North Dakota diet. While they had always eaten their own pasture-fed beef, they endeavored to find year-round food sources from within their own farm or their neighbors' farms. They began by grinding their own wheat flour and serving home-grown barley rather than rice. Their very own biodynamic wheat was available in dried pasta products milled and distributed by Eden Foods. In a half-acre garden, Raffensperger, an author, activist, and director of the Science and Environmental Health Network, raised potatoes, tomatoes, carrots, green vegetables, melons, apples, and other produce eaten either fresh or put up for winter consumption. A neighboring farmer provided vegetable seedlings from varieties particularly adapted to the Prairie Pothole climate, making it easier and more enjoyable to attain near self-sufficiency. Their grand foray into North Dakota cuisine changed course, however, when Kirschenmann took the job at the Leopold Center for Sustainable Agriculture and they moved to Ames, Iowa, for the better part of the year. The couple quickly adapted a plan for community-oriented consumption by joining a local Community Supported Agriculture (CSA) farm that provided weekly deliveries of just-picked produce.

On this August day we don't have the pleasure of eating from Raffensperger's large organic garden. We stop instead at a picnic dinner prepared by a neighbor for a group of agriculture students visiting from the University of Minnesota who are also at the farm that afternoon. Kirschenmann talks candidly to the students about the future of agriculture, including many troubling signs. Decades of applying synthetic fertilizers to farm fields are having the cumulative effect of creating eutrophicated dead zones in aquatic areas throughout the planet, a phenomenon predicted to worsen unless immediately addressed. And most of the world's "biodiversity hot spots," he hastens to add, are threatened by poor and developing human populations that may be forced by political and social forces to convert wilderness to agriculture. "The more our agricultural regions become denuded of their wildlife, the more the farmers will recognize the value of it," Kirschenmann explains. "The pollinators may be the species that turn the tide. Pollinators are absolutely critical to agriculture. Once farmers realize that they are going to have to create habitat to attract the pollinators, change is going to happen. Then they'll have a basis for creating a different kind of consciousness." That change of consciousness between the tame and wild, Kirschenmann believes, is just beginning to appear in field boundaries and places between cultivated areas. The crucial research, he says, is at a stage comparable to where we were when the transition from horses to tractors began. And not a moment too soon.

THE DAIRYMAN'S DIVERSITY

The gravel lane to Enchanted Meadows, in southeastern Minnesota, traverses a ridge just a few miles from the Mississippi River, amid steep pastures, contoured corn fields, fallow Conservation Reserve Program (CRP) plots, and wooded pockets. Almost as soon as we pass the farm's sign, several meadowlarks flush out of the thick, deep grass, their yellow breasts flashing as they tilt toward us. According to our guide, Tex Hawkins, a U.S. Fish and Wildlife Service biologist based at the Upper Mississippi River National Wildlife and Fish Refuge headquarters in nearby Winona, grassland species such as the meadowlark, bobolink, vesper sparrow, and dickcissel have severely declined in recent years throughout the Midwest. With falling milk prices, small grass-pasture dairies are being plowed for subsidized-commodity crops. And rested CRP land is often more suitable for shrub-loving birds, such as quail and pheasant. Farmers like Art and Jean Thicke (pronounced tick-ee) of Enchanted Meadows, who employ "management-intensive" rotational grazing and periodically rest their pastures to provide grassland habitat, are helping to restore a semblance of pre-settlement or perhaps "post-industrial" conditions to the area. In fact, Hawkins tells me, the Thickes tend to refer to their management style as "laid back" rather than intensive, because it involves a good deal of observation, reflection, and adaptive experimentation.

A drizzle descends as we begin our tour of the ridgetop farm. We pass a newly built hay barn (made primarily from the timbers recycled from the original farm house) and walk through the milking barn, where Jean takes a break from feeding cows on this milking shift to greet us. She directs us down a track that separates sloping pastures where her husband is working. Every available fence post along the track has a bluebird house mounted on it. For the second time that day, Art Thicke has moved his cows into a different 2-acre paddock, one of 42 such grazing units in 90 acres of the farm's 140 total acres of open space.

Thicke immediately launches into an animated explanation of his grazing methods. "A lot of people think that cattle are bad for the land," he says, with a decided Midwestern lilt. "And just outside this farm you might see places where people are letting their cattle grub it to the ground, and that gives everybody a bad rap. But I haven't purchased any chemical fertilizers for over 25 years, and this farm is really productive. I haven't plowed any of these pastures for 15 years, and I don't plan on ever plowing again. Also during that

period we've reduced our erosion to zero." By way of example, he points to a pond in a basin some 50 yards below where we are standing. "In a four-inch rain last year that pond only rose four inches," he claims. "There is so much life in these pastures that the water infiltration is just incredible. We need more grass farms in this region to keep the water on the land rather than having it wash down the river taking our soil along with it."

Grazing, especially of the intensive rotational variety, says Thicke, is an appropriate agricultural system for this bluffland country along the northern Mississippi River. The key to success, he says, is increasing vegetative diversity through cycles of rest and activity. He walks us through calf-high pastures almost thick enough to trip in, pointing out the various cool-season grasses, alfalfa, and clovers that he believes benefit both cattle and wildlife, particularly threatened grassland bird species. Over his two decades in the business, he and Jean have developed a preference for smaller Ayrshire cattle, which are hardier, more lightweight and long-lived, and are better grazers than the more common Holsteins. He likes to keep his pasture grass long, moving cattle twice per day. "The most important thing is a rest period. Grasses need adequate rest. Longer grasses help many more birds to fledge, as opposed to pastures that have been continually grazed extremely short."

Enchanted Meadows offers a drastic contrast to the corn and soybean rotations that dominate Midwestern row crop farming and agribusiness. "Corn and soybeans are the dueling banjos of conventional agriculture that amount to little more than subsidized erosion," says Thicke, laughing at his own critique. "When you get a lot of diversity, it's like a symphony. Every time you add another species, it gets fuller and fuller. I don't want to just hear the banjos, I want to hear everything. I think the grass feels happier if the birds are singing and there are a few thistles rather than if you have a guy out there chopping it. But the reason I want a lot of diversity is really because it's a lot healthier for the animals. Our cows are tremendously healthy. We've got 90 cows, it's October 9th, and we haven't spent one penny on a veterinary bill this year."

It's obvious that Thicke could talk all day about the rotational grazing system he has developed for Enchanted Meadows. He demonstrates how he spaces bales evenly in win-

Perennial Pastures

The expansion of grass-farmed dairy and cattle operations like Enchanted Meadows could dramatically help to reduce agriculture's impacts on the Midwestern landscape. Perennial grass systems have proven to be profitable and to halt erosion and reduce the need for vast amounts of farm chemicals and animal inoculations.

Art Thicke (left) and biologist Tex Hawkins (wearing cap) talk about the importance of grass pasture systems to declining species such as Western meadowlarks, vesper sparrows, and bobolinks, whose populations have been decimated in the Midwest.

ter pastures, intentionally directing how the cows will graze the paddock, ultimately managing for increasing productivity. "Wherever you position the hay bales you get the nutrients," he says. "The key is learning to listen to the land. The land tells you what it needs. When pastures get away from me, I'll lengthen the rotations, and sometimes cut and bale extra forage. We graze 90 acres with 90 cows 200 days per year, which in this region is quite astounding. In the first part of April, our farm just goes crazy. And because of the resting and long rotations, we usually have a lot more forage late into the fall.

"I find high production doesn't necessarily mean high profit. Some people are spending so much time and money to eke out every last drop of milk," says Thicke. "We found that with a lower level of milk production our cows are healthier and we're doing better financially and have a better lifestyle. You can't just look at production. You have to look at the whole picture. If you have healthier cattle and aren't constantly reseeding or fertilizing your land, then you can keep your operation financially fit and you don't need that big production. I had a cow that just lived 17 years. I just sold 12 calves and that helps the operation as well."

The rain turns to a steady downpour. Hawkins identifies a pileated woodpecker and the conversation turns to birding. "We once had a fall flock of 65 bobolinks," reports Thicke.

"In summer, we have eastern kingbirds, savanna and vesper sparrows, tree swallows, and meadowlarks. Meadow birds don't like corn and soybean fields. And alfalfa haying is less forgiving than grazing because early season mowing destroys nests. On the other hand, an area being rested attracts meadow birds, and if successful, they can even raise a brood of fledglings in the lush grass." As Thicke talks, Hawkins sights a flock of wild turkeys.

"Nature's always trying to go to biodiversity, why fight it? Hey, I got some thistles, they'll be good for the gold finches, not a big concern. If you have something taking your farm over, you have to change your management. Faster rotations, shorter rests. Different species will be dominant. How you treat it is what you get," Thicke concludes.

I ask them, "What does the phrase 'farming with the wild' conjure in your minds?" Hawkins responds first. "I think that Art is farming in partnership with the wild, because he looks to the wild for reinforcement about whether what he is doing is right or wrong. In turn, the wild responds to his adaptive approach." Thicke's answer is simpler. "If you've got good energy on your place then your product will have good energy. I'm pretty New Agey but you probably don't want to put that in your book," and he laughs like someone content with being exactly where he wants to be and doing exactly what he has chosen to do.

UNCONVENTIONAL CONVENTIONAL

On a chilly June morning, Pete Kenagy is inspecting a plot of native fescue he hopes will someday germinate into a profitable product for a niche market in habitat restoration. The bunch grasses are now blond, with a few seed-loaded stems tied into shocks with color-coded ribbons. In cooperation with a local agency, he has been producing a supply of seed for restoration crops such as native yarrow, goldenrod, and blue wild rye. Admittedly the day that native plants support Kenagy Family Farms may still be many years away, though Pete could easily talk all morning about the complex machinery needed to clean and sort source-identified seeds of all different sizes. He leads our small group—Oregon State University farm extension advisor Dan McGrath, visiting agroecologist Steve Wratten from New Zealand, and local plant breeder Frank Morton—on a morning tour. Kenagy is a fourth-generation farmer in Oregon's Willamette Valley who has developed innovative methods for growing canning corn, green beans, grains, grass-seed crops, buckwheat, and most recently, native plant seed. "With 325 tillable acres," says Kenagy, "I'm classified as a small big farmer."

Looking down on a section of the farm from a high vantage, we see plots of buckwheat, corn, barley, blue wild rye, and green beans just starting to emerge from the tawny stubble of last winter's cover crops. Dividing some of the fields are hedgerows of spirea and ceonothus, punctuated with tall French pussy willows, designed by Dan McGrath. According to McGrath, these hedgerows are among the first planted in a commercial row-crop operation in the Valley in 100 years. Forested riparian buffers create what appear to be fairly wild edges around and the entire perimeter of Kenagy Family Farms. These multi-story riparian woodlots, once cleared for row crops, have been replanted with trees and shrubs some 40 to 70 yards wide between the field edge and the water. Skirting the nearly 500-acre property are the Willamette River and a network of unnamed sloughs that frequently submerge the low-lying fields as part of the annual winter flood plain.

The integration of riparian corridors and hedgerows in combination with a unique farming approach is why McGrath recommended our visit. "Pete Kenagy is an unconventional conventional grower," says McGrath, who has worked with Willamette Valley farmers for 20 years. "You are standing in the most brilliant field in the Willamette Valley, because this is more than just row crop farming, it's a rotation system designed and planted for the specific conditions of this area."

As we descend to the lower field level Kenagy explains some of the general goals of his farming system. "I really have three primary goals," he says. "First is the need to save time, energy, and resources by reducing tractor usage as much as possible. Second is the maintenance of soil quality by limiting tillage to an absolute minimum without sacrificing yields. We also want to protect the critical functions of the floodplain as they relate to the surrounding lands." The Kenagys were among the first in the Valley to experiment with reduced tillage approaches, and over the last 20 years they have been fine tuning no-till, reduced-till, and strip-till techniques to achieve their energy and soil quality optimization goals for various crops and field conditions on their farm. "How do you mimic a natural system with annual cropping?" Kenagy asks rhetorically, then answers his own question. "There is no tillage in a natural system. In a natural system all the organic matter falls and gets worked into the soil. This is my attempt."

In a newly planted field of sweet corn, Kenagy and McGrath explain the method. Between the rows of corn seedlings, now green and six inches tall, are mats of mulching stubble from last season's cover crop. The rotation had begun a year before, with a field of Piper green beans, planted in summer. By early fall the bean crop was harvested, followed by drilling a Sudan grass cover crop directly into the bean stubble without tilling the soil. Winter frost killed that grass, tying up leftover nutrients in the soil and providing additional forage for wildlife. In the spring, the corn was tilled into narrow strips after the field dried sufficiently. Narrow strips (six inches wide) were tilled into the grass stubble and supplemented with a band of carbon-fertilizer and treated with a residual herbicide into which the seed was planted. The conversation immediately shifts to the reliance on herbicides in the reduced tillage system. "If you want to farm ecologically on any scale," says McGrath, who trained with the Biointensive gardening guru Alan Chadwick at University of California, Santa Cruz in the 1970s, "you need lots of labor just at the time when you're most busy. Faced with using biologically rational technologies, such as glyphosate, and not doing anything at all, which makes more sense?"

Kenagy addresses the issue from a seed farmer's point of view. "A weed that goes to seed continues to create problems," he says, admitting that he suppresses weeds with what he describes as a religious zeal. "For one application of herbicides I would have had to till five to six times to get the same amount of weed control," he says. "From my observation and experience, I feel that this is more beneficial than exposing the soil and damaging its structure through extensive tillage."

From the field we walk to the riparian buffer alongside the slough, which in certain places is nearly 200 feet from field edge to the water. Rather than annual-cropping this often wet area for low return, Kenagy instead planted a diverse canopy that increases in height as it approaches the slough's edge. In the buffer closest to the field edge is a thicket of fruit and nut trees mainly for family consumption but also intermixed with medicinal shrubs. Behind it run taller rows of black walnut trees for lumber (an 80-year crop) with an understory of perennial blue wild rye, then stair-stepping higher still to poplar for pallet stock (7- to 20-year harvest), and finally to sizable cottonwoods near the slough. "Maintaining wild edges takes so much time," Kenagy says, "but it wouldn't have been practical to eliminate the riparian buffer, and we like the way it looks."

McGrath is determined that I appreciate the thought and effort that have gone into the design of the farm. "Out in the fields you have an herbaceous cover, followed by a wild woody area, a secondary wood crop, and then one of the finest riparian edges in the Willamette Valley zipped into a reduced-till system—wow! For the time being and scale this is the best we can come up with," says McGrath. "This is a brilliant farming system because it's very evolved and also very beautiful, and that's a good sign."

Low-till Systems Approach

Father and son Cliff and Pete Kenagy's farming practices are adapted to the riparian systems that border their 500-acre Willamette Valley property. Fields are separated by hedgerows and crops grown with low-till methods designed to limit soil disturbance. Riparian borders (between 40 and 70 yards wide) contain numerous tree layers and perennial native cover crops. They also produce seed for local restoration projects.

FARMING BELOW ZERO

Daylight savings time is over and the afternoon light is abbreviated by the time I reach the rocky coves of Cape Rosier. Fishing boats and dinghies bobbing along the central Maine coastline are barely discernable in the twilight. Autumn leaves rush the windshield like giant snowflakes. When I arrive at Four Season Farm, Eliot Coleman and Barbara Damrosch's complex of greenhouses–my tell-tale marker and the reason for my visit–is already swathed in blackness. A note on the living room table directs me toward a path into the woods that I navigate in dim light, curving around to a small shingled house at the edge of a pond. The building is finely constructed, a hybrid of Zen and Scandinavian design. Candles and oil lamps illuminate an enclosed changing area. I peer through the small square window into an amber haze, knock once, then crack the door. I grab a towel and take a seat in the middle of the sauna's top bench, flanked by three other bathers. This visit took place in 1997 and I happen to arrive on the night when it's their turn to host a community sauna. Saunas, I am told, have been a weekly custom here in this area for quite some time. The heat is thick and cedary, and we dive into conversation, about my journey, the weather, the day's farm work. Soon I am oiled with my own sweat and join the others in plunging breathlessly into the pond outside. In hindsight, the experience seems an appropriate introduction into a farm operation predicated on acclimating to subzero temperatures. After a half hour in the wood-fired room, I am ready for rehydration.

Eliot Coleman and Barbara Damrosch are two of American horticulture's most valued practitioners. Both are accomplished writers who have made careers working the soil. Coleman has written two classics, *The New Organic Grower* and *The Four Season Harvest;* Damrosch's *Theme Gardens* and *The Garden Primer* are ever-reliable gardening resources. It's not to talk about books that I've made this pilgrimage, however, but to see their commercial-scale, year-round farming operation. Here at 44 degrees North latitude, they have embarked on a unique agriculture enterprise–growing baby salad greens and root vegetables throughout the Maine coast's formidable winters. But there's something more impressive: they do it in unheated greenhouses, or as Coleman describes, "inexpensive protected micro-climates." As we sit down to bowls of steaming corn chowder, he says, "I'd like to create a new name for what we're doing. Garden farming," he suggests, "or simply the American farm dream."

Barbara emphasizes that what they are doing should not be confused with hobby farming. "People get the impression that because we've written books, that's how we make our living," she says. "But that's not true. We are working very hard to show people that this is a way you can make an honest living and not harm the land."

Throughout our conversations, Coleman often refers to farming as a game, a game that for over a decade has required outcompeting faraway sources of organic produce by emphasizing superior quality and just-picked freshness. It soon becomes obvious that he is as much a sportsman as he is a farmer who likes to challenge what is considered impossible, such as defying Cape Rosier's hibernal temperature deficits. He started farming 30 years ago when he befriended the back-to-the-land legends Scott and Helen Nearing and eventually purchased this farm from them. While he had been experimenting for decades with hothouses, he began his new operation in earnest in the mid-1990s. "It's the fact that we don't have to heat these greenhouses that is most appealing," he says, adding with characteristic New England pragmatism, "and also because we can do it so darn cheaply–$2.50 per square foot." Coleman's game is relatively small-scale and strictly local. The greenhouses and adjoining fields take up two to three acres. All produce is sold within a 30-mile radius of the farm. In the first year of the enterprise, the couple aimed at a gross of over $50,000 with a net of 70 percent–and they would take the summer off. (Since my visit, however, Coleman reports that greenhouse farming has become so exciting, he's been drawn into full-scale summer vegetable and culinary herb production as well. Profits have also far out-paced their early expectations.)

A salad course is served, a fluffy mound of lightly dressed vibrant leaves, multi-colored and variably textured, bitter, sweet, and tangy. Coleman selects a blood-red beet leaf and tells me it looks so intense because the plant is stressed, still struggling outside in the dropping temperatures. Our main course is a hearty French bean soup with homebaked sourdough bread. Now in their mid-50s, Coleman and Damrosch were married in 1991, and they exhibit a sense of open gratitude with each other that you often find in couples who've met later in life. They are passionate about this greenhouse farming business and share in all aspects of decision making. Damrosch now works at least half-time at the farm, handling orders and deliveries, managing the business, making time for weeding, and cooking meals for the farm crew. Coleman is the master of production. Our discussion shifts to a recent product innovation, a winter-hardy stir-fry mix, an assortment of oriental and western greens, that can be tossed together for a quick meal. (I learned later that the stir fry greens were successful for a season but then lost out to the booming demand for higher-value products.)

"'Making good easy' is one of my mantras," says Coleman. "By that I mean if you don't make doing good easy for someone–eating well, for instance–they'll rapidly opt for the alternative." In the case of winter greens in Maine, that could mean buying lettuce grown thousands of miles away in massive operations in California, Florida, or Mexico, which arrives a week or so after picking and leaves behind unknown impacts on habitat. He's even done rough calculations to show the amount of energy saved by producing a pound of salad greens locally rather than importing it from California.

After dinner, Coleman and I withdraw to his study, which at the time is a small room with a desk, a computer, and an astounding collection of books on sustainable agriculture. He has long been in the habit of making monthly journeys to the library to scour the Horticultural Index to review abstracts of agricultural research from around the world. His research at the time is focused on greenhouse farming and what growers across the 44th parallel are planting. An entire bookcase is dedicated to it, and he and Barbara have taken European junkets to talk first hand with 44th parallel compatriots in Provence, the Ligurian Coast of Italy, and Northern Tuscany. He proudly shows off a Spanish text recently published on growing asparagus in winter hothouses, an old French treatise on market gardening, and a classic by American horticulturalist Emery Myers Emmert, a pioneer of greenhouse agriculture. Coleman divulges one of the keys to his winter-harvest game: devising a successive planting regimen beginning in August and on through the fall, so that salad greens and root crops can grow tall enough before the "big stunt" arrives–that period between December and mid-February when growth slows to a halt as daylight hours diminish. During that deep winter interim, the crops remain fresh in the ground, they're just no longer adding bulk.

In the morning I tour the farm and must be content with what little time I have before catching a plane back to the West Coast. Some years ago, after purchasing 45 acres from the Nearings, Coleman determined that–despite his irrepressible love of farming–two-thirds of the land should be left for Nature. Those adjoining wilds include woodlots, swamps, and rocky outcrops that provide habitat for deer, coyotes, foxes, skunks, raptors, raccoons, squirrels, bears, bobcats, and various birds. "Since our winter season production takes place in greenhouses," Coleman explains, "the local deer population is something pleasurable to watch rather than something to fear. During the warmer months, we use movable electric fences to keep them and the raccoons away from our outdoor crops. Small rodents, specifically voles, are a problem when they get into the greenhouses, where we do trap them. But the best control is an abundance of natural predators–coyotes, foxes, skunks, owls, hawks, and bobcats–for whom these creatures are furry little snacks. We aid the predators in their search by mowing the grass short in the areas around the greenhouses and by making sure there are no piles of old boards under which rodents can hide."

A cold rain settles in, and as we walk past the sauna and the pond, through woods and fields newly mowed, I get the overall sense of a working farm with compact production zones embedded in wildness that extends beyond its boundaries. The 15 acres of Four Season Farm that have been developed are immaculately kept and appropriately scaled. There are hay fields planted and mowed for composting. We stop at a small shed where he designs tools that allow him to work upright with the least amount of strain, tools that are now sold at major garden retailers such as Smith and Hawken. I also realize that Coleman possesses what most successful agrarians do: an inexhaustible optimism and tendency to dream. He shows me a hillside where he hopes to establish Cape Rosier's first successful red table wine vineyard; an area to raise ducks for *fois gras* (their livers, he insists, can take it); and a field destined for wheat production.

The greenhouse operation is intensively arranged, a cluster of six large greenhouses, each with an adjoining field. The greenhouses are standard-issue, 50 or 100 feet long and 30 feet wide, with arched roofs to shed the snow. There are also smaller temporary shelters that protect a variety of crops and even compost piles through the winter. The frames are made primarily of galvanized metal joists that are easily assembled, all with simple ventilation systems and operable doors. As we walk inside one, the rain pounds loudly against the plastic-sheeted cover. As I imagined, the beds are practically weed-free. They are about three feet across and mounded just a few inches high, and Coleman explains that the bed mounds are the only soil layer he disturbs, amends, or concerns himself with. He selects a long-handled hoe of his own personal design and begins to demonstrate the upright weeding methods he's developed for this farming system, similar to sweeping the floor.

I recall that in a previous interview I conducted with Coleman he emphasized a farming philosophy he characterized as "plant positive." This approach runs counter to "pest negative" strategies that attempt to eliminate pests from fields through applications of chemicals. His reasoning is that his primary duty as a farmer is to provide and maintain the ideal conditions that any given plant needs to thrive so that it can actively resist pests or disease outbreaks. Proper soil preparation, well-balanced fertilization (particularly of aged compost), optimal supplies of air and moisture, appropriate planting dates, carefully selected varieties, rotations, and most of all—careful observation—are all part of the long-term steps needed to create a healthy system in which plants can prosper. This in turn leads to the optimal quality he is striving for as a grower.

In the unheated greenhouse environment in which Coleman is working, this plant positive approach might seem challenging, but it is obviously working. It is late fall, already cold, and the crops look exuberant. I walk among the leafy rows, planted so densely the soil isn't even visible, with 20 types of vegetables in various stages of growth and a spectrum of luminous red, purple, and green shades. Among the chill-resistant varieties so essential to the winter harvest are spinach, chard, carrots, sorrel, kale, and scallions, as well as the lesser-known mache, claytonia, minutina, tatsoi, and arugula. Coleman points to a bed of turnips and explains, "They produce roots quickly because the fall weather gives them the signals. If it were spring, they'd be thinking that they had all the time in the world to do it. Because of this, we're able to plant them more closely together." Another innovation entails providing the beds with an additional low-cost protective row cover. When necessary a layer of remay cloth, a white, gauzy synthetic fabric, is draped over custom-made wickets about six inches above the beds. This single thin layer creates an additional protective buffer that thwarts drops in temperature even as the weather outside the plastic house plunges to minus 10 degrees F. The combined plastic and remay climate modification ("like wearing a sweater under a windbreaker"), Coleman believes, provides a low-cost, low-input passage to an entirely new way of farming. A zealot for scientific research, he shows me a computerized thermometer that allows him to keep exact records of external, greenhouse, and soil temperatures and then import them into a program for careful analysis. "The hoop house's plastic sheeting places us one-and-a-half USDA growing zones to the south," he says. "The additional remay layer puts us an additional zone and a half to the south. Essentially, we're producing growing conditions similar to those in Zone 8, coastal Georgia."

We wander among the greenhouses and tour the salad packaging area. He explains everything he seems to think is important to mastering his gardening system. In one experimental bed, where he's germinated a dozen or so varieties "from probable to marginal," he reaches down and plucks a few leaves off a blue-green cabbage plant, takes a bite, then hands me a leaf. "This will make excellent color and flavor in a stir fry mix," he says, an entrepreneurial gleam shining through his blue eyes.

Outside, he shows me yet another key element to the winter-harvest system. The greenhouses, oriented on an East-West axis, are mobile. Configured on tracks, they can be hitched to a tractor and moved like giant sleds to cover an adjacent field. That way a field that was planted in late summer can get its start outside and later be protected for winter production. In the mean time, heat-loving crops can be grown in the greenhouse throughout the summer, and uncovered plots can be kept in rotation with nutrient-fixing crops.

I tell him that I think it would be no sin to sell his produce to restaurants in Portland, just three hours by car, to increase his customer base. "Frankly, I'd rather teach someone how to do this themselves, so they could sell the produce in Portland," he says. In fact, the details of the operation have since been carefully documented in his self-published Winter Harvest Manual (1998),[13] including the suppliers of greenhouse hardware, lists and suppliers of cold-hardy varieties, and the technical details of water management, planting schedules, and pest control tips.

More than anything, I admire these farmers' dedication to quality. Organic produce may be shipped in from California, Mexico, Florida, and beyond (Chile, Turkey, and New Zealand, for example) and might undercut Four Season Farm's prices, but imports can't hold a candle in terms of freshness or taste. I am remembering the carrots I ate last night as hors-d'oeuvres, crunchy and index finger-sized with a taste both sugary and earthy. Freshness, taste, perishability, these are the new frontiers of a profound food culture, drawing the circles of our food production ever closer to our tables, requiring zealots like Eliot Coleman and Barbara Damrosch, who embrace the challenge of family farming and understand full well the ultimate benefits. Although it is raining and I have no time to see the Good Life Center or the Nearings' legendary stone-walled structures, I feel that I am taking something fresh back with me, a glimpse at an exciting way to farm, one that seems uniquely rooted in this salty northeastern coast.

High Output, Low-Acreage, Four Season Farming

Top left, Maine farmers Barbara Damrosch and Eliot Coleman.

Winter greenhouse farming begins with beds planted in late summer (bottom left). After the plants have grown for a few months, the greenhouse is moved over the top of the plot like a giant sled (center row, right). A layer of remay cloth draped over the beds provides an additional USDA growing zone of protection (center row, far left). No additional heat is necessary.

THE FARM OF MANY FACES

As we hike up a hilly pasture in an early morning drizzle, Joel Salatin describes the first major management action he undertook upon returning to the family farm in 1978. Inspired by his study of permaculture concepts, Salatin mapped out ecozones–forest, riparian, and open grassland–to establish structural parameters that would allow Polyface Farm to be managed from a landscape perspective. As he talks, he points out particular crop trees, such as American black walnut, cherry, and ash that could eventually be selectively harvested from the predominantly deciduous forest on our right. A simple two-wire fence separates the steep north-facing wooded hillside from the gently sloping south-facing pasture on our left. Ahead, a raptor has pinned some prey in the open field.

"Our rule of thumb is that if it's too steep to drive on, then it ought to be in trees," says the broad-shouldered, professorial Salatin. By defining boundaries that follow and delineate the contours between ridge and slope, and between slope and swale, the Salatins excluded cattle from forests and riparian zones. They reclaimed 60 acres of forest, some by replanting, but most by natural regeneration. Of Polyface Farm's 550 acres, only 100 are in blocks of pasture that weave in and out of southwestern Virginia's forested Shenandoah Valley hills and wetland hollows. Bordered on the north and south by livestock-grazing operations, to the east are diversified farms with woodlands, grass, and cultivated crops, and to the west the farm abuts the forest-blanketed hills of Little North Mountain Wildlife Management Area, which connects to the George Washington National Forest beyond.

"Creating these different zones right next to our open lands invites a lot of wildlife activity into the farming system," he continues. "Many birds don't feel comfortable foraging more than 200 yards away from cover. This way, we benefit tremendously from the natural biological control for grasshoppers, crickets, grubs, and other bugs." There are other advantages. "We're in the livestock business, so we want pasture, but not at the expense of air flow, wildness, and fundamental hydraulic dynamics. The trees on the slope actually pump water up the steep hillside to the top, completing a valuable hydrological cycle." While a mixed herd of three dozen Red Angus, Brahman, and shorthorn cattle graze in an upper paddock, a few hundred yards away a large flock of Rhode Island Red and Barred Rock chickens surrounds two ramshackle covered wagonlike structures. Eggmobiles,

Salatin informs me. They provide nighttime shelter and laying boxes, while the hens free range during the day. "There are plenty of predators in these hills. We see coyotes in packs of ten, but we've never seen a coyote attack a chicken. We've had one fox attack in 30 years. Raccoons, skunks, possums, very seldom. One of the values of these edge habitats is that they produce a lot of voles, moles, chipmunks, and other prey for carnivores to feed on." And because cows have grazed the area before the chickens are put on it, he explains, a great horned owl can easily hunt a predatory weasel in short grass.

The 2,000 square-mile Shenandoah Valley–with its comparatively high elevation (ranging between 900 and 1,800 feet), May 15 and September 15 frost dates, and 31 inches of annual precipitation–falls in the same hardiness zone as North Dakota. Bison roamed this country, and early European settlers recounted being able to tie the Midatlantic prairie grasses in knots above their horses' saddles. Although the heavy limestone soils are unsuitable for high-organic-matter, temperate annual cropping systems, the hills were plowed for hard winter wheat. During the Civil War, the valley was transformed into the breadbasket of the Confederacy, and its forests were cleared to fuel iron ore foundries. When Salatin's parents, William and Lucille, bought the property in 1961, a lengthy history of land use and abuse came with it. Their approach, which evolved over four decades, became pragmatic: let grasslands be grasslands, let forest be forest, and never use a machine to do something that an animal can naturally and contentedly accomplish. William, an accountant by trade who died in 1988, didn't buy into the model of intensive-capitalization being promoted by mainstream agriculture at the height of the postwar Green Revolution. After reading Andre Voisin's *Grass Productivity*, he became an early practitioner of rotational grazing. He eschewed pesticides and other agrochemicals because he viewed them as uneconomical, and he began experimenting with mobile poultry shelters as a way of building a low-cost infrastructure. Although he and his wife never made their living off the farm, they soon paid for the property, giving their son, daughter-in-law, Teresa, and now their grandchildren, Daniel and Rachel, a running start at farming.

Under Joel Salatin's management, the rotational grazing system at Polyface Farm was accelerated and finally blossomed into a kind of free-range ballet, with 60 head of beef cattle,

12,000 broiler chickens, 40,000 dozen eggs, 700 turkeys, and a few dozen lambs in continual motion, not to mention some 200 hogs that graze in permanent forest clearings. Netting an average of between $3,000 and $4,000 per acre, the farm seems remarkably profitable, especially considering everything is sold locally or regionally. One-third of its products are divvied among some 400 local families and the remaining output is sold to restaurants, buying clubs, or farmers markets within a few hundred miles of the farm. It is a family operation; Teresa manages orders and deliveries; their son Daniel helps manage their farm; their daughter Rachel is still in high school. There are regularly a few paid interns, and only two medium-sized tractors, which remain parked in the barn during my daylong visit. The means of production consist of small-scale portable livestock shelters, movable electric fences, the livestock themselves, large-scale applications of homemade compost, and a unique management system Salatin refers to as "stacking."

Stacking starts with the cow herd, which is moved to a new paddock each day, followed three to four days later by the Eggmobile. Salatin stops in mid-step and crouches to inspect a ripe cow patty. "Cow patties are incubators for pathogens in cattle," he says, pointing with his pocket knife blade to what appear to be clawings in the manure. "But the chickens willingly scratch out the fly larvae, sanitizing the pasture and eliminating the need for systemic grubicides and wormicides–and controlling the crickets and the grasshoppers to boot." This model mimics many large herbivore grazing patterns, says Salatin; caribou and wildebeest, for example, mob up in tight packs for predator protection, then move on to fresh forage everyday, often in a synergistic relationship with birds. "By stacking an egg production model on top of a beef production model, we're doubling the pasture return," says Salatin. "Beef plus insects turned to cash in the form of eggs. And we don't have to turn cows through the head gate and lose our religion by shooting them up with Ivomec."

Further down the pasture, following behind the laying hens in the stacking rotation, is a series of low-lying square boxes, staggered corner-to-corner, making a geometric pattern across the hillside. These movable shelters are 10 ft.-by-12 ft.-by-2 ft. high, constructed with a wood frame, aluminum siding material, and chicken wire, and house 70 Cornish-cross broiler hens. The structures have no floor but provide both protective cover and open sides. The broilers are always caged throughout the short eight weeks in which they grow as large as feathered footballs ready for harvest. "Poultry like to be in small groups," says Salatin, "and in this model, they're almost as dense as they are in a confinement house. But since there are only 70 of them, it completely changes the stress element, according

to my own observation." To demonstrate how he rotates a shelter, he slides a dolly under the back end, lays it flat, giving the shelter wheels to slide on; he then goes around to the front and pulls the house along with a large handle. "This is an acquired skill," he says. Because the houses are arranged in a staggered pattern, they can be moved across the hillside checkerboard fashion, "giving the birds a clean, fresh salad bar everyday." Restaurants, he boasts, love working with the free-range birds because cooks don't suffer sore hand syndrome as they reportedly do with conventionally raised birds loaded with toxins.

Although reforestation has been a major goal for some areas on the farm, other areas have been cleared to reclaim pastures, while still using the ecozone system to determine where the fences run. Where they did clear woods, the Salatins made sure they maximized their income from the timber, selling sawlogs and firewood, and storing away prime lumber for on-farm projects, such as the upcoming construction of Daniel's house. (During my visit, a neighboring farmer stops by and orders 20 2-by-4s, which Salatin will cut to order on his portable sawmill.) Ponds were built in low-lying areas to capture winter precipitation that can later be meted out to provide pasture irrigation and water for livestock in the summer. Soils excavated to make the ponds were spread out to fill gullies and reverse major erosion resulting from earlier farm practices.

We walk to a hilltop pasture, a two- to three-acre area recently cleared. At ground level, one can see a scattering of berry canes resprouting as well as short stumps where the woods stood. Just beyond the crest of the hill is a steep, shaded, north facing slope, and Salatin is quick to point out how they purposely fenced around rather than clearing it. A wedge of sloping woods juts out into the center of the pasture, and the grassland wraps around it in the shape of a horseshoe. There were a few reasons for leaving the woods that had as much to do with pasture management as with retaining edge habitat. "North slopes tend to green up more slowly and retain moisture longer," says Salatin. "So we would have had a real damp swale abutting a dry southwestern slope. In a rotational system it is easier to graze pastures that have relatively homogenous conditions." Instead the wooded area serves as a swale that filters winter rains and snow melt, and will produce some future high-value crop trees along the perimeter.

We walk down a precipitous trail through leaf duff beneath luminous hardwoods, our tour momentarily shifting away from pastures as we tune in to a symphony of bird calls, snapping twigs, and forest sounds. Much farther down the hollow, on the outer edge of the woods, we stop at one of Polyface's four permanent pig pastures. A 3-acre patch of woods has been cleared in what appears to be a crude squatter's settlement. The terrain is rough and rocky. Piles of brush have been left to provide habitat for rabbits and other wildlife. (The Salatins trade the privilege of rabbit hunting to some locals who in return haul in free wood chips for their compost operation.) A dozen or so hogs are rooting, lounging, or munching from a large grain feeder. The outer perimeter has been permanently fenced off with a two-strand wire. Inside the pigs have a permanent water system and numerous paddies sectioned off by portable electric fencing that they rotate to every few weeks. "We've learned a lot about pigs," says Salatin. "First of all, never graze pigs in here in the winter time. They just turn everything into brick." Instead, I am later shown, the pigs share barn quarters with the cows in winter, where they turn the silage into compost–"Pigerators," Salatin calls them. Throughout the winter, the cows' bedding is continually cleared into a central holding area into which the pigs are turned loose. "All you can see sometimes are wagging tails as they forage for ears of corn, injecting oxygen and creating humus in the feet-thick livestock bedding. Allowing those pigs to do the composting is not only economically sound," he says, "it's also ecologically sound, and gives the pig a life that is hog heaven. It allows that pig to use its plow as a wonderful asset rather than a liability."

We pass a large pond and cross over to a second pasture, this one with knee-high grass and a flock of some 100 ewes encircled by what seems to be a rather flimsy electrified fence. Within the fence is a high-tech, hooped structure, its frame made of lightweight metal, its roof of stretched white synthetic fabric. "We call this our Ewe-go," Salatin says, with all the bravado of a car dealer. The Ewe-go is actually an off-the-shelf prefabricated 30 ft.-by-48 ft. structure that becomes a sheepfold corral and shelter. It accommodates 100 ewes, providing shade and predator protection, and can be moved with a tractor (with sheep inside it) to a new paddock in less than an hour and a half. He points to a trampoline-like structure not far away and continues, "That portable shade device is our Lamb-borghini." On 20 acres, he predicts, this lambing operation will support 100 ewes and generate $15,000 in income. It can even be used on rented land. "One of our critical challenges right now is to develop the prototypes whereby a white-collar salary can be earned on land that is largely controlled by elderly, discontented, pessimistic, noncreative geezers," he says with a mix of mischief and mission. He claps a few times, and the sheep slowly begin to follow him into the Ewe-go, demonstrating how easy it is to move from pasture to pasture. By the time we've reached the sheep pasture, I begin to understand how the stacking sys-

tem gathers height and dimension. With the continual rotation of cows, laying hens, broilers, turkeys, and sheep, the sky seems to be the limit. (That's not counting the more permanent areas for pigs and rabbits.) "In this pasture where we're standing right now," Salatin says, "we've already grazed it with cows twice in the spring, we've run broilers across it, we've run the Eggmobile across it twice, we've run the sheep across it for the third time, and in the fall we can run turkeys. The point being that the cows make $300 per acre, the broilers $2,500 per acre, sheep $500 per acre, Eggmobile $500 per acre, turkeys $1,500 per acre, and look at the infrastructure! It's the ultimate flexible system, but as you flex this system you also have to emphasize differentiation. For example, we begin our mowing and grazing regimens in a different paddock each year. That allows different species of grasses to reach physiological maturity at different times of the year."

Before the morning is out, we visit an R&D table grape vineyard that doubles as a pasture for turkeys. We pass the portable ram house known as the Rambler and move on to the Feathernet, cousin to the Eggmobile. Where the Eggmobile is as much about sanitizing cow pastures as it is about eggs, this is serious commercial production with a thousand Barred Rocks and Black Austrolorps strutting across a quarter-acre pasture, laying some 120 dozen eggs per day. Every third day, the interconnected complex of feeders, nest boxes, and water troughs is moved to fresh grass on a skid.

I ask Salatin to take me to his favorite part of the farm, and we head back out through the main pasture, then enter the north-sloping forest he had pointed out at the beginning of our tour. We stop at a grove of white pines that he and his father planted 30 years ago. At that time, he explains, this was deeply eroded ground with no vegetation on it. The trees have grown 50 to 60 feet tall and have dropped a bed of needles three decades thick, covering any trace of gullies. One disagreeable winter day, Salatin remembers, it snowed 30 inches, and he went out of his way to stop at this spot and found that there was not a flake of snow on the ground. The diversity of wildlife that had congregated amid their nascent cathedral forest in the tough weather astounded him. For a moment, Salatin seems to have nothing to say, as if he is listening to what these particular trees might offer. Then he nudges his glasses up the bridge of his nose and says, "People say that it's too slow to make land change, but I'm not too old to remember what this land was like. Part of my ministry is that there are some things that are off limits to us, that I am not the dominant force, that there is a force outside me that is beyond my control."

The Art and Science of Grass Farming

Top left, Joel, Teresa, and Daniel Salatin. Top row center, portable shelters made of chicken wire and corrugated metal for broiler chickens. The shelters are easily moved to fresh grass each day (center row, center), and are staggered across pastures (center row, top right). Top right, shows a view of the "stacking" system. Cows graze first, followed by laying hens that sanitize pastures. Broiler shelters, staggered across the hillside, come next. Sheep follow.

Bottom left, some of the more than 400 acres of forest, in which there are three permanent pig pastures of a few acres. Bottom, second from left, turkeys graze within a table grape vineyard.

Mobile structures provide low-cost infrastructure for the egg-laying Black Austrolorps and Barred Rocks (center left) and Rhode Island reds in the Eggmobiles, at bottom right. Polyface Farm produces 40,000 dozen eggs and 12,000 broilers per year alone. The Ewe-Go, center row bottom right, is a portable sheep shelter.

CORRIDORS, WILDWAYS, AND CITIZEN MONITORING

Although the decade directly following the Dust Bowl was one of proactive conservation planting that reintroduced habitat to farming regions, the practice of maintaining shelterbelts, windbreaks, hedgerows, vegetated waterways, and contour buffer strips has long been in decline. Decades of fencerow-to-fencerow "clean" farming have severely fragmented wild habitats in many regions throughout the country, and never has the need for conservation corridors been more pressing.

Envisioning agricultural landscapes interconnected by habitat linkages requires, first of all, accepting that all farms should have "throughways" or "wildways" that encourage the presence and flow of native species. Reestablishing farmland-to-wildland connectivity can begin slowly, yet provide short-term benefits to farmers, native wildlife, and local communities. The reintegration of native hedgerows to attract pollinators, beneficial insects, birds, and bats, for example, is one excellent throughway model that is fundamental to healthy agriculture and can benefit local ecosystems. Research on introduced native hedgerows on farms in Yolo County, California, has shown that beneficial insects attracted to the native plantings outnumbered pests by three-to-one and have posed little or no threat to adjacent row crop farming.[1] According to Gary Nabhan, honeybees and other wild species that transfer pollen between flowers now contribute more than $10 billion a year to fruit and seed production on North American farms.[2] Across Great Britain, where over 100,000 miles of hedgerows have been removed since the early 1980s, farmers are now in the process of replanting them for their aesthetic, agricultural, and ecological values.

The Adirondack-Boquet-Champlain Valley Forest and Farm Project has been working to create a "wildway" between Lake Champlain and the nation's largest protected wilderness area, the Adirondack State Park.

In addition to biological pest control and pollination, habitat corridors can provide many other direct functional advantages or ecosystem services to farmers: soil conservation, water filtration, suppression of weeds and invasive species (once native cover is reestablished), protection from noise, dust, wind, and snow. Game species attracted to the nesting, brooding, and loafing habitats provided by corridors can create recreational opportunities in farmlands, as long as mowing and other disturbance activities are carefully timed to respect nesting cycles. Restored woodland corridors can offer economically competitive alternatives to row cropping and pasturing, with agroforestry products like fruits, nuts, mushrooms, and veneer and pulp woods, medicinal and herbal plants, hunting, fishing, bird-watching, and agrotourism. At best, these woodlands attempt as much as possible to mimic and draw from native habitat and are most effective when plantings have complex horizontal and vertical structure.

Around the country, watershed stakeholder groups have formed to reclaim and protect threatened river corridors. Of the country's 3.2 million miles of rivers, for example, only 5 percent support high levels of their original native fish species. Riparian corridors are used by over 70 percent of all terrestrial wildlife species during some part of their life cycle, including many threatened and endangered species.[3] They are particularly valuable in arid and semi-arid zones because of the species complexity they support. Yet the function and the structure of riparian corridors in areas throughout the country are in a catastrophic decline, even in agricultural areas that depend upon them for their very survival. Researcher Gary Nabhan has found that of all habitat restoration efforts designed to attract native pollinators to farms in the Santa Cruz River area of southeastern Arizona, restoring riparian zones is the most effective.[4] In the California wine-growing counties of Sonoma, Napa, and Mendocino, growers have begun replacing exotic species such as Himalayan blackberry in riparian corridors with natives, as exotics have been found to host the blue-green sharpshooter, a vector for the dreaded Pierce's disease, which could decimate this multibillion dollar industry.

Such initiatives will falter, however, if individual farms remain islands of diversity in seas of industrial monoculture and development. The extent to which corridors can be arranged and connected to one another will ultimately determine their value to ecosystems and wildlife. While there is little doubt that bigger is better in the pursuit of habitat preservation, regions can be transformed on a collaborative basis, farm by farm, creek by creek, woodlot by woodlot. This is the gritty, on-the-ground work of citizen democracy. Restoring the unraveled fabric of North American ecosystems requires landscape-level imagining, connecting corridors at the watershed level.

For the past decade, organizations such as the Wildlands Project have been setting forth bold initiatives and wilderness design principles to restore and rewild the native biodiversity of North America from Canada to Central America. The Wildlands Project's unique vision entails identifying and connecting "nodes" (core wilderness reserves) via corridors surrounded by compatible-use areas with an emphasis on maintaining habitats sufficient to sustain populations of wide-ranging carnivores. The monumental task of mapping and strategizing this wildlands network is now ongoing in most regions of the country. Corridor projects have been launched to create travel routes for the Florida panther, Mexican wolf, and jaguar. "Stepping stone" corridors are being planned to allow for the cross-country migrations of many species throughout a fragmented landscape. In 2000, California scientists and activists compiled *Missing Linkages: Restoring Connectivity to the California Landscape*. Complete with maps and project descriptions, this impressive document charts the on-the-ground routes needed to heal and reconnect the flow of wildness in this heavily developed state.[5] This report is nothing less than a 21st century priorities list that should be replicated by every state in the country.

Research on corridors in agricultural lands, however, is both lacking and urgent. The term *corridor* itself may be part of the problem, as it suggests a narrow passage, which may not adequately address the biological requirements needed to support the full range of native species or the pulses of natural processes within a given area (migration, predation, pollination, nutrient cycling, fire, flooding and groundwater recharge, carbon sequestration, among others). The term is also used to describe a number of distinct and sometimes conflicting landscape features. Ecological corridors link fragmented habitat through areas of nonhabitat and can vary greatly in size, from stepping stones as small as a few meters in length to a conduit that spans several counties. Disturbance corridors, such as powerlines and the more than 2 percent of the country that has been paved, fragment otherwise continuous habitat, change patterns of wildlife movement, and may serve as death traps for certain species. Remnant corridors represent the vestiges and mini-repositories of pre-settlement ecosystems and therefore preserve essential clues and native biological elements necessary to mimic natural structures in a given area. Introduced corridors such as hedgerows have been part of agrarian landscapes for centuries, planted and maintained to provide habitat for game, delineate property boundaries, protect fields from wind and erosion, and numerous other functions.

Corridors can function first and foremost as habitat. They become passageways for the flow of plants and other wildlife, allowing for migration, the dispersal of seeds, and the transfer of genes. Corridors can act as filters and barriers between fields, catching windborne or water-driven resources, such as snow, soil, spray drift, or even attracting weeds and unwanted exotic species. Depending on their structure, they can provide source materials for local restoration efforts (and for that reason restoration ecologists often travel strips of undisturbed habitat in search of seed plants). The species mix within a corridor can be complex or simplified, native or exotic, thereby affecting its depth of function.

"The science of corridors is in its infancy, and presently there are a lot of misunderstandings," says John Davis, a cofounder of the Wild Farm Alliance and the initiator of a landscape-scale corridor project in upstate New York's Boquet Valley region. "However, there are two safe rules with corridors. First, the wider the better. Second, the wilder the surrounding landscape, the better." The true ecological values of corridors, he goes on to explain, depend on width and the type of landscape they pass through. A narrow corridor may allow for genetic exchange and migration among some, but not all species. Hedgerows and narrow bands may primarily provide edge habitat attractive to only a small number of species. It is argued that narrow hedgerows may in fact serve as a "population sinks" where predators and opportunists find it easy to victimize sensitive species in the early succession or edge habitat. "In the highly fragmented landscapes we are now dealing with, however, almost any wildlife corridor is better than nothing," continues Davis, "but they need to be very broad and connected to one another to serve the full range of native species." He refers to the type of broad connectivity needed as a "wildway" rather than a corridor, and "hedge thicket" rather than hedgerow.

In their award-winning document on corridors, *Conservation Corridor Planning at the Landscape Level: Managing for Wildlife Habitat*, Craig Johnson, Gary Bentrop, and Dick Rol have enumerated several guidelines of corridor planning: large reserves and patches are better than small ones; connected reserves are better than isolated ones; united reserves and patches are better than fragmented ones; several redundant reserves function better than one; natural connectivity should be maintained or restored; two or more corridor connections between patches are better than one.[6]

Wildlife corridors on farms present valuable opportunities to reintegrate Nature into agricultural systems and to restore lost ecological and aesthetic values to the rural landscape. While shelterbelts, hedgerows, grass belts, and other corridors have often been installed with exotic species or single species in the past (and still are), today's emphasis is on creating native habitat using locally sourced ecotypes, grown within a complex vertical structure that includes understory, shrubs, and canopy plants. Such a vision transforms farmers and landowners into restorationists, involved in the interdisciplinary task of reassembling pieces of pre-settlement or pre-agricultural habitat and fluidity to the landscape. It also represents a challenging opportunity for landscape nurseries that specialize in natives as a way to diversify their operations.

Biodiversity corridors are the focus of educational programs and agricultural services at the Heinz-Watties Kowhai Farm at Lincoln University in Canterbury, New Zealand. There, researchers established a 1.5-kilometer-long corridor through the 150-acre working row crop farm. Dubbed the Biodiversity Trail, it fulfills a number of different functions. For the monocrop organic vegetable production, these native plantings—rare in this type of agricultural setting—harbor beneficial insects and pollinators. A 1.5-meter-wide "beetle bank" runs the length of farm fields, for example, and becomes an insectary refuge throughout the year. Along the trail, placards teach visitors about the different habitat types and human interventions and how they interact with the field crops, including bumble-bee motels, weed suppression through native plantings, underground diversity, and bird habitat. "We're trying to demon-

strate the dozens of reasons that biodiversity can further benefit organic farming operations," says Steve Wratten, a professor of agroecology at Lincoln University and one of the creators of the Biodiversity Trail. "And this high-profile collaboration is visited each year by thousands of interested citizens and influential politicians and business people alike."

Understanding wildlife migration patterns is yet another key to installing effectively functioning corridors. For that reason, collaborations between landowners and nonprofit organizations and citizen scientists are being established to track the presence and patterns of species throughout the landscape. Among the many portraits of wildlife movement is the annual Christmas Bird Count, the longest running database of ornithology in the country. Each year more than 45,000 volunteers in every region of the country assemble a census of early winter bird populations, which provides invaluable baseline information. (See *www.birdsource.cornell.edu/cbc.*) Keeping Track Inc., a Vermont-based organization, trains students and volunteer naturalists with the skills to identify tracks and signs of wildlife in their regions. The organization believes that the consistent presence of wide-ranging animals is an excellent indicator of healthy land. Another nationwide citizen monitoring campaign focuses on the hundreds of thousands of monarch butterflies that journey between Canada, the United States, and Mexico. At least nine different citizen-based data observation programs help compile and share invaluable data on the plight and flight of both eastern and western monarchs and their threatened habitats.

In some cases, citizen monitoring programs can help provide landowners with a deeper understanding and appreciation of the wildlife on their own farms. More broadly, observing and documenting the paths and strands of habitat connectivity to larger breeding areas can also be absolutely crucial to town and regional planning and to the conservation easement process. It may also inspire initiatives that can lead to the construction of underpasses, overpasses, and routes around existing bottlenecks and choke points that effectively eliminate wildlife connectivity.

One thing is clear: we have lost so much, and are losing so much still, that we do not even know what is now gone forever. The efforts toward creating wildlife linkages must become national priorities to hold together and restore what still remains—meaning that funding, research, and other resources must be brought to the table.

LINKING FARMSCAPES, LANDSCAPES, AND HUMAN COMMUNITIES

John Davis is one of those truly iconoclastic Americans, cut from the philosophical cloth of Henry David Thoreau, John Muir, Rachel Carson, and David Brower–devoted to the wild and its preservation by a nearly spiritual compulsion. Now in his late 30s, Davis is known to cover vast distances by hiking, biking, cross-country skiing, or by rowing across Lake Champlain. As a founding editor of *Wild Earth* journal and as the biodiversity program director for the Foundation for Deep Ecology, he spent the 1990s helping to usher grassroots conservation into the mainstream. In 1994 Davis invested his hard-earned savings in a 50-acre parcel of forest and wetlands on what's known as the Adirondack Coast of Lake Champlain. There he moved into a rustic log cabin surrounded by a beaver clan and established a wildlife refuge. By 1997, he and others had sprung a plan to create a broad wildway that would connect Lake Champlain and its valley with the wild mountains to the west–all part of the largest conservation area in the Lower 48: the 6-million-acre Adirondack State Park.

Davis didn't have to look far to find collaborators. From the conservation expertise and leadership of such organizations as the Adirondack Nature Conservancy and Land Trust, the Adirondack Council, the Wildlands Project, the Boquet River Association, and the Eddy Foundation, the Adirondack-Boquet-Champlain Valley Forest and Farm Project was born. (We'll call it the Forest and Farm Project for short, here.) Mike DiNunzio, a former organic farmer and now the director of science and education programs for the Adirondack Council, saw the wisdom in the idea and quickly became an inspirational spokesperson for the effort. "The first thing groups interested in creating a wildway need to do is begin looking around and asking a few simple questions," explains DiNunzio. "Where are we? What are we trying to do? Who owns the land? Can we align them with our vision, or perhaps purchase their property or a strong conservation easement on it?"

The new wildway team began searching the area for potential routes that would "functionally link" the lake and its valley westward to the Jay Mountain Wilderness and other large wild areas of Adirondack Park. Such a link would have to cross roads and wind through or between active farms, dairies, orchards, hobby farms, maple sugaries, and managed forests and yet provide safe and contiguous habitat for the region's many sen-

sitive or wide-ranging species–including imperiled freshwater mussels, landlocked salmon, 193 species of nesting birds, black bear, bobcat, fisher, mink, river otter, and snow geese on their way from the Arctic to wintering grounds in the Dominican Republic. Maps and aerial photographs, displayed in a dedicated campaign room in the Eddy Foundation Essex, New York-based headquarters, allowed for study and strategizing. By process of elimination, it was soon decided that the most promising wildlife corridor was via the already protected 4,000 acres of Split Rock Wild Forest, west through Hemlock Rock Wildlife Sanctuary, over Coon Mountain, across the Boquet River around Little Falls, north to Boquet Mountain, then west toward the High Peaks. In just five years, the Forest and Farm Project has protected nearly 3,000 additional acres. Added to existing state and Adirondack Land Trust holdings, these preservation purchases have brought roughly one-half of the project area into wildlands protection.

It soon became obvious to this group, however, that this was more than just a wildway project. "We realized quickly that we had to develop community involvement, such as local products, local markets, and local participation to make such a plan work," says DiNunzio. "The concept of creating a whole region that was known for the integration of conservation and small-scale, value-added agriculture was very exciting. Then there were the issues of citizen involvement, public education, and further conservation initiatives outside the wildway."

By 2002, under the direction of Jamie Phillips, the Eddy Foundation had purchased more than 1,500 acres within what is now called the Split Rock Wildway. The Eddy Foundation intends to place most of this land under the same "Forever Wild" protection status afforded state-owned lands in the Adirondack Park, protection enshrined in the world's most advanced conservation law, the Forever Wild clause of the New York State constitution. Some of this land–including part of Black Kettle Farm–had been in agricultural production for many decades, and Phillips wants to keep many of those acres in production, but with an emphasis on wildlife compatibility and value-added foods for local consumption. "Historically, these fields have been barriers to movement of most wildlife," says Phillips. "In the future, these same fields will be set in a matrix of wild forest, allowing free flow of wildlife and criss-crossed by broad hedgerows or 'hedge thickets' of native early succession and fruit-bearing species. Black Kettle will also produce a diversity of fruits, vegetables, herbs, mushrooms, grains, and fibers—all organic and for local and regional consumption. In addition to value-added products and services to locals and visitors, these lands will support native pollinators, grassland birds, raptors, and small mammals." It must be emphasized, however, that most of Black Kettle Farm will become Forever Wild forest. This will be a gain for wildlife that requires a small amount of restoration and a large amount of restraint—curtailing logging and just letting Black Kettle's 300-plus acres of forest go wild.

Another key element of the Adirondack-Boquet-Champlain Valley Forest and Farm Project has been the creation of a citizen monitoring program. Sue Morse, founder of the nonprofit organization Keeping Track, has conducted several workshops in the area, helping locals monitor wildlife movement in the area as well as increasing awareness of the needs of wide-ranging predators. Another monitoring program will involve school children in the tagging and assessment of monarch butterfly populations.

The Adirondack-Boquet-Champlain network has broadened its vision to include developing a regional certification or ecolabel that combines small-scale organic agriculture, certified green-forestry, heritage tourism, and other ecologically sustainable products and services. "In addition to wildways for all species, we have to also develop wildways for food distribution and other products," says DiNunzio. "We have to capture local markets as well as the support of urban consumers in outside areas like Burlington and New York City. Clean, green, local and wild are the future of farming with the wild. Explaining the benefits to producers and local communities is a key part of that." Other public outreach activities encourage preserving and restoring as much native vegetation as possible, in as connected a fashion as possible; protecting broad riparian buffers and ladder forests leading to uplands; accommodating native predators; avoiding toxic pesticides and heavy machinery; adopting Forest Stewardship Council certification and standards for timber harvest on private lands where full protection is not yet possible; and renovating farm houses and barns.

"Why is this wildway so important?" asks Davis. "Habitat connectivity is crucial for many shy, sensitive, and wide-ranging species, yet many of the protected areas in the Adirondacks are isolated by roads, reservoirs, towns, or other fragmenting features. Split Rock Wildway is the most robust connection, the surest wildlife corridor, between the biggest mountains and the broadest valley in the largest park in the largest cluster of states in the country!"

Forever Wild

Top, a landscape perspective of the farming region between Lake Champlain and the mountains of the Adirondack State Park. Much of the land in the wildway will be provided Forever Wild status. Center left, Saw-whet owl captured by Gary Randorff. Bottom right, Adirondack fall splendor. Bottom left, John Davis and Tom Butler of the Wildlands Project take a break on Split Rock.

CENTRAL COAST FARMSCAPING

To those who've ever driven through the flat belly of the Salinas Valley or read heavy doses of John Steinbeck, the scene may sound familiar. Row after row of sprinkler irrigated salad, vegetable, and strawberry production. For an hour and a half, the ordered, geometric fields and vineyards are interrupted only by paved roads, warehouses, and the increasing march of urban development. The fertile soils, broad valleys, and mild maritime Mediterranean climate have made the central coast of California one of the world's fruit and vegetable producing powerhouses. It is home to some of the state's largest agribusinesses—both conventional and organic—but also the locus of an innovative "farmscaping" initiative that may one day more closely integrate Nature and food production in the region.

Farmscaping, explains Sam Earnshaw, usually begins with a farm plan: a set of maps, aerial photographs, and lists that details both the physical attributes of a property and the many goals that a successful agricultural system requires. Maintaining noncropped areas of the farm with native plants is one excellent tool that landowners are now using to achieve many of their farm system goals, such as pest control, soil management, water filtration, wind protection, and aesthetic enhancements. Trained in forestry and ecology, Earnshaw spent the 1980s running an organic farm in Santa Cruz with his wife, Jo Ann Baumgartner, now the project director for the Wild Farm Alliance. Since the early 1990s, he has served as the Central Coast Program Coordinator for the Community Alliance with Family Farmers (CAFF). A tireless activist, Earnshaw has split his time between fieldwork and organizing to encourage large and small growers to learn biological practices, protect open space, and establish on-farm native habitat.

On a balmy May morning we tour a number of his early farmscaping efforts, projects scattered throughout the Pajaro and Salinas watersheds. They range from small tailwater ponds to beneficial insectary plantings amid intensive row croppings to hedgerows and a major wetlands and open-space protection area along the Harkins Slough. At the Foster Ranch-Pinnacle Brand farm in San Juan Bautista we walk along a hedgerow adjacent to a diverse operation of vegetable production and orchards. Planted six years earlier, this now well-established hedgerow runs the entire length of the cultivated fields.

The larger plants are already ten feet across and more than ten feet tall. Jutting above the hedgerow and facing the fields are several pole-mounted barn owl boxes. As we walk and talk, Earnshaw points out the numerous native plants that make up the insectary—coyote brush, California lilac or ceanothus, toyon, and coffeeberry. This hedgerow, he explains, has been specifically designed to provide plentiful pollen and nectar sources throughout the year as the plants bloom sequentially, so that the full potential of beneficial insects could be realized. Indeed, the heavy, conical purple-blue blooms of the ceanothus are swarming with honeybees and other insects. Birds are darting among the branches. From the aesthetic point of view, the hedgerow visually softens the impact of the farm operation on the landscape, providing a sense of connection to the buff-brown hills to the north and the forested Coast Range to the east. Farther down is a windbreak of redwood, incense cedar, California pepper tree, strawberry madrone, giant sequoia, Monterey cypress, and soapbark tree.

Reintroducing native habitat into farmscapes is not without challenges, chief among them being the need for additional management. Once installed, hedgerows frequently suffer from inattention, says Earnshaw. Weeds, lack of water, deer, or even careless tractor operators are just a few of the damaging ends to which hedgerows can succumb. When they do survive, lack of management may allow undesirable species—pest birds, mice, and other rodents—to move into to the new habitat. "A couple of dead mice in a bin of salad mix or a gopher infestation in an orchard could be devastating," he explains. Another pressing concern throughout the state is the potential to introduce plants, mulches, or any other materials that may spread or host epidemics such as Sudden Oak Death syndrome (which affects oaks and certain softwoods) or Pierce's disease (a bacterium lethal to grape vines).

"Increasing diversity in the farmscape brings with it a whole new range of challenges," says Earnshaw, "but it also offers a deeper philosophical way of looking at things. For many farmers it just means learning to live with birds rather than going back to clean farming," he says. "The most interesting thing about this work is that there are no general formulas. Every situation is different. There are no silver bullets. But at least in the short term, habitat must be managed just like any other on-farm resource."

Through trial and error, careful monitoring, and close collaboration with scientists and farmers, the hedgerow plant list is becoming more expansive each year with inputs from entomologists and ecologists about California natives. Plantings can be designed to attract beneficial big-eyed bugs, syrphid flies, ladybeetles, minute pirate bugs, parasitic and predatory wasps, and other species that prey on such crop pests as aphids, mealy bugs, leafhoppers, scale, mites, whiteflies, thrips, and stinkbugs. The next phase of the farmscaping program may require locally adapted plant materials specifically sourced from the individual regions, rather than relying on faraway established nurseries that offer "generic" native plants for restoration projects. Fortunately, a number of regional nurseries are specializing in the production of local plant materials. On the Central Coast, the internationally renowned restoration biologist, Paul Kephart, runs Rana Creek Habitat Restoration ranch in the Carmel Valley, with over 100 acres of native-grass seed production and an additional four acres of native plant propagation. Rana Creek and several other nurseries are now producing local ecotypes for Central Coast plantings.

By mid-2002, interest in creating on-farm habitat within the region has increased exponentially. With financial assistance from USDA's Environmental Quality Incentive Program (EQIP), the National Fish and Wildlife Foundation, and the State Water Resources Control Board, Earnshaw has received full or partial cost-sharing for at least 15 separate farmscaping projects, from grassed waterways to hedgerows to vegetated buffer strips along fences and roadsides. Describing his vision for farmscaping, Earnshaw says he takes both a short-term and a long-term view. "I plan to keep working, learning, and developing more locally oriented solutions as more farmers subscribe to the concept," he says. "But in the long run, I see a landscape in which, farm by farm, watershed by watershed, Nature and food production are far more seamlessly intertwined. As a former ecologist and farmer, the integration of agriculture and ecology has really brought my work and my interests full circle. The farmers we have been working with are very enthusiastic about reconnecting their productive farming with natural habitats. This is an extremely exciting time and despite all the challenges, it is obvious that we are breaking new ground."

Habitat Central

Photos at top, Paul Kephart, restoration biologist with plant flats and his native grass plots at Rana Creek Habitat Restoration.

Center right, 5-year-old hedgerow with owl box integrated into row crop and orchard operation.

Bottom left, Steve Pedersen of High Ground Organics and habitat advocate Sam Earnshaw with the protected Harkins Slough in the background. Bottom right, the wild field margins at High Ground Organics Farm.

WASHINGTON'S METHOW AND SKAGIT VALLEYS: BUILDING CONSERVATION COMMUNITIES

When the Methow Valley Conservancy's Katharine Bill mailed 225 letters to landowners seeking permission to survey their properties for the presence of songbirds and quality songbird habitat, her boss was skeptical. In the winter of 2001, a controversy was roiling over the endangered species listing of bull trout, steelhead trout, and spring chinook salmon in the Methow River watershed. Maybe it was the Sibley's bird guides that she offered to the first 25 participants. Perhaps it was the opportunity to see their land through the eyes of a youthful Yale-educated biologist. In the end, 72 landowners signed up for the survey, and this rural northwestern community received a well-timed injection of conservation consciousness.

The Methow Songbird Survey

Four hours northeast of Seattle along one of the country's premier scenic drives, the Methow Valley lies between the eastern slope of the Cascades and the upper Columbia River Basin. It is a landscape of extremes, of upland shrub steppe and forest that give way to valley bottom grasslands transected by the winding, forest-banked, snowmelt-fed Methow River. Winters are chilling; summers can be brutally hot. An 80-90 day growing season, 13 inches of annual rainfall, and isolation from markets and processing facilities are limiting factors for farming. Ninety percent of the surrounding uplands are controlled by either the state or the U.S. Forest Service, and within the past decade, the former agricultural lands have been discovered by Seattlites, ratcheting up land values and the pressures for subdivision. Descending into the western side of the valley around the time of the summer solstice, one is initially greeted by three and a half miles of fields and river habitat protected in the mid-1990s by a Washington Wildlife and Recreation Coalition bond initiative. Entering the narrow Methow Valley, one finds a pastoral scene of round hay bales and almost surrealistically green fields of irrigated alfalfa that dominate what agriculture remains. Most of that hay is sold outside the valley, although there is a growing effort to develop a local market for organic grains grown on both dryland and irrigated farmland.

The decline of songbirds in riparian areas throughout farming regions in the United States, particularly where extensive amounts of chemicals are applied, had been one of Bill's main concerns in launching the project. With support from the National Fish and Wildlife Foundation and Partners in Flight, she, Kent Woodruff, a Forest Service biologist, and Brad Martin, the former director of the Methow Valley Conservancy, developed a methodology for the Methow Songbird Survey. A study of aerial photographs identified all owners with more than ten acres in the riparian areas, which make up approximately 1 percent of the land in the watershed yet support 80 percent of the valley's wildlife. Each received a letter, inviting them to participate in the baseline study. Woodruff and Bill then devised a scorecard to qualitatively rank various habitat types. "We used six different indicator species in the riparian lowlands and uplands to identify where the best habitat areas were, such as redstarts in the cottonwood canopy or yellow warblers in the understory," explains Bill. "We weren't just looking for one cavity nester or one duck species, but a whole complement of birds that indicated layers of habitat to assemble a complete picture of the landscape."

Bill spent six weeks in the summer of 2001 observing nearly 7,000 acres, focusing on vernal pool riparian habitats in shrub steppe uplands ("they function as mini-oases") as well as on the cottonwood-forested riverbanks of the bottomlands. Almost from the start, the songbird survey struck a chord among residents. "The phone began ringing off the hook," she remembers. "'The turkey vultures are back today,' they'd tell me, and I'd say, 'We're surveying songbirds, but that's okay.' One of the things I did was spend a lot of time admiring snags. I'd stop with the landowners and say, 'Wow, this is great habitat!' I think people perceive cottonwoods as a hazard when they die and we are trying to encourage people to leave them where they fall on the ground or in the river."

The scorecards allowed Bill to generate a color-coded map, identifying the most valuable habitats. The next step was to analyze that data to prioritize key properties and draft an outreach strategy for conservation easements and restoration projects, with the ultimate goal of protecting all pristine habitats and connecting the lowlands with the uplands through corridors and patches of contiguous habitat. "Our hope here is to keep common birds common while also protecting what is rare," Bill explains. "In the Methow, meadowlarks are common, and sharp-tailed grouse are in decline." When the original 72 participating landowners were contacted, 28 expressed a willingness to pursue conservation easements. Fortunately, the timing of the songbird protection plan coincided with an influx of funds for salmon habitat recovery. In the time between the songbird survey in 2001 and the summer of 2002, the Methow Conservancy received nearly $2 million to purchase perpetual easements for development rights and to assist landowners in restoring habitat. Luckily, active restoration and protection for songbird and salmon habitat are often complementary. "The songbird survey became a launching point and spread exponentially through the valley as one landowner talked to another," says Bill. "It has proven not only a good way to teach about bird habitat but also a good way to educate landowners about easements in general and to talk about our three listed salmon species." A year after the survey, 11 perpetual easements had been negotiated. Bill expects all 28 to ultimately be completed.

On a balmy late June morning I accompany Bill and Pete Vogt, a Seattle documentary film maker and Methow resident who participated in the songbird survey, to a property with which the Conservancy has recently negotiated an easement. The 523-acre Stean farm has been awarded priority status through the survey because it spans riparian habitat, prime agricultural land, and vernal pools in the upland shrub steppe. We walk toward the river through part of a 35-acre knee-high organic grain field. The field is separated from the river by a narrow grassy floodplain that gives way to the forested riverbank. Above the field, the terrain quickly steepens as it rises toward the uplands. A project is underway to broaden the riparian buffer by planting shrubs and grasses in the floodplain. Serviceberry, wild rose, willow, cottonwood, snowberry, elderberry, chokecherry, and Great Basin wild rye were reintroduced to increase complexity in the understory for mid-level nesting species. Efforts like these benefit from the nearby Methow Natives nursery, which specializes in local ecotypes. And, as Bill points out, "The fact that there is already an irrigation system existing is essential to the restoration project. There's no point in planting natives unless there is an irrigation system to get them established through the hot summer." As we walk through the recently mowed floodplain toward the tall cottonwoods by the river's edge, we pass numerous marmot burrows–circular mounds with an entrance tunnel. In less than a half hour, we've identified warbling vireos, sandpipers, western tanagers, and a Lewis's woodpecker. On the rocky, root-strewn riverbank, a young raccoon pokes its head from behind a cottonwood. The handiwork of beavers is evident on various trunks and fallen timbers, and Bill speaks about their importance in reestablishing the cottonwoods. "Trees resprout when beavers cut them and the trees they do fall help to create pools. So it's always important to understand the whole system that you are farming in. I think that there is a lot of hope for working with farmers to integrate deliberate habitat plantings with sustainable forms of agriculture." Evidently other communities find their approach compelling. Already

West of the Cascades

Top left, Katharine Bill conducted a songbird survey that resulted in more than 1/3 of landowners expressing interest in conservation easements.

Top right, the western entrance to the Methow Valley was preserved by a state initiative.

Center right, the native sunflower after which the valley was named.

Bottom photos. Sam Lucy grows organic grains as a way to suppress the spread of noxious weeds on leased farms. His own 30 acres are dry farmed.

the Inland Northwest Land Trust, 200 miles to the southeast in Spokane, has borrowed their songbird survey model to stimulate conservation consciousness in their community.

Dry Farming for Weed Suppression

From the river bottom Pete Vogt escorts me upland to glimpse another dynamic of the Methow conservation and restoration effort. Sam Lucy is a 35-year-old transplant from western New Hampshire, where he grew up on a family farm held for seven generations. He began working with the valley's largest farmer when he arrived in the Methow a decade ago, and for the past five years he has been farming in formerly plowed areas in an attempt to reverse the invasion of weed species such as knapweed (aka Barnaby), cheatgrass, and white top, by using plantings of self-seeding organic grains. "Long ago they scratched away the soil, then ran cattle, and now we have a salad of noxious weeds," he says. With some persistence, Lucy has found that grains such as barley, rye, and red wheat can outcompete the invasive weeds, slowly improving soil conditions, and demonstrating new possibilities for formerly farmed fields in decline. His ultimate goal is twofold: to develop a source of organic GMO-free grains on viable arable fields under a regional Methow ecolabel; and to restore other targeted areas to native grasses, wildflowers, and shrubs.

Lucy's modest farm spans 30 hilly acres of stunning upland territory, a mosaic of dry-farmed barley fields and patches of native habitat that swathe the land in a cloak of sage green. The region is experiencing the fourth year of a dry cycle, and the present crop is thin, occasionally interspersed with lupine, sunflower, yarrow, or wild celery between the rows, native successional plants that the farmer doesn't mind. The surrounding rangeland, Lucy says in a salty New England accent, is teeming with weeds. He stops to yank out a tumbleweed as we trudge through the thigh-high barley field, cussing while he demonstrates his point. "That's why the neglected public lands are such a concern. All the bad guys gather on the public lands, then threaten all the other landowners!" After the agencies launched a campaign of overhead chemical spraying in a futile attempt to bring the weed problem under control, Lucy finally decided to take matters into his own hands. "My first step here was to plow under the Barnaby and to overplant with rye. For three or four years I built up the soil and got organically certified. I've harvested some sections, green-manured others, and planted native grasses wherever I could. And the populations of quail, grouse, deer have all responded. They weren't around when I first moved here. Grain is better than Barnaby. What I'm doing here is what the game department should be doing. They've got some of the best ground in the valley. And what do they do? Let the same farmer overgraze it year after year!"

In addition to his own land, Lucy has extended his experiment to contract farming on 200 more acres. Some is dry-farmed uplands, most is irrigated bottomland, and all is organic. He has also forged a partnership with second-home owners from Seattle, such as Vogt, who organized this visit for me. "Being a second-home owner is an embarrassment of riches," says Vogt, "but working with Sam and the Conservancy to restore the land allows me to put my money where my heart is." At present, landowners pay Lucy to plant fields to winter rye or winter wheat in order to suppress weeds and help restore soil quality. He harvests what he can, and they reap the aesthetic and stewardship rewards and maintain their agricultural tax status. "This wouldn't have gone anywhere unless you had second-home owners who love this valley, because they love the land and they want to keep the land healthy, and they can afford to support an organic restoration program."

Lucy admits that his is a frenzied business, and that he lacks machinery to do his job better and perhaps expand his operations. Looking toward the future, he sees the Methow's isolation as a potential benefit. "The only advantage to being so far in the middle of nowhere is that you can be in the middle of nowhere. Very soon they are going to introduce genetically engineered wheat, and then where are you going to be able to grow organic wheat? Right here under the Methow label. To do that you've got to be isolated from drift," he says, his arms outstretched toward the vast openness. "What's more isolated than this?"

Across the Divide and Into the Buffer Battles

Returning west over the glacial peaks of Washington Pass and Rainy Pass, descending the slopes of the Cascades and following the (wild and scenic) meandering Skagit River through the lush Skagit Flats toward Puget Sound, one comes to an area with distinctly different circumstances in both agricultural production and regional politics. There are some similarities: salmon species are in decline; upstream forests have been abused; small-scale agriculture is being challenged by large industrial operations moving to the Columbia Basin; communities are poised for action; and farmlands are threatened by suburban encroachment, from Seattle and Vancouver, British Columbia. But in what is known as the Magic Skagit—a farming area with some of the earth's most productive soils and up to 70 different crops, including 90 percent of the world's cabbage seed—the struggle between agriculture and conservation has become far more contested than in the Methow Valley. The Swinomish Tribe, the Department of Fish and Wildlife, and other conservation groups have been battling for 150- to 200-foot riparian buffers along farmlands in order to restore fish habitat. Farm advocacy organizations, such as the Mt. Vernon-based Skagitonians to Preserve Farmland, argue that while they are willing to expand and protect buffers, riparian zones of more than 75 feet would put some already struggling farmers out of business. In addition, the upland habitats of the eastern Skagit differ greatly from the broad lowlands near the sound, a former estuary that was drained and diked in the early 20th century by Northern European immigrants. One-size-fits-all buffers could be appropriate in one area, but might force out many conservation-minded farmers in another.

The issue of bird habitat in the Skagit is far less divisive. The broad valley in which the Skagit River meanders, known as the Skagit Flats, is a winter haven for raptors, owls, and migratory waterfowl. This is some of the most prized territory for birds of prey in the Pacific Northwest, if not the entire United States, attracting large numbers of bald eagles, red-tailed, rough-legged, and sharp-shinned hawks, northern harriers, and five species of falcons. With encouragement from the local Barley for Birds Program, Skagitonian farmers have for some time used a winter cover crop rotation of barley to enhance already sound habitat for snow geese, widgeons, and other migratory waterfowl journeying south along the Pacific Flyway.

If the nonirrigated, diverse, and highly productive farms of the Skagit are lost to the pressures of globalization, population growth, and conservation buffer battles, it won't be for lack of trying. While admitting past mistakes, the directors of the Skagitonians to Preserve Farmland are attempting to deeply address all these issues simultaneously. Their main argument is that farms *are* buffers, and that working with private landowners to accomplish mutual goals is preferable to losing farmland to development. In 1996, Skagit County passed a property tax that annually raises approximately $400,000 and empowers the Skagit County Farmland Legacy Program to purchase development rights from willing farmers. A mapping program is underway with The Nature Conservancy to prioritize and ultimately protect and connect valuable habitat in the region. In response to the exodus of vegetable processing facilities, markets for local produce are being boosted by a Skagit regional label. On both sides of the Cascades, then, farmers, scientists, locals, and outsiders all seem engaged in a struggle to reshape their future. Creating communities of conservationists holds a key to embracing a partnership ethic between the human and the wild.

World-class Topsoils

Top left, Anne Schwartz of Blue Heron Farm. Her CSA farm includes buffers of native trees for restoration as well as a robust riparian margin.

Center right, winter stubble provides foraging habitat for snow geese, swans, and dabbling ducks.

Bottom row, the Mauer family operates a dairy farm on the Upper Skagit. Wetland habitat is inter-mixed throughout. Kim Mauer has a reputation for breeding rare domesticated animals, particularly poultry.

THE FARM AS PARK VISITOR CENTER

In the spectacular fjord country of southern Chile's Palena region, agriculture has long been a challenging endeavor. For decades, pioneer settlers have been burning and carving small homestead farms into the region's densely forested valleys and slopes, eking out a lean existence on a diverse mix of livestock grazing, fishing, woodcutting, and gardening. Among many limiting factors for farming is water; not too little, but too much—over 200 inches per year on average, the perfect climate for a temperate rainforest. This is the land of the fabled alerce, a member of the cypress family and southern cousin of the coast redwood, that frequently reaches diameters of 10 to 12 feet or more. Alerces and other species make up extremely rare old-growth forest systems that spread from the fjord's edge, into valleys and lower mountains beneath the glacial peaks and volcanic cones of the Andes. Many alerces even grow on the slopes of the volcanoes.

In 1990, adventurer and entrepreneur Doug Tompkins bought an 18,000-acre cattle ranch in this region with the intention of settling into an ecological lifestyle surrounded by remote, undeveloped wilderness. He had recently retired from an extremely successful career as co-founder of the Esprit clothing company, and shifted his talents and resources toward environmental philanthropy by starting the Foundation for Deep Ecology. A lifelong pilot, mountain climber, and kayaker (with many first ascents and descents to his credit), he immersed himself in learning everything he could about conservation biology, ecology, and sustainable agriculture. During this time, he met a fellow outdoor adventurer, Kris McDivitt, who was also retiring from a career with the eco-conscious Patagonia corporation. They married not long after and over the next decade, channeled their collective genius for organization building toward the establishment of two of South America's most ambitious wildlands philanthropy organizations, the Conservation Land Trust (CLT, in Chile and Argentina) and more recently, the Patagonia Land Trust (PLT, in Argentina). In Chile's Palena region, the CLT began slowly and methodically purchasing holdings in the mountainous temperate rainforest for the purpose of conservation. Their initial focus was a fairly pristine area between Hornopiren and Caleta Gonzala, where the gravel highway that transects southern Chile stops for 30 miles. The only way to travel the undeveloped wilds in between is by air or sea, a journey often accompanied by sightings of dolphins, sea lions, and orcas. A decade later CLT had acquired an area totaling over 730,000 acres, roughly the size of California's Yosemite National Park. What they have named Parque Pumalin (or Pumalin Park) is now one of the world's largest private park initiatives. Provided that CLT receives full assurances from the Chilean government that the land will be permanently protected, it will eventually be incorporated into the Chilean National Park system.

While Parque Pumalin's primary focus is the protection of native biodiversity—about 98 percent of the area is undeveloped wildlands—the remainder is in pastoral farms. These privately owned farms, in fact, are an integral component of the project's design and represent a unique model that is now being studied by park officials throughout the world. Each in its own watershed, they fulfill a number of functions. They act as ranger stations, establishing a strategic presence in each valley, helping visitors, discouraging poaching, and providing services such as cafes, information centers, cabins, and camping facilities. They are diversified operations now undergoing whole-farm organic certification with the Institute for Marketecology (IMO) and as such serve as demonstration centers for sustainable agriculture. The visitor center at the southern ferry station of Caleta Gonzala, for example, is one of Parque Pumalin's seven agricultural areas. Visitors can walk raised wooden pathways through highly productive organic gardens graced with utility and artistry. Throughout the spring, summer, and fall growing seasons, the beds swell with an astounding bounty—carrots, peas, strawberries, lettuces, artichokes, chard, herbs, local potato cultivars. Fava bean cover crops and insectary flower plantings vividly span the length of the gardens. Ingeniously designed, rustic greenhouses, assembled from locally milled lumber and plastic sheeting, protect plants against wind and rain and create warm miroclimates. Beyond the production gardens are hen houses and plots of trellised blueberries, gooseberries, and raspberries. Sheep and horses graze in pastures between the fjord and the forest edge. Farther out are stations of colorfully painted bee boxes. Many trees in the surrounding forest support bees, particularly the native ulmo, a flowering hardwood that produces an exceptional honey. All of the farm's organic food production is directed toward feeding the local community as well as the increasing number of visitors passing through each year, eager to experience this new ecotourism destination. Rather than the institutional fare doled out in national park concessions throughout North America, Caleta's cafe serves healthy meals consisting largely of the farm's fresh fruits and vegetables, meats, eggs, as well as locally caught seafood. Local artisan products such as hand-knit woolen goods, hand-carved bowls, honey, and preserves are offered as well. Despite challenges of rainy weather, the park farms have rapidly emerged as Chile's fifth-largest honey supplier, and the leading supplier in the Tenth Region, and visitors can tour honey production facilities.

"Conserving bioidversity is our primary goal," says Doug Tompkins, "but we are also working very hard to compatibilize agricultural production with conservation." While he admits that the farms depend on the introduction of exotic species such as honey bees and sheep, these have been chosen for their light impact on the ecosystem and are monitored as carefully as possible. Cows, traditionally pastured throughout the region, have been removed from the farms in favor of sheep, which are more lightweight and have far less impact in extremely wet conditions. Sheep sheds provide both predator protection and manure collection for farming operations. In agricultural areas, erosion has been arrested and animals kept out of the forests. Low-lying areas in valleys that were previously cleared by settlers for pasturing have been dramatically rejuvenated. Stumps and debris were cleared, grasses rested, and no-till seeding equipment imported to enhance pastures. "Restoration is a third objective," says Tompkins, "and we are attempting to bring degraded ecosystems back to health." At Vodudahue, an impressive section of Parque Pumalin with granite domes and peaks reminiscent of Yosemite Valley, the park farm has a native tree nursery. Thousands of seedlings and saplings of numerous species grow in raised beds under the protection of large shade structures to be used for reforestation projects throughout the park.

Although farther north, Chilean agriculture is quickly adopting California's Central Valley industrial practices, the efforts at Parque Pumalin's demonstration farms have not gone unnoticed. Tompkins and other employees increasingly field inquiries from regional landowners about organic gardening, pasture restoration, and reforestation techniques. As important as agriculture is to the project, however, the farms exist only as portals to wilderness. Parque Pumalin's primary objective will always be to allow the species-rich forests and valleys to continue evolving as they have for millennia. The park's namesake, after all, is the puma, whose exploits occasionally result in the loss of a lamb or sheep, but whose territory here will most likely never be adversely affected by a human presence.

Farming at the Edge of Wilderness

Top left, a gardener at work in one of the world's premiere organic gardening operations. Top right, sheep grazing at sunset. Center left, the park's native flowering trees and shrubs support a growing honey operation. Parque Pumalin spans from inland bays to the Andes Mountains. Visitors can explore rare temperate rainforests as well as organic farms and restoration projects.

WILD GARDEN FARMERS

In "Song of the Gavilan," an essay of near sublime inspiration from *A Sand County Almanac*, Aldo Leopold recounts a journey through stony and precipitous country in which he is overcome by a profound sense of ecological harmony. Ironically, perhaps, in painting that picture of a once self-willed, balanced and biologically diverse landscape, Leopold emphasizes the role of the human presence. For thousands of years, he surmises, prehistoric farmers had built stone check dams and terraces to irrigate and contain their gardens and fields, carefully guarding them from their hilltop perches. Pines, oaks, and junipers had long ago overtaken these plots, revealing how many centuries ago such a culture had existed. At one point, Leopold aims an arrow at a buck lying in the shade of an oak whose roots are entwined in the ancient masonry and overshoots. "It was appropriate that I missed," he writes, "for when a great oak grows in what is now my garden, I hope there will be bucks to bed in its fallen leaves, and hunters to stalk, and wonder who built the garden wall."

Around the country today there exist smaller-scale agriculturalists who have, at heart, the earth wisdom of the "old terrace-builders" in the "Song of the Gavilan." A major part of this movement has taken a decided turn toward "pre-European conditions," including the embrace of native species. Several examples readily come to mind—Cannard Farms (Glen Ellen, California), the Occidental Arts and Ecology Center (Occidental, California), Ecology Action (Willits, California), the Long Branch Environmental Education Center (Leicester, North Carolina), Shoulder to Shoulder Farm (Philomath,

Oregon), Wolf Berry Farm (Yacava Valley, Arizona), Native Seed SEARCH (Patagonia, Arizona), Molino Creek Farm (Davenport, California), and the Chadwick Gardens (University of California Santa Cruz) among many others too numerous to list. For the convenience of categorization, we might call them "Wild Garden Farmers."

The principles of sustainable farming—organic, Biointensive, and Biodynamics—were the launching points for these efforts decades ago. What these practitioners share is the drive to bring knowledge based in place, ecosystem, and habitat back into modern agriculture. The wild garden farmers share a solemn if unspoken pledge to devise a farm's scale according to what the land will allow, rather than making the farm conform to predetermined goals and notions. This can take the shape, for example, of rainfall-based, rather than fossil water-driven (aquifer) cropping. Off-farm nutrient and pest control inputs are relied on only as a last resort. Climate-adapted food, fiber, and medicinal plant types are sought out, as are native ecotypes for restoration and conservation. Perennial cropping systems, fruit forests, harvesting and wildcrafting (cultivation in wild settings) of native plants, and permaculture designs can be emphasized. Such operations are often best described as large-scale, intensively managed gardens. They are obviously not hobby farms but engaged in serious production on anywhere from a few to a few dozen acres. Yet because of their scale and integration into the surrounding landscape, the boundaries between wild and cultivated are blurred to such an extent that the farmscape begins to evolve and function as a natural system. In place of total control is a faith and knowledge in the self-regulating function of extreme diversity and the fundamentals of biologically based agriculture. Nature fills in the gaps between the cultivated and wild areas. Self-seeding food crops over time become weed

"South Garden," an exceptional canvas by Adam Wolpert, resident artist at the Occidental Arts and Ecology Center. Garden landscapes are a continual subject for this highly talented, hardworking painter.

species. Walking the rows of some of these operations, one might be tempted, at certain times of the year, to ask—Why are there so many flowers and legumes and grasses? Where is the food? On closer inspection, one is stunned by the intricacy, ingenuity, and gutsiness of the wild garden farmers at work.

By virtue of the scale and local orientation, one might dismiss wild garden farms as marginal contributors to the nation's food production. This is far from the truth, particularly when one factors in the growing number of such farms around the country and their contributions to local food systems. A number supply foods to some of the country's finest restaurants. Others are highly profitable and productive operations that show how with hard work but sound management, an honest yet challenging living can be made on the small farm. Many function as educational centers with activist orientations. Yet it is exactly by finding ways to create cultures that value and are informed by the natural world that we move toward the light touch of agriculture that Leopold admired on the banks of the Gavilan so many decades ago. It is only by allowing the wild to influence agriculture that we move away from what California farmer Bob Cannard describes as "hollow food grown with discontent," and recognize "the difference between food grown for quality rather than obscene volume." Finding ways to enhance and incorporate this essential work into our mainstream agriculture ranks among the key challenges of this new century.

Joanna Divine, a graduate student at the Center for Sustainable Environments at Northern Arizona University, Flagstaff, has been studying the advantages of using superbly acclimated Navajo Churro sheep on southwestern ranches. She sums up the wild garden farmers' approach this way: "Farming with the wild is juxtaposed with farming against the wild, which is what we tend to do here in the United States—replacing what's here with what we think agriculture should be. It's a destructive practice that's digging us deeper and deeper into a hole that's going to be harder and harder to get out of the longer we do it. Farming with the wild encourages people to look at native biota as a source of food, as a source of aesthetic value, as compatible surroundings, as well as the basis of all life. What we can learn from what's here is how to live here. What grows here is how we should grow here. So in a sense, farming with the wild is a way to learn how better to adopt agricultural practices that are less destructive and more in sync with the natural rhythms of any place."

There once were men capable of inhabiting a river without disrupting the harmony of its life. They must have lived in thousands on the Gavilan, for their works are everywhere. Ascend any draw debouching on any canyon and you find yourself climbing little rock terraces or check dams, the crest of one level with the base of the next. Behind each dam is a little plot of soil that was once a field or garden, sub-irrigated by the showers which fell on the steep adjoining slopes. On the crest of the ridge you may find the stone foundations of a watch tower; the hillside farmer probably stood guard over his polka-dot acrelets. Household water he must have carried from the river. Of domestic animals he evidently had none. What crops did he raise? How long ago? The only fragment of an answer lies in the 300-year-old pines, oaks, or junipers that now find rootage in his little fields. Evidently it was longer ago than the age of the oldest trees.

–Aldo Leopold, "Song of the Gavilan," *A Sand County Almanac*

Path through the north garden at the Occidental Arts and Ecology Center in Sonoma County, California.

SANGIN' IN DANIEL BOONE'S FOOTSTEPS

Walking down a steep path ankle-deep in papery yellow and red fallen leaves not too many miles the way the crow flies from Daniel Boone National Forest, Syl Yunker displays his familiarity of the woods with a deliberate reverence. As we descend, he points out how the pine, oak, and beech of the sandstone ridge gradually give way to cedar, maple, poplar, and, along the creek, sycamore. The wiry, gray-haired, and white-goateed Yunker uses a "seeding stick" to steady himself–a wooden tool handle with a length of half-inch PVC pipe (to drop seeds) and bowie knife (to dig holes for seeds) duct-taped to the handle. When we reach moss-covered limestone outcrops at the top of a deep draw, his pace slows. "Limestone soil is the key to where you locate wild ginseng," says Yunker, pronouncing "soil" like "soul" and "ginseng" like "jen-sang." "Ginseng loves calcium!"

For the 72-year-old Yunker, ginseng cultivation has been a longtime preoccupation. He learned about the plant while serving in Korea following World War II and was fascinated to observe that the price and demand in Asia, particularly for the highly prized wild roots that grow in the forest, never wavered–not even during crises such as the Communist takeover of China in 1949. As the yeoman small-farm scene in his native Kentucky began to unravel throughout the 1970s and 1980s, he began to see ginseng wildcrafting (cultivation in the wild) as one of several potential alternatives to tobacco, a traditional economic mainstay in an area also heavily exploited for timber and coal.

The medicinal herb *Panex quinquefolius* thrives as an understory plant on northern slopes of the mixed mesophytic Appalachian temperate forests and related forest types, which spread from Georgia to Maine and as far west as the Ozarks. Indeed it is a rather ordinary vine with extraordinary roots, that has connected Appalachians with Asians and Native Americans with New Agers. According to Yunker, it is believed that ginseng was brought across the Bering Strait land bridge, just as many of what we now consider native species of plants and animals, including bison, arrived on this migration route. French traders were shipping ginseng to the Orient by the early 1700s. New York's Astor family started its fortune with a shipment of ginseng to the Orient. Documents and legend recount that Daniel Boone was an inveterate "sang" gatherer, roaming the Appalachian forests, hunting more ginseng than bear, delivering it by the 15-ton raft-full to Fort Pitt for eventual export to Asia.

Today, with most of the Asian temperate forests gone, the slow-growing, knobby roots of North American ginseng are revered for their various salubrious effects.

In Yunker's beat-up Ford Ranger, we headed east from the bluegrass thoroughbred estates around Lexington toward the Appalachians–from one of Kentucky's wealthiest to one of its poorest regions. We passed bottomlands divided up into trailer lots and small farms with creosote-blackened barns where tobacco hung drying, then climbed a ridge looking out over verdant valleys and wooded mountains now radiant in fall foliage. So fearful was Yunker that his sang might be poached, we spoke only in hushed tones during a coffee stop in a local fast-food restaurant.

His caution is understandable. Wild ginseng cultivation is a long-term investment to say the least and poaching is considered a regional pastime if not an entitlement. It takes 18 months for the seeds Yunker plants with his seeding stick to germinate, five years for a plant to bear seed, and another five years before it amasses a root significant enough to harvest. Once a patch reaches harvesting age, 10 percent of the annual crop–about a half pound per acre in Yunker's case–can be sustainably collected indefinitely. A pound of those roots will fetch $450-1,000 in the United States; a broker will resell that same amount for nearly $2,000 in Hong Kong. A deer hunter or opportunist, then, who stumbles upon and cleans out a carefully cultivated crop, literally hits pay dirt–and spells the end to a decade's work.

We reach an optimal 18 percent north-facing gradient where Yunker has an 11-year-old patch. The sang is sown in terraces, made of deadfall limbs, specifically designed to capture moisture and nutrient-rich leaf litter. Soon we see the bright yellow horse chestnut-like leaves of the plant rising about calf-high in the mottled beds. The plant has a tell-tale cluster of three major and two minor leaflets per leaf, and a set of red berries by midsummer. "The wild turkeys cleaned me out of seed this summer by beating me to the berries," Yunker says, still harboring a tinge of resentment. "The stem is the best indication of root size," he adds. "When you get one that approaches the thickness of a pencil, you know you got a good old root that is nine or ten years old."

With a spade, Yunker digs up a plant he deems of a worthy age. He starts with side cuts about a foot away from the spindly plant and, once the soil is loosened, angles the spade deep under the stem. He ends up with a pointed root ball, and carefully crumbles away the soil, exposing a pocket knife-sized main root with more than a dozen hairy sideshoots. Holding up the ginseng, he shows how the forest growing conditions create tight horizontal compression rings as well as a "multiplicity of shape"—in other words, a gnarled rather than a uniform carrot-like root. "Most valued of all is a 'man shape,'" he says, "with two arms, two legs, and a male member, said to enhance sexual vitality."

A patch can be seeded in the fall after a summer harvest of berries or grown from seedlings started in a sand medium. Yunker frequently uses goldenseal as a companion plant, he says, because it can actually feed off and neutralize pathogens that a ginseng plant naturally gives off, which can prevent new ginseng plants from growing in the same spot for ten years. "This way you can replant it continuously, not as densely perhaps, but the higher price of the wild over cultivated and continuous cropping every year make it just as feasible to grow it this way."

It is the economics of sustainable ginseng harvesting that occupy Yunker as much as the details of cultivation. "We need to build enough production—about 3,000 pounds or 6,000 acres worth—for brokers to take us seriously, and get the prices up to $1,000 per pound." Even in a best-case scenario, he explains, it will take the Asians 60 years to regenerate forest conditions that would allow them to grow ginseng in the wild. So he estimates that there is at least a half-century market for this plant. Kentucky forests could also potentially supply a great diversity of native herbs, nuts, fruits, mushrooms, and quality hardwoods. Organizations, such as the Forest School in Constantine, Kentucky, argue that wild mushrooms, wild game, walnuts, chestnuts, pecans, butternuts, pawpaws, persimmons, and many other products could be harvested at a significantly higher per-acre return than the state's grain-dominated agriculture.[1] Commercial-scale wildcrafting, however, should be done with great care not to disturb wildlife or rare or uncommon native species.

A bird calls out across the forest, teer teer teer teer teer teer. "The copperheads and eastern timber rattlers," Yunker says, "have now gone underground with the colder weather." It is obvious he is always listening to his land, looking for signs and opportunities. For the people living in the margins of rural Appalachia, one can sense a logic in what he hears, and perhaps appreciate Syl Yunker's ginseng tune.

Little Person of the Forest

Top left, a ginseng plant in its fall colors.

Center left, wood terraces catch leaf litter and slow runoff. Center middle, the blade and tube on a seeding stick allow for digging and seeding while standing. Syl Yunker, ginseng crusader.

Bottom left, a mature root, carefully harvested to preserve all natural features.

Bottom right, a ginseng bloom.

BASINS OF RELATIONS

Encircled by oak and conifer woodlands, and exhibiting a diversity that borders on chaos, the terraced gardens at the Occidental Arts and Ecology Center (OAEC) embody a dialog between tame and wild. Insects and birds whir and dart amid nectar- and seed-laden amaranths, sunflowers, and wildflowers. The ecotones between cultivated and noncultivated are permeable—with the exception of perimeter deer fencing around garden and living areas. Exuberant colors and forms impressionistically fill the landscape. Vegetable gardens, irrigated by pond-captured rainfall, suggest a bounty of almost idyllic proportions. Gardeners move meditatively about, intent on the morning's chores, as a cassette tape of world beat music plays counterpoint to the sounds of winged and crawling creatures.

For three decades, this 80-acre site nestled on a ridge above western Sonoma County's Coleman Valley has been the locus of unique forms of activism. Formerly housing a sustainability think tank known as the Farallones Institute, in 1994 it became home to a community of wildlife biologists, wilderness and watershed activists, permaculture and agroecology practitioners, educators, artists, and teachers. The ninth oldest farm certified by the California Certified Organic Farmers, its gardens and orchards were eventually placed in a permanent organic agricultural easement with the Sonoma Land Trust in 1994. In an agricultural area where small-scale family farms, dairies, and ranches have increasingly been subdivided or converted to industrial vineyards, OAEC has, among other efforts, established production-scale gardening practices particularly suited to the wet winters and arid summers of northern coastal California.

As is fitting for a teaching environment, the intensively managed gardens embody a daring horticultural inventiveness, and an October tour offers the opportunity to graze in this botanical library. Inspired by the principles of agroecology and permaculture, as well as by indigenous Pomo agriculture, OAEC produces up to 500 crops annually, with an emphasis on open-pollinated heirloom varieties and perennials. Among these are numerous Andean vegetables that perform surprisingly well in local north-coastal California conditions. Pepino is an eggplant-shaped perennial that tastes like a cross between a melon and a tomato with a zing of cucumber. Mashua, a relative of nasturtium, produces turnip-like fingerling tubers and edible flowers that are both honey-sweet and piquant. Oca is yet another tuber, which, according to the veteran OAEC gardener Doug Gosling, "melts in your mouth when roasted—we just can't grow enough of them." Mediterranean crops also proliferate in the gardens, including lupini, an Italian lupine prized for its edible seed. Cape gooseberry fruits have a lantern-like papery shell and an almost tropical coconut flavor. Uncommon corn varieties, including teocinte, the early wild relative of maize, are sown. Even the clover and grass paths themselves have nutritional value and purpose: the clippings provide a primary nitrogen source for the center's many compost piles.

The horticultural library is an appropriate metaphor for this decades-old garden. Through OAEC's Mother Garden Biodiversity Program 3,000 varieties of heirloom open-pollinated annuals and 1,000 varieties of edible, medicinal, and ornamental perennials are propagated and inventoried in a living plant and seed collection. "Conventional farmers who visit here often ask why we grow so many flowers," says Gosling. "This has been a seed-saving garden for more than 20 years, and in a way, we are working in the opposite direction of most gardeners. Instead of trying to harvest crops before they go back to seed, each of the garden beds is literally a seed bank. Rather than fighting the diversity, we work with it. And most of the time it's a very exciting conversation in terms of harvesting the weeds for food, for mulch, for compost, and for increasing the diversity of the system by allowing the gardens to select what comes up."

Among the goals of maintaining such diversity is the establishment of a natural gardening environment that is resilient and independent of off-farm inputs. Farming with such wild edges, however, also has distinct challenges. "We struggle with the birds at times," says Gosling, dragging his fingers through his unruly curls. "We have to cover everything under netting until the plants are established, especially along the edges. And it sometimes seems like we are growing gophers." Yet when a red-breasted nuthatch alights on a drooping 12-foot-high sunflower head and plucks a seed, Gosling's face lights up. "This is really extraordinary. They rarely come out into the open like this."

Successful gardening at OAEC is predicated upon biological indicators such as the red-breasted nuthatch, as well as the wrentit, Douglas squirrel, Pacific tree frog, and other species that dwell or pass within the property's diverse microhabitats. With both gardeners and biologists on staff, as much effort is placed on understanding the ecology of this upland habitat as on growing the food for the 20 full-time residents and seasonal workshop attendees. OAEC maintains impressive vertebrate and vascular plant species lists to monitor that biodiversity. Under a grant from the U.S. Fish and Wildlife Service's Partners for Wildlife Program, resident wildlife biologists Brock Dolman and Carol Nieukirk are now studying the behavior of neotropical songbird migrants on the property—including warblers, tanagers, grosbeaks, and vireos—with an eye toward the maintenance and restoration of the vegetation communities that support them. As a consequence of decades of fire suppression and unsustainable forestry practices in much of Northern California, the late-successional evergreen habitats (which include hardwoods) necessary for many species have been diminished. OAEC's study is focusing on reducing fuel loads in their fire-prone area, thinning Douglas fir to promote new hardwood growth, and removing exotics such as French and Scotch broom in order to restore pre-European conditions in grasslands.

"If we're going to talk restoration, however," cautions Dolman, "we literally need a revolution at the watershed level." That revolution, he says, must be predicated on a shift from water rights to water responsibilities and on restoration of the pre-development hydrological functions of the area. Intensive forestry and development have resulted in increases in both volume and velocity of runoff. The lack of vegetation facilitates scouring, erosion, and sediment loading. Compacted and paved areas make the soil impervious. Recharging the groundwater and keeping streams clear of sediment, full of water, and well shaded have become nearly impossible struggles. "Endangered salmon and steelhead are merely the canaries in the coal mines of our endangered watersheds," says Dolman.

Along contours and stream channels of its own lands, OAEC has constructed gabions and brush swales to collect debris and slow runoff. Twenty years ago, when it was still the Farallones Institute, a 6-acre-foot runoff pond was constructed by damming an eroding gully. That pond today provides all the irrigation water for OAEC's three acres of gardens. A second small ephemeral pond outside the north garden is a wildlife watering hole. It's only a small puddle on the day of our visit, after the first autumn rain. But it will soon become a catch basin that controls erosion, and the winter venue for deafening choruses of Pacific tree frogs, as well as a harbor for dragonflies and damselflies in summer.

OAEC's work also extends far beyond the boundaries of gardens, orchards, and property lines, addressing the cultural aspects of agriculture by reaching out into local communities. The Basins of Relations Program trains community watershed groups—multi-stakeholder groups of farmers, ranchers, landowners, and environmentalists—to conduct local watershed assessments and craft short- and long-term restoration plans. Expert panels focus on best-management land-use practices pertaining to agriculture, forestry, roads, and home building. Each group then participates in the ongoing Sonoma County Watershed Network, coordinating restoration work and collaborating on local land-use and farm policy changes. The OAEC School Garden Teacher Training and Support Program establishes organic gardens in schools throughout the Bay Area and North Bay. These gardens serve as outdoor laboratories where children can learn about and explore the art and craft of growing food. (In one such garden, for example, where my children attend elementary school, students grow all the necessary ingredients to make pizzas.) They also provide supplemental culinary and nutritional values in the form of just-picked, locally grown produce.

Dave Henson, OAEC's executive director, is an articulate activist who is at once idealistic and pragmatic. Henson is not optimistic about the direction of an economic and political system dominated by transnational corporations. But he is optimistic about the ability of communities to make dramatic adjustments and avert the worst case scenarios many environmentalists and others are concerned about. For that reason, he directs the Center's Corporations and Democracy program and serves on the steering committee of a national group called the Program on Corporations, Law, and Democracy. Part of a solution, he insists, lies in reviving an agrarian culture that has its soul in soil and community, which is the antithesis of the current global food system that has become increasingly dominated by intensive machinery, toxic chemical inputs, and genetic engineering. "Our challenge," Henson states determinedly, "is to restore a community-based family farming culture that has been dismantled by industrial agribusinesses and life science corporations whose goal is to control the global food and agriculture system.

"We're the ones in our area of Sonoma County who bring people together to talk about how we want our community to be," says Henson, in an office piled with paperwork. "This boils down to nothing less than reimagining our democratic rights. That drives us to create programs such as seed saving, the 'No Spray Action Network,' school gardens, and community events that bring together people who have a stake in their future and want to discuss their quality of life. If our communities are educated about ecological, agricultural, and democratic literacy, we can remake our world, by redefining our local laws and culture in ways that reflect the values of ecological agriculture, sustainable food systems, and a restored native biodiversity."

It is a sweeping, radical, almost overwhelming mission, but also a rational critique being lived out by the members of the OAEC community. Throughout the year, waves of visitors arrive at the Center to imbibe its information and inspiration, attending workshops, conferences, training seminars, and plant sales. They stay in the Center's humble yet comfortable yurt quarters, work in and eat from the gardens, attend seminars conducted by experts in permaculture, natural building, community organizing, and democratic decision making. Painting and art classes are conducted by Adam Wolpert, OAEC's resident artist, who can be seen most days out on the land or in his studios, working on various canvases. There are compost piles to be turned, greenhouse starts to be watered, natural building projects underway, forests being carefully thinned to restore some of their former species distribution. The Center's annual catalog artistically and intellectually reflects and documents these activities, complete with four-color photographs and reproductions of Wolpert's canvases. Walking the gardens, forests, and grasslands, and engaging in this dialogue of tame and wild, one can begin to believe in the transformation in such a positive vision.

FARMING WITH THE WILD—Wild Garden Farmers

Community with a Wild Heart

A group photo outside the kitchen and dining hall at the Occidental Arts and Ecology Center in Sonoma County, California. The gardens, established more than 20 years ago, were inspired by the late Biointensive gardening guru Alan Chadwick. The gardens have become particularly adapted to their wild surroundings. The harvests supply year-round produce for the Center's residents as well as frequent retreat visitors.

Top, third from right, bay nuts were a staple of indigenous peoples in much of Northern California.

Center right, a sampling of heirloom potato varieties. Numerous Andean crops are grown and do well in the OAEC gardens.

Bottom left, a Pacific tree frog makes itself at home in cress.

Center bottom, shows a view of the north garden, with a perennial insectary running through its center.

SAVING THE SEEDS OF ENDANGERED AGRICULTURE

When we catch up with Bill Fowler, manager of the Native Seed SEARCH Conservation Farm, on a July afternoon, the monsoon sky was darkening ominously. He was out driving metal stakes and setting wire in a row of Tohono O'odham pink beans. The 60-acre farm is located in Patagonia, Arizona, just 20 miles from the U.S.-Mexico border, near one of the world's birding meccas. It is dramatic country, with the floodplain-level farm encircled by a higher desert plateau and a Sky Island mountain peak looming like a monument to the south. Whistling-ducks, vermilion flycatchers, and crested caracaras pass through the farm borders frequently, Fowler told us, as do javelinas, pumas, bears, reptiles such as the rosy boa, and "all kinds of neat bugs." When the drizzle turned to a steady rain, we retreated under a thatched open-air shelter to talk about the organization's operations and mission.

"How they got the acronym SEARCH into the name was actually an amazing feat," says Fowler, dressed that afternoon in a T-shirt, shorts, sandals, and a baseball cap. "It stands for Southwestern Endangered Arid (Lands) Resources Clearing House." The "resources" are more than 2,000 domesticated crop varieties, developed over centuries and millennia by traditional farmers for the arid short-season growing conditions of northern Mexico, New Mexico, Arizona, and part of southeastern California. Included in the bank are the native triumvirate of corn, beans, and squashes, dozens and dozens of chiles and their wild relatives, the chiltepines, tobaccos and sunflowers, amaranths and melons, tomatoes and tomatillos, to name just a few. Gourds, dye plants, herbs, and basket-making materials are also represented. By rule of thumb, these seeds must be grown out at least every ten years or lose their potency, so the bank is caught in a perpetual race against time to preserve the material it has acquired.

Starting in 1983 with just a handful of seeds entrusted to the organization's co-founders, Gary Paul Nabhan and Mahina Drees, by Native American farmers, the seed bank has since been collecting, organizing, and conserving an invaluable repository of domesticated traditional crops. Nabhan and Drees, Fowler told us, were attempting to help people on reservations to grow their own gardens and provide their own nutrition through a program called Meals for Millions. "They were planting broccoli and carrots and other vegetables, and they said, 'This is great, but we'd love to be able to grow the varieties that our grandparents grew.' They didn't want just any variety. They wanted a specific bean that they associated with their heritage." As a result, the fate of cultural traditions as well as agricultural wisdom now lies with Native Seed SEARCH. Such collections could one day help counteract the intensive monoculturalization and hybridization of the world's staple and minor crops by offering naturally pest-resistant plants and cultivars with characteristics of adaptive value in a period of anthropogenic climate change. These collections may also play a crucial role in the gradual revival of traditional food and dietary systems throughout the Southwest.

Seed preservation, however, is a risky business. Change is a constant, and every time seeds are grown out, the potential exists for contamination or random selection to alter the seed's genetic composition. The farm takes extraordinary precautions to keep lines pure and prevent unwanted cross-pollination, including adequate spacing between plants and plant types, careful timing to prevent simultaneous flowering, and the use of isolation cages and hand-pollinating for specific plants. In a row of common beans we inspect, buckwheat has been interplanted as a foil to attract any pollinators that might go from one bean type (or accession) to another and cross-pollinate.

"When you're growing for seed, you have to understand the reproductive variety of the plants you're growing," says Fowler. "In the case of the beans, they are self-pollinators with a perfect flower, meaning they have both the male and female component contained in one flower. They're very small, so it's not really conducive to bees pollinating them. You can plant them together if you have a little bit of separation without them cross-pollinating. With corn, on the other hand, we can only grow one variety per year. They are wind pollinated and the pollen travels for miles."

There are further complications. Seeds grown out at the Conservation Farm have the benefit of ample water, cover crops, and organic soil amendments—at least enough to provide a vigorous start on life. When grown under less favorable conditions—that is, in their traditional circumstances—the survival rate could be lower. "We talk about this all the time," says Fowler. "You can minimize that, and it's going to be very slow genetic drift, but every time you grow these out on a modern organic farm, there's a possibility that you can alter their genetic makeup, either through cross-pollination or if some of them survive that otherwise might not have.

"Our goal is to preserve the seeds in the exact condition we got them in, and then let growers and farmers and native peoples decide what to do with them," says Fowler. "We try not to do any selection at all. If we have some that are growing both tall and short and the taller is yielding more beans, then we collect them from both, because we want the entire genetic picture. Somebody else can take the next step and say, 'Well, this one that's tall produces a lot more, and it can survive on a month and a half of summer rains.'"

When the rain breaks, we walk to the back of the property, through rows of brilliantly flowered scarlet runner beans, tall stalks of blue corn, over to net-meshed isolation cages, where open-pollinated crops, such as chiles, tomatoes, and tomatillos, are housed. A flock of a rare breed of domesticated turkeys and a dozen Dominique chickens (the original American breed that came west with the covered wagons) strut among the plots, pecking and offering pest control. As harsh as this arid clime may seem, Fowler says it is an ideal place to do his work. "You baby the plants until they get going and then stand back and watch the summer monsoons take over. It's an incredible process." In dry years, they have the benefit of supplemental water. Native pollinators are never in short supply. The previous year, however, they suffered a major grasshopper invasion. "I'm talking biblical," he says, "little baby grasshoppers and then a plague."

One would assume that one of the perks of being a small-time seed producer would be a generous bounty of unusual garden fresh foods flowing into the kitchen. No such luck. "Everything we produce is so valuable, we're not allowed to eat the food," says Fowler. But that might not be a permanent condition. "One of the ideas of the seed bank is to put ourselves out of business. If we were able to distribute these seeds to the people who were originally growing them and they were able to continue an agricultural tradition, these seeds wouldn't be endangered."

Desert Seed Bank

Bill Fowler, manager at the Native Seed SEARCH Farm in southeastern Arizona inside a tent where rare pepper varieties are being grown for seed.

Top right, the view of a Sky Island mountain range south of the farm.

Center, right, bean blooms.

Bottom left, the farm grows out an impressive collection of native squashes.

Bottom right, heirloom turkeys.

THE APPALACHIAN FOOD FOREST

The headwaters of the Long Branch of Sandy Mush Creek traverse the forested uplands of western North Carolina's Appalachian Mountains, and as we walk the steep, wooded hills, the rippling and babbling of its running waters are always within earshot. We have journeyed to the Long Branch Environmental Education Center (LBEEC) outside Leicester (near Asheville) to speak to its founder, Paul Gallimore, who has spent the past 20 years developing a farming and foraging system he refers to as a food forest. "The inspiration for the food forest came from the southern Appalachian bioregion," explains Gallimore. "We live at the northernmost extension of southern species and the southernmost extension of northern species and as a result, we are blessed with what some consider to be the most biologically diverse region anywhere on the planet outside the tropical rainforests. Because all of Nature's wildlife species are taken care of by the forest ecosystem, we wanted to model our system of meeting human needs after that of the forest." (LBEEC was set aside as an ecological sanctuary in 1974 including over 1,600 acres of forest and 5 acres of farmland.)

In this part of rural Buncombe County, it is not uncommon for landowners to clear and plow the steep slopes in order to raise cattle, tobacco, corn, or the latest over-produced cash crop, tomatoes, known locally as "maters." Toxic fungicides are typically used on row crops to combat the region's high humidity and wet conditions. And with 50 inches of annual rainfall combined with hilly terrain, these regional agricultural practices have resulted in high levels of erosion and stream sedimentation.

The LBEEC's approach has led them primarily to establish perennials in order to minimize or eliminate the need for plowing or other soil disturbances. Hundreds of fruit and nut trees, large patches of strawberries, blueberries, blackberries, raspberries, asparagus, and rhubarb, as well as medicinal and culinary herbs have been integrated into gardens and the surrounding forest. Gallimore leads us to an area where numerous back-crossed 15-year-old American chestnut hybrids share the forest canopy. It is late October, and many of the nuts have dropped. Their spiny hulls are dried and split. Using a pocket knife, he shells a few of the chocolate-colored nuts and offers them to us. They are incredibly sweet, not bitter, with green and nutty flavor. Once an integral component of the eastern deciduous forests, the American chestnut was wiped out by blight beginning in the late 19th century and is only slowly being revived through horticultural triage. The tall trees are loaded with nuts and seem to be thriving in these woods, which are now just beginning to show signs of autumn color in their foliage. We explore another area farther back in the forest where Gallimore has interplanted native ginseng and goldenseal in an attempt to develop a diversity of additional wild crops in the understory. The forests also supply firewood and construction materials for the Center's buildings. At one point we stop at a small pond fed by the year-round flow of the creek. Gallimore throws out a handful of dried kibble-like food, which elicits a flurry of splashing and slashing at its black, mirrored surface. The pond is 30 feet in diameter and produces nearly 3,000 pounds of trout per year, much of which is sold at an annual fund-raising event. At the end of the year, the pond is drained so that the waste can be harvested and returned to the gardens in the form of compost.

As with the small fish pond, every attempt has been made to keep capitalization costs at a minimum. "In much of our agriculture today," Gallimore says, "the debt burden is enormous, and the stress of that economic system has been transferred on to the land. There are many crops, however, which can produce a sustainable yield and at the same time minimize the necessary labor and mechanization." The real challenge, he believes, is putting together a diversity of crops and markets to support a lifestyle.

In a hillside clearing is a maturing orchard with hundreds of apple, cherry, nectarine, and plum trees planted on a series of terraces that step down the steep slope. We sample a few of the heirloom apples and take a moment to sample the sounds of the surrounding forest as well. "The wild is the deepest part of human nature that we are tapping into," says Gallimore, "and farming is the cultural part of our lives. What that brings up for me is how we can integrate nature and culture so that we meet our needs in ways that minimize disruption. If we look at our food crops of today, we know that they all had their origins in wild ecosystems. Now we are tracing some of the origins of our crops and trying to figure out the habitats in which they prospered and perhaps mimic some of those habitats in our own food production systems. This is something we can all do, and we can spend our whole lives researching and applying. This is the cutting edge of where we need to be going in our research pursuits and day-to-day efforts in practicing survival on Planet Earth."

Appalachian Diversity

Top, Paul Gallimore and canine companion in a terraced fruit orchard, part of his unique food forest system that includes hundreds of fruit and nut trees and thousands of berries.

Top right, a trout pond, fed by a year-round stream, produces food for the Long Branch Environmental Education Center and helps raise money in an annual fund raising event.

Two photos bottom right are of the back-crossed American chestnuts, which are thriving throughout the property. LBEEC collaborates with the American Chestnut Foundation to revive the blighted species.

LEADING EDGE LETTUCE

The way Frank Morton tells it, he stumbled on plant breeding by accident. One day, while walking beds of specialty salad greens on his Shoulder to Shoulder Farm, he noticed an errant red-colored cross in an otherwise green crop of Salad Bowl lettuce. Morton, who possesses a predilection for color, decided to let the plant go to seed.

Shoulder to Shoulder Farm sits on a 55-acre parcel in the eastern foothills of the Oregon Coast Range and includes a remnant of Willamette Valley prairie. The farming operation surrounds the homestead cabin and straw-bale barn that Frank and his wife, Karen, and their two children call home. The farm is the antithesis of monocrop farming. Its complex plantings of insectary crops and hedgerows are so diverse, that it's hard even to locate the gourmet salad green crops that the Mortons have specialized in for nearly 20 years.

As a plant breeder, Frank Morton has taken a unique path, focusing on and selecting plant varieties for the particular challenges of organic farming—in addition to favoring outrageous and unexpected colors and textures. "In the old days, every locality kept its own seeds, varieties adapted to their life in place," he writes in Shoulder to Shoulder Farm's Wild Garden Seed catalog. "Today, we grow varieties adapted to some other place, judged on merits that may have little to do with our needs, like herbicide resistance or shipability."

Morton intentionally grows seed crops in order to develop varieties with particular values to organic gardeners and farmers. He grows cultivars in chemical-free settings, observing and selecting those that exhibit resistance to common challenges in organic farming, such as downy mildew; he also selects for unusual colors and for slow-bolting varieties. As we walk a field of seed crops, he points out a number of varieties to his credit: Blush Butter Cos, a beautiful red butter crunch; Frankenshpeckle, a red-and-green-speckled oak leaf; and Triple Purple Mountain Spinach, a velvety, almost crimson spinach with a salty taste.

Dan McGrath, a long-time Oregon State University Extension Farm Advisor, who arranged the visit, notes that Morton's farm operation represents the unconventional frontier of organic farming. "It takes a lot of guts to have this much diversity in a farmscape and still make a living. In fact, this is profound from a biological point of view, and only this extreme amount of diversity could create such a balance of biological control. This garden is just full of information. The focus is on beauty, not a fixation on control, and it reflects the philosophy of the family living here."

Beyond Morton's lettuce and spinach beds, yet another accidental discovery has determined the direction of his botanical energies. "When we bought this land," he says, "we had no idea it contained an intact fragment of upland prairie, an amazing community of plants that might hold the key to future restoration projects in the Willamette Valley." For a number of years now, Morton has been slowly familiarizing himself with the native grasses, wildflowers, trees, and shrubs on his land and collecting their seed. The walk around Shoulder to Shoulder Farm is peppered with Morton's identification of the plants endemic to the piece of ground where he and his family have made their home.

Finding machinery for cleaning small lots of hand-collected seed has posed quite a challenge to Morton. He has three different machines but none of them seems to measure up to good old fashioned hand-cleaning. Planting out hand-collected materials has posed another challenge. "As you get into polyculture and you are confronted by the complexity of the crop mixture, it's hard to mechanize and scale up your cultivation. It's easier to resist pests but harder to farm. You quickly come to understand why people do monoculture," Morton says. "Part of what we need to understand is the complexity of these natural conditions." But something in his strong presence indicates that farming embedded in truly wild environs is the only way he would have it. And if he has his way, farms will become more diversified, not just with native perennials, but with annuals bred for local conditions and fabulous colors, and with native vegetation preserved wherever possible.

"When we were looking for a name for our products, my wife, Karen, and I were standing in our farm, and she said spontaneously, 'Wild garden salad,' and I looked around, and there was every kind of diversity around, and it seemed totally appropriate. With our big role in the earth ecosystem, we are wild gardeners."

Wild Selection

Plant breeder Frank Morton and son filling trays with some of their gorgeous lettuce varieties. For two decades, Morton has been selecting varieties for their unique colors, taste, and performance in organic growing conditions.

Unbeknownst to Frank and Karen Morton when they bought their remote Willamette Valley farm was that it contained a remnant of upland prairie. They are now growing and collecting native seed in addition to their catalog company, Wild Garden Seed.

DRY FARMED TOMATOES

In enclaves of the Central Coast of California, where winter rainfall averages 30 inches, where clay predominates over sandy loam, and where hot summer days yield to foggy nights, dry-farmed tomatoes have become legendary. Biting into one of these vine-ripened, water-starved Early Girls delivers a mouthful of flavors. A slightly thick skin gives way to juicy flesh that is at once sweet, tart, acidy, and robust. These climate-tailored specialty tomatoes offer a fitting contrast to many of their Central Valley counterparts, some of which have been genetically engineered with flounder genes for frost protection or selected for their ability to survive transcontinental shipping rather than taste.

Molino Creek Farming Collective lies four miles up a dirt road into the Coast Range east of Davenport. The farm itself has 137 acres, most of which are forest and chaparral surrounding a bowl into which a sloping 15-acre field is nestled. The tomato operation is supplemented by cut flowers, peas, and other vegetables and is conducted on the large end of the gardening scale. Only 5 of the 15 acres are planted in any given year, allowing the remaining ground to rest two years out of three. The process is labor-intensive and yields are low, with plants four feet apart and rows on eight-foot spacings. Among the rows of vines on the day we visit, workers are trellising the stunted waist-high shrubs to boost production.

Joe Curry has been at Molino Creek since its origin in 1982, when 14 people bought the property jointly. (Only he and two other founders have stayed.) With a scant water budget of just one gallon per minute from the creek, creating an irrigated farm operation was not an option. Dry farming became the practice early on. Fortunately, it was readily apparent that dry-farmed tomatoes tasted like nothing else in the supermarket. "People tried them and immediately said, 'That tastes like a homegrown tomato!'" remembers Curry. "That's the key experience that most people associate with the old days when grandpa used to grow tomatoes. We've heard from more than one retailer that when our tomatoes are in the store, all the vegetable sales pick up."

As we walk the gently sloped and generously spaced rows, Curry explains the growing cycle. Tomatoes are started in the greenhouse in February, then transplanted into the field in May, after which they receive no supplemental water at all unless it rains, which usually happens at least once in June but is not necessary. After the initial transplanting, the tomato plants are shocked when they no longer get water, and don't put on new growth for at least three weeks. By then their roots have developed enough to take advantage of the winter rains retained by the clay. As the growing season plods along, the lack of water and moisture results in intensely concentrated flavors as well as a delayed harvest. These are the latest, and arguably the most flavorful tomatoes to come in to market.

There are, however, disease problems that dry farming exacerbates. "A major challenge with dry farming is that tomato plants can't use calcium unless they're in moisture, so even though there might be enough calcium in the soil, a lot of times you'll see blossom end rot, which is a deficiency problem," said Curry. "There are other disease problems too—molds, mildews, and late blight, our biggest challenge." They typically try to compensate for these with compost applications. "I think if tomatoes had feelings they would tell us we're abusing them," admits Curry. "I draw the analogy that if you work your way through college and you have to struggle a bit to learn what's available there, you probably end up with a better education than the person who had a free ride. So the irrigated tomato is the one that is getting the free ride. It has all of the necessary components of what it needs to grow big and vigorous and strong, but it doesn't develop character along the way."

In addition to growing some world-class-tasting tomatoes, gorgeous cut flowers, and sugary snap peas, Molino Farm prides itself on its wildness. There is an extreme sense of quiet that suggests the farm is open to flow of natural elements: wind and fog blowing in from the nearby Pacific; the visitors to and dwellers in the forest that encircles the cultivated fields. "One of the reasons that I'm here at all is because I'm surrounded by the wild," Curry says. "We have owls that help with gopher, rat, and mice control. We have coyotes and bobcats that are inside our fields nightly. So the hawks, the owls, the coyotes, the bobcats, not to mention the native vegetation all around that harbors beneficial insects—all that surrounds us here—helps to make this a farm. It would be different and more difficult if I had to be an organic farmer right next to a commercial farmer. For me it's just a part of the way I want my life to be."

Water Saver Tomato

Chaparral and forest surround Molino Creek Farming Collective on the central coast of California. Tomatoes are started in a greenhouse, but after their planting in May, receive no supplemental irrigation. This coastal area, however, typically experiences foggy evenings. Spaces between rows and plants are generous, and plants are hand-trellised. Fields are rested two of every three years. Farm co-owner Joe Curry (top right) says retailers report that produce sales go up during dry farmed tomato season. Molino Creek also produces cut flowers and shelling peas.

INGRAINED TRADITIONS

Gull Creek provides a soothing background hush as Anishinaabeg tribal member Dan Leu pushes our canoe out into a small lake. We are somewhere near the heart of the "rez," the White Earth Reservation that is, in Minnesota's north woods. On a late August morning, we're getting a firsthand tour through wild rice country. The lake is not an expansive body of water like those you often find in this angler's paradise. In places it's hard to see the water, there are so many lily pads, cattails, and wild rice wands, now swooping and laden with grain. What I soon discover is that this brief foray connects me with a deep tradition of *manoominike*, the annual Ojibwe wild rice harvest, and to modern debates about biodiversity, culture, and globalization.

"I've never seen a combination of such high water and beautiful rice," says Leu, skillfully paddling the dinged and battered canoe toward a thick curtain of overhead rice stems. A week from now, he will be part of a two-man ricing team. While the poler steers the boat into ripe patches, the pounder, wielding two sticks, sweeps an armful of plants into the belly of the boat and knocks off poundfuls of wild rice kernels. "Two guys working will get up in the dark and be off the lake by noon," explains Leu's colleague, Ronnie Chilton. Depending on the season, prices can range between $1 and $1.50 per pound. "I know ricers that can harvest 500 pounds in that time, and others that can pound 200."

Leu glides into a patch, gathers in a bundle of plant wands with a sweep of his powerful arm, and knocks a large pile of dark rice kernels into the canoe with his paddle. His technique is one coordinated motion, like a skillful archer retrieving an arrow from a quiver, notching it into the bowstring, pulling back, and releasing. About half of the kernels fall into the lake, part of a natural reseeding process. Yet the work is anything but easy. "It ain't no joy ride," says the good-natured Chilton, "there's work involved. You can get a rice burr in the eye or mouth. Worms can be so thick sometimes you can see the whole boat move. And they bite too. That's why you wear the rubber bands and plastic bags around your ankles and wrists to protect yourself."

"Or if you have an unbalanced poler," says Leu, from what sounds like experience, "you'll take a swim once in a while and lose all your rice." One can only imagine the skill needed to navigate a skittish canoe through the vegetation-smothered lakes with a quarter-ton of grain ballast. For the Anishinaabeg, wild ricing follows summer gardening and comes just before deer season, providing cash for their children's back-to-school clothes and other necessities, as well as grain for the winter. "I'm an Anishinaabeg," says Chilton, "I know what wild rice tastes like. I don't know what paddy rice tastes like."

As Chilton is implying, native-harvested rice, in the process we've just witnessed, has suffered under the reign of industrial agriculture. After the University of Minnesota developed a domesticated version in the 1950s, Minnesota farmers launched an aggressive expansion in paddy-grown, industrial "wild" rice by the late 1960s. Paddy production increased annually, ultimately gaining the attention of big distributors such as Uncle Ben's, Green Giant, and General Foods. While this product established a mainstream perception of wild rice among the consuming public, traditional harvests slumped into a steady decline. Ironically, by the mid-1980s, California, not Minnesota, led the nation in production, and 95 percent of all wild rice was paddy grown. According to Winona LaDuke, executive director of the White Earth Land Recovery Project, "When the glut of wild rice hit the market in 1986, the price plummeted, not only affecting the newly domesticated market, but devastating the native wild rice economy."[2]

Back at the headquarters of the White Earth Land Recovery Project, LaDuke, a Harvard-educated author who twice ran as Ralph Nader's vice presidential candidate, puts wild ricing into a cultural perspective. "People need to understand that you can buy wild rice from a huge plantation in Northern California that is organic. But you know what? It is not the same as buying wild rice from a lake in Minnesota [she pronounces the ota like ooda] that somebody put their hands to the harvest. It is a different thing. There has to be a market for native wild rice that ensures a premium and fair price, the same way we now market and purchase fair trade and shade-grown coffee. I pay that price for my coffee because I want to support those people and those places. Our rice does not taste the same either. What we want to tell them actually is that paddy-produced rice is not what wild rice is supposed to taste like."

Rice is one of many products the organization markets through a mail order operation called Native Harvest, which includes handcrafted birchbark and leather goods, jams and jellies, maple syrup, buffalo sausage, and hominy. "Our people selected this area largely because of its biodiversity," says the dark-haired, strikingly featured LaDuke. "It spans from prairie to the maple hardwoods to the pines to the 47 lakes that include the vast wild rice resources. Our traditional land use pattern involves noncontiguous parcels with collective ownership and individual or family use rights, which is very different than private property concepts." The Anishinaabeg harvest has traditionally taken place year-round over a wide staging ground, beginning with maple syrup in spring, followed by mushroom and medicinal plant gathering, then fishing and berry production in the sandy soils. By summer, pumpkins, beans, and other traditional foods such as the Flint corn varieties (Oneida white, Bear Island, and Mandan used for hominy) are farmed, with wild ricing, corn harvesting, deer hunting, and fishing and trapping as major fall activities. The restoration of such a food system is the mission of the White Earth Land Recovery Project. "Our relationship with the ecosystem has always been heavily managed," says LaDuke. "We are trying to establish a fair price for resources at market and to encourage consumption within the community because these are foods that the Creator has given us to eat." Forty percent of the adult population on the reservation, she says with a heavy sigh, suffers from Type II diabetes, and much of that is due to changes from the native diet to "modern" high-sugar processed foods.

On this particular afternoon, she is concerned about the state of school lunches and their effects on children. "What do institutionalized lunches do to a kid's taste?" she asks. "It's a form of colonialism! They come back with a really bad sense of taste. So we are trying to reinfuse traditional foods into the lunch programs at these schools, helping them remember how they are supposed to eat." In addition to her already overcrowded plate of issues and activism, LaDuke rattles off a long list of pressing concerns she must relentlessly pursue. Acquiring sufficient land to secure production. Building partnerships for long-term forest management. Advocating on issues of water quality to protect ricing and fishing habitat from agricultural runoff and airborne contaminants. Campaigning for human rights and fair trade issues, including defending the cultural and intellectual property rights of her people.

She mentions NorCal Wild Rice Company, a California corporation that holds two patents on wild rice. "We found that interesting," she says ironically. "California is the largest rice-producing area in the world so they get to represent wild rice as such in the market. Not to be disrespectful to those farmers, but this is a fair trade issue that needs to be closely scrutinized. We are a community by and large below the poverty level, and rice is a cultural inheritance as well as an income source. This is the commodification of what is sacred."

From wild ricing we follow the dust cloud of Chilton's truck along dirt roads through dense woods of aspen, poplar, maple, and pine, finally arriving at a clearing. "We have 220 acres on this side of the road and 80 on the other side all dedicated toward maple sugaring," says Chilton, who has spent the past few years clearing trails throughout the tracts to make the operation possible. "The sap runs when the snow melts, and we tap and collect it in 5-gallon tanks. Then we use our horses to pull it out on skids to our holding tank."

Like the antiquated infrastructure for husking, cleaning, and sorting rice, the sugary is a bare-bones operation. A few dozen cords of split wood up to three feet long lie in giant piles in the clearing. In addition to the firewood are long timbers, ready to be milled for the reservation's planned straw-bale office project. Beyond stands a complex of structures, including a small warming hut and an open shed that houses a wood-burning boiler. Yet for Chilton and Leu, the "sugar bush" is a source of great pride. Chilton explains that 40 gallons of sap are boiled down to make one gallon of syrup. "It takes a third of a cord of wood to get the boiler up to temperature, and you have to really hump when you're loading it, because the faster you get that thing filled up, the faster you can get away from the heat." After it goes through the evaporator, the syrup is filtered, bottled, and sold via the Internet. "All over the world really," says Chilton proudly. "Twenty-one hours was the longest day we put in last year. We boiled 2,500 gallons down to 60 gallons of syrup and burned six or eight cords of wood."

As we begin our return journey along winding roads and isolated lakes, something LaDuke mentioned earlier resonates. "Coming from an Anishinaabeg perspective," she said, "there is an order in the woods—its own order. What our instructions have always said is that our responsibility as humans is to live within that order, and that's how the Creator allows us to feed ourselves. That's traditionally how we have related to the broader ecosystem. This project is really about continuing that process on a larger scale, whether it is maple syrup harvesting and doing it in the woods in a way that is good, or whether it is growing corn or wild ricing."

Non-contiguous Native Harvest

Ronnie Chilton and Dan Leu (top left) demonstrate wild ricing in a remote northern Minnesota Lake, part of the Anishinaabeg White Earth Reservation. Ricing is an early fall pursuit and provides valuable food and income for the tribes. Wild ricing is a tag-team endeavor. The poler propels and steers the boat through the often dense stands of tall rice. The pounder knocks the rice kernels into the belly of the canoe. A day's haul can reach upward of 500 pounds.

Winona La Duke, bottom left, is an Anishinaabeg tribal member and director of the White Earth Land Recovery Project. A Harvard-educated author, La Duke has twice run as a vice-presidential candidate with Ralph Nader.

The non-contiguous farming, fishing, and harvesting practices of the Anishinaabeg require large areas and diverse habitats. In addition to the wild rice wetlands, they grow crops such as native corn, berries, beans, and other vegetables.

The maple syrup operation (two photos on top right) is another important activity at the White Earth Land Recovery Project. The maple sap runs in the spring, is hand-collected and transported with horses, then reduced in the wood fired boiler. Products such as maple syrup, wild rice, honey, and preserves are sold through the Project's own label, Native Harvest.

In the photo at bottom second from the right, Chilton (seated left) and Leu (right) pose atop a pile of logs selectively harvested and scheduled for milling into dimensional lumber. The wood is slated for use in the construction of a new administration building..

ECOLABELS AND LOCAL MARKETING INITIATIVES

For decades, the food industry has thrived upon the premeditated omission of product histories. What bacon producer, for example, would be willing to acknowledge on its packaging that its hogs were raised under despicable conditions of confinement that necessitate excessive injections of growth-promoting antibiotics? That they were fed genetically modified corn silage or that, as a result of intensive overcrowding, their fecal waste lagoons dangerously contaminated surrounding waterways and rendered the air in local communities intolerable? Ecolabels (seals that certify standards of production and uphold social and environmental values) and local marketing initiatives (programs that directly link consumers with farmers) are predicated on closing that information gap. Rather than an absence of disclosure, where and how something is grown becomes the selling point. One might learn that hogs ranged freely in conditions where antibiotics are avoided or used only as a last resort, or that the farm on which they are raised was protected by a land trust organization. The product history takes on meaning, one that connects it to a place and to standards of stewardship.

In *The Farm as Natural Habitat*, Laura Jackson made the case that the food-consuming public must begin to make profound and enduring correlations between its grocery lists and the Endangered Species List. Today, communities and consumers around the world are beginning to understand their powers and responsibilities, and are mobilizing to reshape the fate of biodiversity through their everyday purchasing and dietary habits. This can include supporting local producers and eating in rhythm with the seasons, finding alternatives to feedlot intensive diets, seeking out wild-harvested products, "buycotting" genetically modified food items, and choosing products that support efforts to limit impacts on biodiversity. In a global marketplace where societally harmful production "externalities" such as water contamination, pesticide pollution, soil erosion, uncontrolled genetic alterations, fishery depletion, and transportation impacts have for decades been passed off onto communities and taxpayers, ecolabels and local marketing initiatives are attempting to put a face, a history, a price, and a practice of accountability on goods and services. While still a David-versus-Goliath struggle, the union of producers on the one hand with ideologically motivated consumers on the other, has established market mechanisms that attempt to pay for many of the true costs of production, rather than adding them to the ever-expanding "tragedy of the commons."

In elbowing their way toward the mainstream, ecolabels fall subject to the chicken-and-egg growing pains of the marketplace; should they ultimately persevere, they also pay the consequences of their success. First, there is the need to develop scientifically rigorous standards for production that can be practically and economically applied to small-scale operations. These standards are then followed by consumer education campaigns to generate market demand. That demand must in turn be matched by sufficient and consistent supply, and monitored by a third-party certification system throughout its production cycle. The premiums required to fund these activities–ecological growing practices, education, organization building, chain-of-custody certification–must compete with the subsidies and massive scale that underpin the already established global commodities markets. In the global supermarket culture, success is linked to mainstream supply and distribution, which favors large producers. Within ecolabel organizations, clashes between "purists" and "mainstreamers" over the terms of success are inevitable. Purists want to keep standards as high as possible, even if it means having a smaller number of producers. Mainstreamers want to encourage a larger number of producers through more flexible standards in order to have greater impact in the marketplace and on the landscape. As a concept goes the way of mass production, small producers are often squeezed. The example of the organic foods industry springs readily to mind.

Thirty years ago, a generation of pioneering farmers launched a revolution to develop an alternative to a food system that was increasingly dependent on toxic chemicals known to have decimating effects on the environment, wildlife, and people. In the decades between the publication of *Silent Spring* and the turn of the 21st century, these farmers developed (and often openly shared) the craft of producing superior quality food and fiber using biological methods, and slowly attracted a significant number of consumers to the organic marketplace. Contrary to what many pioneers had ever dreamed was possible, by the mid-1990s vast multithousand-acre organic monocultures of nearly every major crop were being cultivated. A victim of its own hard-won success, the movement fledged into an industry on the verge of going global, growing at a phenomenal annual rate of 20 percent, supplying year-round certified organic produce to consumers nationwide and worldwide. Many organic farming operations were shipping their harvests across the country and abroad, a distant remove from the locally grown roots of the movement's origins. According to the University of California's Agricultural Issues Center, for example, in the mid-1990s, 50 percent of organic production was controlled by just 2 percent of certified producers. Corporate expansion of organics forced many small farmers into high-end or boutique niche markets, with prices that further alienated the poorer sectors of our society. Small- and medium-sized organic food producers, processors, and distributors fell prey to Wall Street mergers and consolidations, undermining the community orientation of the movement's origins. Chlorine rinses on salad mixes, hydroponic production, and the use of "permissible" food additives were all symbolic of an organic industry lurching toward mass production, long-distance transport, and even fast food.

The U.S. Department of Agriculture spent most of the 1990s drafting and negotiating a watered-down and limited national organic standards policy, which would have benefited large exporters. Their early standards included the allowance of "the Big Three"—genetically modified organisms, sewage sludge fertilizers, and irradiation treatments. Outraged citizens barraged the USDA with over 200,000 letters of protest, and none of the Big Three were incorporated into the national law, which went into effect in late 2002. By this time, however, many in the organic community had already realized that original organic standards hadn't gone far enough in the protection of biodiversity. Conserving habitat for endangered species, using water responsibly, protecting and restoring riparian zones, using non-lethal predator controls, managing livestock humanely, providing living wages, and many other practices that connect the food system directly to local communities were being acknowledged as necessary measures to create a more sustainable form of organic agriculture. Beyond the successful battle to establish more acceptable organic standards from the USDA, ecolabeling programs and other marketing initiatives began shifting the issues of sustainable food and fiber production to a new frontier—local food security and biodiversity protection. Some focused on limiting agriculture's impacts on targeted species, such as salmonids, native predators, or migratory songbirds. Others were process-oriented, advocating grass-fed dairy and beef, Biodynamic farming, or wildcrafting. Still others were devising standards specific to farmers in a given region, such as Marin Organic in Marin County, California. In Europe, products were coded with Food Miles in an attempt to educate consumers about the vast distances between farm fields and supermarket aisles. Emerging meat safety crises, such as mad cow and foot and mouth disease, as well as active resistance to U.S. pressures to force overseas markets to accept its genetically modified products on the basis of fair trade, helped increase support and demand for these product differentiations.

As we enter the 21st century, a wave of secondary labels and initiatives signals a shift in the maturing of consumer values. These add new layers of ideologically motivated production concerns to already accepted purchasing decisions like organic, fair trade, or Forest Stewardship Council (sustainable forestry) certification. The primary benefit to producers from these ecolabels and initiatives may not necessarily come in the form of direct sales. Rather they may provide an additional value or product differentiation, thereby helping to gain coveted recognition in an ever-growing conscious-consumer movement. Ecolabels intended to reward growers who reduce the impacts of agriculture on endangered salmon and steelhead habitat have been established for a few years now, most notably the Portland, Oregon-based Salmon-Safe and the Sonoma County, California-based Fish Friendly programs. Both are directed at disconnecting a farm's sediment and agrochemical runoff into the local watershed, as well as engaging consumers in supporting regional conservation efforts. In a more controversial move, Farm Verified Organic (FVO) certified the 1999 native salmon catch in Bristol Bay, Alaska, as "Certified Wild." According to David Gould of FVO, the Bristol Bay communities have been living and fishing in this remote Bering Sea ecosystem for centuries, but are now losing what outside business they do conduct to the disastrously polluting salmon fish-farming industry in Canada. The harvest of the salmon–which FVO determined was identifiable, non-contaminated, and inspectable, among other variables–was certified as wild; the processing was certified as organic. Other products that could potentially be certified as wild include honey, wild rice, berries, mushrooms, and herbs.

Such local initiatives, particularly the economically successful ones, says Mark Ritchie, the founder of the Institute for Agriculture and Trade Policy in Minneapolis, can perform a great service in protecting the wild, but they will not go unnoticed by the forces of economic globalization. "If you or somebody you know has started something to make the world a better place and it cuts into someone else's ability to make more money, there's going to be a fight about it," says Ritchie, who grew up on an Iowa corn farm and cut his activist teeth in California in the 1970s in the emerging food co-op movement. "We got so successful in the '60s and '70s kicking some behinds that multinational distributors went to international agencies that set rules that take precedence over local, state, and federal laws. Those institutions are now set up to globalize production, drive down prices, and increase imports. Successful ecolabels make these global institutions very frightened," he explains, "partly because of the clout of large procurement institutions that can get behind them, such as universities and government purchasing agencies." He cites the Dolphin-Safe tuna initiative, which has been challenged in the World Trade Organization by Mexico as an unfair trade restriction, as just one example.

Fostering a local organic food ethic does not mean life without trade. There are excellent examples of region-specific "luxury staples"–coffee, tea, and wine, for example–that are being produced with attempts to limit impacts on biodiversity. The coffee growing region that spans the Caribbean and Central and South America is one of vast biodiversity, and shade-grown farms can provide much-needed habitat for many species, including endangered orioles, warblers, and other feathered migrants. Rapid deforestation has been driven in no small part by the industrialization of coffee farming, which radically transformed production from forest farms to chemical-intensive sun plantations. Only by securing market premiums for organic, fair trade, and shade-grown beans can the hundreds of thousands of small producers continue to provide habitat and fuel our habit for caffeine.

Not all of these movements operate under the official sanction of an umbrella organization. Indeed, because of rising certification costs, increasing amounts of red tape, dissatisfaction with a "lowering of the bar," a growing number of producers are choosing to not continue organic certification. This should drive more and more consumers toward familiarity with local producers. According to "Food, Fuels, and Freeways," a report published by the Leopold Center for Sustainable Agriculture, only 1.5 percent of the fresh produce sales in the United States are a result of direct marketing enterprises. Instead, produce commonly travels 2,000 miles or more on its way from the field to our tables.

Community Supported Agriculture (CSA) is one such powerful but unofficial movement that pairs local farmers with an investing corps of members. The CSA movement gained great momentum throughout North America in the 1990s and introduced the value of eating locally grown, organic, in-season produce to tens of thousands of tables across America. CSA is a nearly revolutionary partnership arrangement in which members pay a fee to a farm to help cover the actual production costs in exchange for a share of the harvest. The genius in the CSA concept lies in reducing the number of barriers that stand between farm fields and dinner tables, as well as in trying to pay the full costs of keeping farming alive within the community. For the farmer it means guaranteed sales, higher profit margins, and interest-free "loans" before the growing season begins. Members, meanwhile, receive high-quality, reasonably priced produce, typically organic or Biodynamic, delivered within a day of being picked.

While exact figures are hard to come by, there were approximately a thousand CSAs operating throughout the country by the late 1990s, with at least one in every state. Some are best described as mutual farms, in which members enter a partnership with the farmer, investing between $300 and $900 in shares at the beginning of the growing season in return for edible dividends paid on a weekly basis throughout the growing season. Other CSAs are more participatory, using pick-your-own operations or relying on members to help with bookkeeping, distribution, and newsletter writing. While most CSAs are organic, many tackle additional social or environmental missions as well, such as supplying fresh produce to less fortunate constituencies, preserving land in perpetuity through purchases and easements, or farming with horsepower. Already, many CSAs embody the principles of farming with the wild, inviting members out to experience and appreciate the habitat values on farms firsthand.

Another type of regional financial mechanism that can play a role in funding wildlife protection are pools that compensate farmers for predator-related crop or livestock losses. In many instances, such partnership programs could take the place of USDA wildlife-damage-control eradication measures that have proven costly, cruel, and often ineffective. Defenders of Wildlife launched the Wolf Country Beef ecolabel program in southern Arizona and New Mexico in the mid-1990s, offering to compensate participating ranchers for any livestock losses suffered from reintroduced Mexican wolves, in return for a commitment to nonlethal predator controls. One of the United States' premier environmental reporters, Ted Williams, documented the economic value of restored wolf populations in the farming and ranching communities of Northern Minnesota, despite what some might consider significant losses. "In 1999 Minnesota paid $64,918.50 in wolf damage claims verified on 87 farms, or about one percent of the farms in wolf range," he wrote in *Audubon Magazine*. "Known livestock losses (and there were surely many others that were unreported and unverified) amounted to 20 cows, 7 yearlings, 70 calves, 3 sheep, and 897 turkeys. Meanwhile, in 1999, about 50,000 tourists who came to the North Woods town of Ely visited the International Wolf Center. ... Each non-member adult paid an entrance fee of $5.50."[1] In another report, Williams suggested a similar program in place of a USDA Animal and Plant Health Inspection Service plan that would, each year between 2002 and 2004, kill up to 2 million redwing blackbirds that feed on sunflower oilseed crops in the Upper Midwest. He wrote that Venezuelan rice and sorghum farmers who had been poisoning dicksissels en masse to little effect, were about to launch an alternative nonlethal initiative. "While funding has yet to be procured, an insurance-style model is being set up in Venezuela in which the farmers' co-op, with the support of government and nongovernment organizations, would compensate farmers who suffer major losses," reported Williams. "In our Upper Midwest, such a system would probably be far more cost-effective than trying to effect population control on superabundant blackbirds, especially if it were combined with aggressive [exotic] cattail reduction."[2]

Food offers us perhaps our most direct and spiritual connection with the Earth, one that can engage us on a daily basis with the seasons, the soil, and the soul of our surroundings. As farms become more distinctly rooted to ecosystems and water-sheds, we must learn to become more adept foragers of our respective "foodsheds." In *Coming Home to Eat*, Gary Paul Nabhan wrote of a one-year commitment he made to gathering the majority of his diet from within a 250-mile radius of his home in Tucson, Arizona. He described this culinary journey to me in his home over a delicious breakfast of blue corn pancakes with prickly pear syrup, and included an account of eating rattlesnake roadkill during the quest. Chefs are also at the forefront of this movement, among them Odessa Piper, owner and founder of the L'Etoile restaurant in Madison, Wisconsin, who has relationships with 200 regional small farmers. In search of something fresh and green in February, Piper relies on a local farmer who forages watercress from an icebound creek on his property. "We can call California like everybody else, but it wouldn't feel right," she says.[3]

The flourishing of a diverse and vital food culture that clearly values and protects biodiversity within farming and ranching regions requires the active participation and acceptance of responsibility by all of us—consumers, chefs, gardeners, producers, nonprofits, retailers, coops, government agencies, and more. Our goals must also branch out beyond farm borders to farming communities that may one day be recognized and appreciated for their wild characteristics. We might do well to embrace the French concept of *terroir*, which translates loosely as "the essence of place" and resonates a sense of quality and pride in both production and stewardship. Rural communities must be vital places to live as well as providers of better sources of food, fiber, energy, carbon sequestration, recreation, and many other services. The coho salmon, prairie chicken, California live oak, and gray wolf cannot speak for themselves in the global and local marketplace. We have to speak up on their behalf and in so doing, proactively create a different relationship with agriculture and with Nature. There is no way we can ask for "too much," as many would like us to imagine. The following examples represent some of the best on-the-ground programs that address the practice and marketing of farming with the wild.

MAKING PEACE
WITH PREDATORS

It's a whopping eight degrees above zero on a Tuesday afternoon in late February, and ranchers Dave Tyler and Becky Weed are feeding their more than 200 sheep as if it's just another day in paradise. While Dave unravels a bale of organic barley pea hay with an implement mounted on the back of his John Deere, Becky forks it around the snow-blanketed pasture, and the ewes hungrily flock to the fodder. Head and neck above the sheep is Cyrus, one of two guard llamas; intently shadowing Becky's every move is the couple's border collie, Taiga. The snow-swept, jagged peaks of the Bridger Mountains seem so close to the outer paddocks of Thirteen Mile Farm, you feel you can almost reach out and touch them. The only remnant wildness in between is a half-mile-long tree-lined creek corridor, well traveled by elk, deer, coyotes, mountain lions, and the occasional black bear. On the opposite side of the farm, a resident pair of bald eagles is perched in a massive cottonwood. It's a fitting setting for one of the focal points of the country's "predator friendly" ranching movement.

Tyler and Weed came to the grass-fed ranching scene by a circuitous route, but it's obvious that the lifestyle's long hours and demanding physical labor suit them. Together, they are a striking pair: he dark-haired, with a woodsman's build and an intellectual demeanor; she blond, with a tomboyish charm, piercing eyes, and high energy. Between them, they've earned five college degrees. Tyler is a former civil engineering professor who started and recently sold a successful agricultural electronic equipment business to go into ranching full-time. Weed holds a master's degree in geology and worked for years as a field consultant. In 1987, after a prolonged search, the pair purchased an 80-acre farm in southwestern Montana's Gallatin Valley about 13 miles northwest of Bozeman. Originally homesteaded in 1864, the property included a rundown log cabin farmhouse, a classic hay barn, and numerous outbuildings—an ideal place to live out their dream of making a living off the land.

By 1993, Weed and Tyler were able to devote themselves to the ranch, although Tyler worked full-time through 2000. They purchased a small flock. "We literally started with just a dozen sheep," Weed says. Shortly after, they learned about a locally forming "predator friendly" ranching group, the brainchild of Dude Tyler (no relation to Dave) and Lil Erickson in nearby Livingston. "We didn't really want to get involved in some cutesy marketing gimmick, but we went and talked to this group of people. The more I talked to them, the more I really became convinced that they were interested in what I see as the real issues, that is habitat preservation for wildlife, but also—equally important—preserving viable agricultural communities. We don't want to ranch if it means waging war on native species," says Weed persuasively.[4]

Like others gaining certification from Predator Friendly, Inc., Weed and Tyler signed an affidavit that they would not kill native predators (coyotes, mountain lions, bears, or wolves) that threatened their livestock. While they'd already had some experience using burros as guard animals, they purchased two llamas and began improving and electrifying fences

Dave Tyler, Becky Weed, and Taiga outside their home in Belgrade, Montana. Thirteen Mile Lamb and Wool Company supplies organic and predator friendly meat and fiber.

("an expensive and never-ending task") and learning the ropes by hands-on observation.

"The llamas keep the coyotes at bay. It's the occasional mountain lion or bear that does the damage. Last fall we had a lion come down from the Bridgers and along the creek corridor," she says. "The llamas cannot fend off the mountain lions, so we ended up going out in the middle of the night at intermittent, unpredictable intervals." When an animal is lost, there is no compensation, unlike with the Defenders of Wildlife program, which pays for losses due to wolves and grizzly bears. In the case of losses to coyotes, usually in and around the lambing season, Weed will take the carcass to the far end of the farm as a "peace offering." Although the carrion remains within a quarter mile of their animals, they have never suffered further loss as a result of this ritual.

Thirteen Mile Farm's predator friendly practices are hardly the norm in the arid West, where ranchers have viewed coyotes as an archenemy for more than a century.

Guard llamas, guard dogs, well-maintained fences, and hands-on monitoring form the backbone of predator friendly wool, which has its own ecolabel.

Estimates place the number of coyotes killed by the U.S. Department of Agriculture's "Wildlife Services" (formerly Animal Damage Control) in the West at more than 80,000 a year—an average of 220 per day—at a cost of $10 million. In addition to the government campaign, organized coyote killing contests are held annually throughout the U.S., such as Montana's Coyote Derby, Arizona's Predator Hunt Spectacular, and the Pennsylvania Coyote Hunt.[5] Mike Finkel has written that "Coyotes are the most maligned mammal in the United States....Despite almost a century of uninterrupted killing, despite increasingly sophisticated hunting methods, despite hundreds of millions of government dollars devoted to coyote removal, today more coyotes are living in more places than ever before. And coyotes are spreading not just in ranching country but in metropolises nationwide, from the suburbs of Los Angeles to the streets of New York City."[6]

Weed doesn't deny that the wool industry suffers losses due to predation. According to the National Agricultural Statistical Service, up to a quarter million lambs and sheep fall victim to predators. But, she argues, coyotes are not to blame for vanishing margins on commercial sheep operations. Multiple factors, including competition with New Zealand and Australian exports, with synthetic fibers, and with other domestic meats such as pork and chicken, as well as the complex pressures of eco-

nomic globalization, have been slowly crushing the U.S. lamb and wool industry since the 1940s. Coyotes, lions, and wolves have become convenient scapegoats.

In nearly every corner of the Weed and Tyler homestead, books are shelved and stacked, and part of their hefty reading diet is studies on predator dynamics. Tyler recently told a reporter: "If you have a pack of coyotes living in the area, they tend to establish what I think of as an equilibrium condition with the food that's available, often the natural food, whether it's gophers or mice. That group will live in the area and tend to breed and adjust the size of the pack to the food source that's available, and things will work out fine. And within the pack, there's often only one male and female that will breed. But if you shoot them, they will typically all start breeding. You could actually shoot a few coyotes and end up increasing the size of the pack and disturbing that equilibrium, upsetting the apple cart."[7] This is the consensus of several biologists, including Rob Crabtree, the founder of Yellowstone Ecosystem Studies in Bozeman and a co-founder of Predator Friendly, Inc. It's also consistent with what many ranchers have experienced.

At the same time they were learning their ranching practices, Tyler and Weed also had to develop a marketing strategy for a small-scale operation. "We knew if we really wanted to make a living at this, we couldn't survive on the conventional market, taking our lambs to auction, selling fiber to the wool pool." They turned to direct marketing of value-added products—grass-finished, hormone-free lamb, and home-knitted woolen goods—primarily through local accounts and a Web site. Weed had no ties to the fashion industry, but she had been knitting since her childhood and became involved in the production of hats, sweaters, blankets, vests, sheepskins, raw yarn, and raw fleece. The blankets are made out of state, while a local artisan produces the other goods, working full-time on a home knitting machine. Occasionally, Weed has purchased other producers' fiber from within the Predator Friendly wool co-op, but the market has been slow in responding. Using U.S. raw materials and labor is expensive, and consumers still need to be educated about the link between large carnivores in the ecosystem and their sweaters. In the middle of their living room stands a drying rack drooped with skeins of yarn, destined for an upholstery project. "We have our moments when we say to ourselves, we are so stupid to be trying this! And then a customer inevitably comes by and excitedly buys a sweater for all the right reasons."

While not yet a fashion or food rage, predator friendly certification has been highly popular with the media and the agricultural community. "Even though I'm not crazy about the somewhat sappy and confusing qualities of the term, predator friendly has definitely made it into the vernacular," says Weed. She has become the movement's spokesperson ("by default") and was cited by *Time Magazine* as a "Hero for the Planet" in 2000. Requests pour in weekly from interested parties around the country, and she has been contacted for help on snow leopard predation in Tibet and cheetah attacks on ranches in Namibia. And at one point the Predator Friendly, Inc. certifying organization received a call from an attorney aggressively cautioning against copyright infringements on the Arnold Schwartzenegger blockbuster movie "Predator."

Nearly ten years into the effort, Tyler and Weed have doubled their owned acreage on Thirteen Mile Farm, grown their flock to 250 ewes, and acquired a few dozen cows as well. Their most successful marketing boost has come from increasing demand for grass-finished, organically certified meat, particularly the tender, high-quality lamb they specialize in. "With the outbreaks of foot and mouth and mad cow disease," says Weed, "people are interested in a clean food supply." It took five years to leap through all the hoops to receive organic certification from Organic Crop Improvement Association (OCIA), but the effort seems to be paying off. While many ranchers are selling out their stock, demand for Thirteen Mile Farm's hormone-, antibiotic-, and chemical-free organic meat is steadily expanding.

Tyler is in fact preparing a delivery that afternoon to a restaurant in Big Sky, about an hour away, and our conversation shifts into the challenges of small-scale meat distribution and butchering regulations for organic processors. At one point, Weed bemoans the temporary surplus of chops and ground lamb in their freezers. "They only want the legs," she says. And Tyler responds jokingly, "We'll just have to grow lambs with more than four legs."

Clouds shroud the valley, and flurries whirl down in spirals and helixes. Thirteen Mile Farm, we learn, recently received a $20,000 open space grant to cover the costs of placing its development rights in a permanent conservation easement. (The bond, attorney's fees, appraisal, assessments and other out-of-pocket expenses will soon consume this.) With two adjoining properties under similar arrangements, there are now 400 contiguous acres under protection, including the wildlife corridor to the Bridgers. "We feel so lucky to have been able to live here," says Weed, exhaling puffs of frost as she speaks. "We know we won't be here forever, and it's nice to know that it can remain a working farm or open space long after we're gone."

SALMON-SAFE: EVOLUTION OF AN ECOLABEL

"When consumers in the Pacific Northwest consider the fate of imperiled native salmon runs," says ecolabel pioneer Dan Kent, "they are usually thinking about sea lions, El Niño, clearcuts, or dams on the Columbia River. They are not thinking about the impacts of farming or urban parks, golf courses, and storm runoff. One of our primary goals has been educating the public about agriculture and the decline of wild salmon."

"Salmon-Safe" certification began in 1997 as a project of the Pacific Rivers Council (PRC), an Oregon-based think tank with a history of forest activism. The organization was founded by a group of concerned river guides, and their early activism focused on the upper reaches of watersheds. It soon became clear that private lands in lower watersheds were absolutely critical to salmon habitat recovery as well. "Eighty percent of the non-point-source pollution on the Willamette River comes from agriculture—nurseries, grass-seed farms, orchards, dairies, and vineyards," says Kent. "We knew that changing farming practices could dramatically reduce that."

PRC started the program with the basic objective of promoting agricultural conservation on private lands. After considering a number of strategies, PRC settled on the establishment of an ecolabel and certification that could be both voluntary and market-driven. With this more refined concept in mind, certification development was the next—and most significant—hurdle. PRC convened what it considered to be a forum of the best Northwest fisheries biologists, stream ecologists, and other scientists, led by its staff salmon biologist. So much information was gathered in that start-up phase that it threw the project into a stand-still. PRC finally called in a sustainable forestry certifier with the Forest Stewardship Council to distill the moun-

BUYING THIS PRODUCT CAN HELP MAKE SALMON LEAP

When you buy a product that displays this salmon safe logo you are supporting healthy agricultural practices that help keep our rivers clean enough for native salmon to spawn and thrive.

SALMON SAFE

tains of data into a practical methodology. Using a framework of five working areas—riparian buffers, irrigation, chemical use, erosion control, and animal management—Salmon-Safe created a scoring system by which third-party certifiers could assess farms.

The system was discussed with farmers to find a middle ground between ecological priorities and economic realities. According to Kent, there was a chasm of mistrust between Oregon farmers and environmentalists that had to be bridged by literally going door-to-door. "We told them, 'In this situation, we need a hundred-foot buffer between the fields and the stream.' They came back to us and said, 'Hah!'" remembers Kent. Ultimately, a flexible landscape-based system evolved that enforces standards on a farm-by-farm basis. In the program's first year, PRC certified a dozen Northwest farms totaling 10,000 acres. A few large-scale operations such as Organic Valley Dairy and Lundberg Family Farms signed on, but most early participants were the region's "low hanging fruit": small organic vineyards that were not threatened by the idea that non-organic growers would also be allowed in the program. AgroEcology Northwest was contracted to conduct the annual third-party evaluations. Today, certification costs range between a few hundred dollars for a small Oregon vineyard and a few thousand dollars for a large barley grower on Idaho's Camus Prairie.

Along with developing farming standards, PRC was equally focused on public education and marketing outreach. A Portland agency, Dalbey & Denight Advertising (now Livengood/Nowack), championed Salmon-Safe as a pro bono client, designing a logo, retail campaigns, in-store displays, and public service announcements. As the education campaign evolved, Salmon-Safe learned to communicate its message simply. But they also came face-to-face with the marketplace realities of package design. "Initially wineries just placed the logo on the bottle label," explains Kent. "And most consumers thought that the symbol meant the wine must go well with salmon."

Since endangered salmon was—and remains—a contentious issue, media interest in the 1997 launch was phenomenal. Articles appearing in *Newsweek, USA Today*, and the *San Francisco Examiner* created sufficient momentum for grocery chain Fred Meyer (later acquired by Kroger) to join the cause, rolling out Salmon-Safe products in its 100-plus stores. After two high-profile years, however, keeping up with the same level of public interest proved daunting. Salmon-Safe bumped up against the typical challenges of sustaining an ecolabel, says Kent. The foundations that initially funded them for their novel approach soon stepped back, expecting them to make it on their own in the marketplace.

Generating an ever-increasing number of certified products for local consumption was difficult in an agricultural region that specializes in export commodity crops. Perhaps most frustrating was the growing realization that scattered certified farms wouldn't create the watershed-level impacts essential for PRC to succeed in its mission.

Meanwhile, on the ground, Oregon vineyards and wine makers constituted Salmon-Safe's largest member group. To begin with, most of these growers dry farm rather than irrigate. Many also use permanent cover crops to fertilize and help curtail erosion. But not all are organic. Herbicide use is common in spring to limit competition around the vines. Limited use of synthetic chemicals (a part of most Integrated Pest Management schemes) is permitted by Salmon-Safe, as long as the impacts on aquatic life are minimized. Certifiers annually check participants' pesticide application records, nutrient containment, and other management practices.

"We really struggled with whether a farmer had to be perfect or not and whether we would work only with the small organic growers or try to include larger conventional operations," says Kent. "But we knew that no matter what we did, there was still going to be agriculture in salmon watersheds. So we tried to include a wide variety of farms in the program." The challenge, he insists, is attracting larger and larger operations to the cause, not just the relatively small-scale vintners who have a much easier time meeting Salmon-Safe standards.

The extensive use of cover crops is the most significant step that Salmon-Safe farmers take to limit riparian impacts. These include clovers, beans, and other plants grown during and in between seasons. In combination with buffer strips along creeks, streams, and river banks, cover crops reduce runoff in spawning grounds. Cover crops also naturally fix nitrogen in the soil through their roots, helping to curtail the use of synthetic nitrogen, which has led to extensive groundwater contamination over decades of heavy applications. Throughout the growing season, flowering cover crops also serve as a natural pest control by attracting a diversity of insects. Although cover cropping is recommended under most of the country's organic certification programs, it is not a required practice. This means that a grower farming near a stream could be harming salmon habitat, even while farming organically. So the Salmon-Safe program (or other regionally based watershed and endangered species initiatives), in tandem with organic certification practices, can help to elevate an organic farm to an even higher standard of sustainable agriculture.

Transforming Salmon-Safe into a self-funding entity has presented an even more pressing goal. "Anyone interested in building an ecolabel has got to be ready to survive the marketplace," says Kent. For Salmon-Safe, survival has meant diversification, outside of agriculture and outside of the Willamette Valley. "There has been a lot of interest from many different entities in the label's concept," says Kent, which has meant a shift toward collaborative efforts. The City of Portland along with Seattle, the nation's first municipalities directly affected by the Endangered Species Act with the listing of species within the urban area, contacted the organization for potential collaboration in restoration efforts for imperiled chinook salmon and steelhead. These discussions culminated in the development of an urban parks and natural area certification program to be launched in 2003. Salmon-Safe standards are currently being developed for public parks and golf courses. Nursery and greenhouse industries, Oregon's highest value agriculture, are also seeking Salmon-Safe's endorsement for the application of new fish friendly practices. "They want consumers to know about their efforts to protect water quality when they purchase a plant or tree for their garden or landscaping," says Kent.

In order to broaden its influence, Salmon-Safe is also forging some innovative partnerships to complement other already established certifications such as the Food Alliance, Oregon Tilth (organic certification), and the nation's leading Forest Stewardship Council–endorsed certifier of forestry products. In 2002, Salmon-Safe teamed up with the World Wildlife Fund to work with growers and landowners in the Klamath-Siskiyou region of southern Oregon and northern California, starting with a pilot project in Oregon's Applegate Basin. In the Applegate River watershed, where low-elevation stream systems have been degraded by agriculture, Salmon-Safe is being used as one more tool to promote conservation and particularly to help small organic farmers to rise above the competition in the marketplace. According to Tim Franklin of the Applegate River Watershed Council, the additional market-based mechanism has provided an entrée to promote new techniques to regional farmers, such as off-channel livestock watering, rotational grazing, natural habitat plantings in cultivated areas, riparian and oak woodland restoration, and native plant system identification.

As to the ecolabel's actual impact on the salmon population, Kent believes it will still take some time before any direct effects can be measured. "I do see a day when native salmon will thrive in the Willamette," he says, "but I'm not hopeful for the near future."

ON HABIT AND HABITAT

Coffee, the East African bean that once bolstered nomadic Ethiopian warriors into battle now wields tremendous power over agricultural economies, human habits, and threatened habitats. Grown in nearly 80 tropical and subtropical countries, coffee has become the most valuable component of international trade for those nations after petroleum (and perhaps illegal drugs).[8] Worldwide, twenty million people work on coffee plantations, which cover a total of more than twenty-six million acres (an area larger than Portugal).[9] Two pounds of beans are produced for every person on Earth; 20 percent is sold to the United States. An Old World crop that has transformed New World economies and agriculture, coffee farming has fanned the flames of colonialism and deforestation throughout Latin America, while many small forest farmers raise coffee for cash and food crops for subsistence. Hawaii is the only coffee producing region of the United States and is rapidly adopting industrial farming practices at the expense of critical rainforest habitat.

Despite many social and environmental transgressions, the coffee industry ranks among the few in the world in which third-party organizations are simultaneously addressing issues of sustainability including biodiversity, living wages, and chemical-free agriculture. In many mountain regions, high-quality coffee can be produced with minimal impacts when cultivated organically and planted in a natural forest canopy of about 50-percent shade. This is particularly important, since the coffee growing region that spans the Caribbean and Central and South America is one of vast biodiversity. Many of these shade grown farms retain desperately needed habitat for many species, including increasingly endangered orioles, warblers, waxwings, and other feathered Neotropical migrants.

From a bird's-eye perspective, the ideal forest would probably have no coffee production. Even the best shade-grown coffees–in the rustic forests at mid-elevation ranges of Mexico and Peru, for example–are farmed in highly managed settings. Trees are both thinned and replanted to accommodate coffee crops. Some species, such as leguminous trees that fix nitrogen, may be favored over the natural species mix. "Coffee is not *that* shade tolerant," admits biologist Russell Greenberg of the Smithsonian Migratory Bird Center (SMBC), "and not all shade should be endorsed, either. I would not feel comfortable [certifying shade-grown coffee] below a certain level of diversity." Shade spans a continuum from the high-altitude, rustic forests with a high degree of species diversity to clearcut plantations where trees are replanted and intentionally pruned, offering little if any wildlife value. According to Greenberg, "As the level of shade diminishes from rustic forests to mono-layer maintained operations, then to canopy-less sun coffee plantations, species are lost every step of the way."

Traditionally, coffee was grown in mixed forest shade, where the berries mature slowly, enhancing aroma and taste. Then in the 1960s and 1970s the "Green Revolution" transformed cultivation practices to technified sun plantations that destroy the species-rich canopy in order to make room for high-yielding hybrids that require heavy inputs of fertilizers and pesticides. Forest coffee was replaced by industrial monocultures of clearcut coffee. Sun coffee operations, promoted heavily by governments and international aid organizations, turned out to benefit very few parties. They produce large crops of low-quality (robusta variety) beans. Overproduction means that the small growers (there are as many as 250,000 in Mexico alone) who work the land lightly and cultivate a quality bean, are squeezed by the sinking prices of flooded international markets. Then in the early 1990s, Vietnam launched an aggressive coffee production program, contributing 12 million more bags (10 percent) to an already bloated supply by the end of the decade. In 2001, the global price bottomed out at between 40 and 50 cents per pound, down from the boom year of 1997 at $1.60, when Brazilian producers suffered a damaging frost. According to David Griswold, founder of the Portland, Oregon-based Sustainable Harvest Coffee Importers, one of the country's largest importers of organic, fair-trade, and shade-grown coffee to the specialty industry, $1 per pound is the break-even threshold for most growers; $1.25 is a living wage. "It's a difficult time to be in coffee right now. There is so much suffering going at the grower level that in turn affects villages and the surrounding communities."

Given the brutal boom and bust nature of the global marketplace, a variety of third-party certification programs emerged over the past two decades to address the human and envi-ronmental costs of coffee production. More than 40 organic agencies certify that coffees are pesticide-free and generally ensure that a 30 percent premium over the current global commodity price goes to the farmer. (The USDA is now enforcing certification at the roaster level as well.) International labor groups such as TransFair and Equal Exchange audit the trail of coffee purchased from select cooperatives, eliminating middlemen, and enabling farmers to benefit directly from the fruits of their labor. While it can cost thousands for groups to join the certification process, the results can be significant. Fair Trade coffee, purchased through democratically organized cooperatives, guarantees a $1.26 per pound premium price; the combined organic and Fair Trade premium is $1.41 per pound.

Shade-grown programs, however, have not developed the same depth of participation and represent the next, urgent territory in third-party certification. While shade-grown coffee was promoted for its high quality in the 1930s, it was in the mid-1990s that biologists from the Smithsonian Migratory Bird Center began to make the connection between migratory Neotropical songbirds in the North, and habitat and mid-elevation coffee farms in Central and South America where the birds wintered. In 1996 the SMBC held a seminal conference to release their findings on the importance and value of forest-grown coffee. The report included a scientific explanation of what qualified as biologically beneficial shade. Coffee importers at the conference, some of whom were already activists in their own rights, were convinced by the idea. Mendocino, California-based Thanksgiving Coffee founder Paul Katzen quickly became a champion of the concept, and sent importer David Griswold out in search of shade grown coffee that he could market as a high-quality product under a Songbird label.

As of early 2002, only two U.S. organizations independently certify shade grown-coffee: the Smithsonian Migratory Bird Project (through its Bird Friendly label) and the Rainforest Alliance (through the Eco OK label). Bird Friendly shade must have several components: a diversity of at least ten different noncrop species; differing vertical structure; a 36-foot minimum canopy; and 40-percent coverage of the sky. Bird Friendly certification returns a $.25 per pound premium to the Migratory Bird Center, and currently has agreements with a dozen importers and more than forty roasters. SMBC's long-term goal is to integrate high ecological standards for shade into the already existing organic movement. This would make certification more efficient and more affordable, a constant challenge to ecolabels regardless of product or industry. In 2001, the SMBC held a number of workshops to initiate more than 70 organic certifying practitioners into their approach to shade.

The Eco OK approach hinges on the strategy that working with larger producers with less stringent standards is the best way to shore up tracts of contiguous habitat. Their standards take numerous aspects of farm management into account, though organic is a long-term goal rather than a requirement for certification (a clear differentiation from Bird Friendly). Eco OK combines shade-grown management with worker welfare issues, integrated pest management (with a preference for organic production), clean-water processing, and riparian and forest protection.

Outside of Bird Friendly and Eco OK certification, shade-grown coffee marketing functions, for the time being, on a certain degree of consumer faith. Conservation International has teamed up with Starbucks and launched a shade-grown coffee project within the buffer zones of a biological reserve. Thanksgiving Coffee's Songbird Coffee is a cause-related marketing program that returns 15 cents per pound or package to the American Birding Association. Sustainable Harvest supplies many specialty coffee retailers and makes their own on-site assessments and documentation of the certified organic producers they market as "shade grown," paying the extra costs of shade certification only when a customer demands it. "Nine out of ten times when you buy both Fair Trade and organically certified," says Griswold, "your chances of benefiting wildlife are high. Fair Trade means you're dealing with small, subsistence growers, and without chemicals, farmers need the leaf litter of shade trees for mulch. But I would love a low-cost, high-demand way to make it 10 out of 10 triple-certified coffee."

Shade-Grown Coffee Country

I journey to the remote village of Pluma Hidalgo in Oaxaca, Mexico, an area as famous to coffee gourmands as Bordeaux is to wine lovers. (As of late 2002 this region was in the process of Bird Friendly certification.) The town of Pluma Hidalgo is a cluster of tin shacks and stuccoed buildings tonsured around a mountain ridge in the Sierra Madres. At 1,300 meters, this is the ideal altitude for the high-quality Arabica coffee plants. It is also the mountain zone hardest hit by deforestation throughout Latin America. On a rutted dirt road that scales a ridge a few hundred meters above the town, children tote bundles of firewood on their backs. At the time of my visit in spring 2000, many of the chicken coops are more accommodating than the rusty corrugated aluminum-sided structures villagers are living in, the recent handiwork of Hurricane Pauline. Pools of dark coffee beans lie drying on cement patios. I spend the afternoon hiking with certified Fair trade and organic coffee farmer, Pablo Perez Ramos. Short, stocky, and with a thick bushy mustache, Ramos looks like a character right out of Pancho Villa's brigade. Ramos farms three hectares (close to seven acres) with two full-time workers and a seasonal crew of eight migrant pickers, who travel from as far away as Guatemala to earn eight to ten dollars a day. He and I set out on a burrow trail that traverses a steep grade toward the mountain. He has paved the first half-mile with ridged cement slabs that allow him to pack up and down to his mountaintop farm regardless of heavy rains. The sharply pitched trail, about six feet wide, is impressively maintained. The cement trail, Ramos says, was only achieved through a number of years of arduous labor. "Mucho sacrificio," he says simply, "much sacrifice."

As we walk, Ramos swings his large machete in a cadence, rhythmically nicking the outer seam of his pant leg, creating a steady zing, zing, zinging sound. Flocks of exotically feathered chickens roam the forest, as do donkeys, whose occasional braying breaks the silence. Trees 90 feet tall tower above the shoulder-high coffee plants. The hand-sized leaves on the coffee plants are thick and shiny, white flowers emerging from bud break. Three varieties are growing in the forest—*bourbon*, *tipica*, and an unidentified modern type—each with different characteristics and yields. Though harvest season has passed, many of the bushes are still studded with bright red berries. Ramos identifies many smooth-barked, deciduous trees he calls *henequil*, (most probably of the *inga* species), the perfect complement for coffee plantations because they provide much needed shade and fix nitrogen into the soil, which in turn helps fertilize the plants. As part of his organic practices, Ramos mixes the leaves with coffee hulls, burrow dung, ash, and other matter to create compost, which is lavished at the base of every coffee plant to maximize seasonal output. At one point, he sights a bird in an upper branch of the forest. *"Pajaro del norte,"* he says, "a bird from the North." It is a cedar waxwing. He then picks up a stone and expertly hurls it at a palmlike plant 30 yards away. It is a direct hit into a mass of black berries smothering the plant. "That fruit is what the birds are after," Pablo says. Back at home we are anticipating the northern flight of songbirds that are overwintering in the south, an annual pilgrimage that should be revered as miraculous. And every day, consumers around Western nations turn, out of ritual and habit, to the bean that could consciously link us to our broader relationships and responsibilities throughout the planet.

COMMUNITY SUPPORTED AGRICULTURE: LINKING FARMS AND TABLES

Wings a-blur, a pheasant glides over rows of waist-high late season brassicas, then descends and disappears into the thick brush in an uncultivated corner of Common Harvest Farm. Dan Guenther's eyes follow the bird's path for a moment, and he is reminded of a hope he has for the land he and his wife, Margaret Penning, have managed to save as an organic farm in perpetuity.

"Last year we had 45 nesting species on the property, including an orchard oriole," says Guenther, a compactly built, dark-haired, bearded man, wearing canvas work clothes and a baseball cap. "But this relatively small piece of ground is too complex for my wife and me to understand and keep track of. We would like to invite people to do annual biological inventories on the farm, including the birds, frogs, toads, and insects. Just as we have a financial audit of the farm, we'd also like to create a monitoring schedule to understand what is going on here ecologically. But I'm not a fan of GIS satellite mapping as an information source. I would rather have people out on the land–'more eyes to the acre'–observing the patterns of wildlife."

Located in Osceola, Wisconsin, Common Harvest lies in former tallgrass prairie territory about an hour east of Minneapolis. It is one of dozens of farms in the state that has turned to Community Supported Agriculture as a way of direct marketing to a corps of loyal member customers. Throughout a growing season that runs from April to October, this CSA produces 220 "farm in a box" shares of up to 50 different vegetables. Because many members share weekly deliveries, perhaps 400 households partake of Common Harvest's artisanally grown, organic, just-picked produce. In addition to supplying a market for his produce and providing interest-free, pre-growing-season share payments, the Community Supported Agriculture model has brought an additional layer of stability to Common Harvest. Ten members agreed to advance 7-year fixed-price shares to help the farm operation capitalize the purchase of the land, which is now protected as an organic farm through a permanent easement established with the Wisconsin Land Trust.

Its value as a working organic farm is even more significant when placed in the context of the broader landscape. On the east, the farm is bordered by a swath of forest, while in an adjacent field on to the south, a huge dust cloud swirls above a combine harvesting genetically modified Roundup-Ready soybeans. To the west lies a single-lane road, and beyond it is Standing Cedars, protected land all the way to the St. Croix River. Immediately to the north is a former farm, recently purchased by a Common Harvest CSA member, which is presently being rehabilitated. Numerous tallgrass prairie restoration efforts are ongoing directly around the farm, including work by the Western Wisconsin Prairie Enthusiasts and the Earth Partnership. Common Harvest has contributed expertise and machinery to those conservation efforts, helping with plantings, mending fences, mowing trails, and other tasks. CSA members have also begun contributing funds to protect land around the farm. In addition, the Western Prairie Habitat Restoration Area is attempting to protect and restore up to 20,000 acres of tallgrass prairie in St. Croix and Polk Counties, from Osceola all the way to River Falls. And nearby, restoration farmer Sean Shotler, of Gentian Farms, has been striving for 15 years to develop the seed supply necessary to reduce the price of habitat restoration to an affordable level of say, $50 per acre. One day, in addition to visiting Common Harvest to participate in harvesting or farm days, perhaps CSA members will come to see reintroduced prairie chickens, trumpeter swans, and Sandhill cranes, or to appreciate plants such as cream gentians, prairie blazing stars, and big blue stem in the restored grasslands.

The "farm-in-a-box" concept of Community Supported Agriculture has helped hundreds of small farmers serve a corps of customers and remain on the land since the late 1980s.

On this October afternoon, Guenther has been eagerly awaiting the visit of the Wild Farm Alliance steering committee and is revved up and prepared for dialogue. Unrolling a bundle of carefully hand-rendered farm maps, he explains his annual planning and record keeping. Throughout the farm, different areas have been named after authors and leaders

in the sustainable agriculture movement. A few catch my attention—Wendell's Berry Patch, Sand County (after Aldo Leopold), and Bromfield (after the novelist Louis Bromfield). In addition to details on the annual rotations of fruits, vegetables, and cover crops, there are notes on what species have been observed during different times of each year, reminiscent of a similar practice written about by the Ohio Amish farmer David Kline in *Great Possessions*.

The intensively cultivated fruit and vegetable plots at Common Harvest span gentle slopes. While the cultivated fields are fenced to keep deer out, Guenther explains that he has plans to expand the borders surrounding his fields to increase habitat. He points to one modification in his cultivation practices to accommodate wildlife. "Have you ever seen the number of snakes chopped up inside a hay bale? It's disgusting," he says. "I usually begin mowing from the middle of the field and drive slowly so that reptiles have time to fan out and get away."

By late October, production is limited to a few rows of broccoli, cauliflower, and a deep purple kale. A tractor cart loaded with pumpkins awaits delivery. A mother donkey and her foal graze in a pasture. On a classic old red barn, William Carlos Williams's poem about being at a dying child's bedside, "The Red Wheel Barrow," has been stenciled in white paint: "so much depends / upon / a red wheel / barrow / glazed with rain / water / beside the white / chickens."

As we walk and Guenther talks, he continually alludes to authors and their contributions to the sustainable agriculture movement. He is clearly a deep thinker, a passionate devotee, and a creative force in staying on and making his living from the land. "I think we need to be continually questioning humanity's relationship with the soil," he says, squinting into the rays of a descending October sun. "Maybe we need a balance between feeding plants and feeding the soil. Clearly, we need to accept chaos, and take what Nature will give us, and release some control over certain variables. Weeds are a good starting point," he says, pointing out some messy borders around his fields. And one parting thought as we are piling into our van. "Farming with the wild?" He repeats my question, then answers, "No-till and no-chemical are where we need to go as conservation farmers."

A NEW BRAND FOR BEEF

When Will Holder helped then-Secretary of the Interior Bruce Babbitt release the first reintroduced Mexican Wolf into the Blue Range of Arizona, a family circle was completed. Will's grandfather on his father's side, Cleveland Holder, was a well-liked district game warden credited with shooting the last Mexican wolf known in Arizona. (At that time, any university publication would have affirmed and reinforced that he was doing exactly what a good steward should have. Apparently, Will's great aunt still has the pelt.)

"I was raised to shoot coyotes and wolves," says Holder, who left the family ranch to work in advertising in Phoenix, then returned with his wife Jan to raise their children outside the city. "But after a while we began thinking, hey, we've been shooting coyotes for 100 years and it hasn't really been working. When we got into researching mountain lions and other predators, we found that when you do shoot a lion, the situation can actually become worse. When you take that lion out, you disrupt the boundaries between the lions, bears, and other predators and now something has to come in and kill to reestablish the boundary. You've almost forced another predator incident by doing that."

Arizona ranchers Jan and Will Holder are direct marketers of healthy meat products.

The Holders began changing some of their traditional approaches. "Mostly cow whisperer stuff," says Holder, "low-stress management techniques where you still herd the cows but allow them to stay together, similar to the behavior of buffalo herds. It's easier for a lion to take out one stray animal than for it to take on four hundred." They also adopted a more traditional herdsman approach, camping out with the herd on and off, especially after any sightings of predator tracks. By July 2001, the Holders hadn't shot anything for 12 years and hadn't had a predator loss in five. "During the same time our neighbors experienced the status quo of four to eight predator losses per year. So that's pretty economical in itself," says Jan.

The Holders' ranch management innovations had actually taken root with Will's father, who initiated a number of changes, such as discontinuing the use of pesticides or antibiotics on animals and the adoption of Holistic Range Management. His challenge was recouping the extra costs of more careful and conscious stewardship.

The neighbors' responses to the Holders' changing management techniques were less than favorable. "Have you ever heard the term 'death threat'?" says Jan, her eyes widening. "Have you ever heard of all your neighbors not speaking to you for four years? One local rancher killed a lion on our property right in front of Will's grandma's house and was proud of it," she says.

Despite the local animosity, the Holders pushed ahead, attempting to build value-added awareness for their beef. They launched their own label to put their product to market—Ervin's Natural Beef, named after Will's grandfather on his mother's side, known for his passion for the land and compassion for animals. "We were frustrated by an industry that places six different businesses between producer and consumer," says Will. "None of these segments work together toward quality or accountability. It's all based on speed and volume. Bigger is better. This is a mature industry and it's a difficult nut to crack."

They began direct marketing by talking one-on-one with customers who wanted more of a connection to their food and to the people who produced it. The going was slow but they achieved steady suc-

cess. After devoting considerable time and energy to their own ranch brand, however, the Holders found they were spending most of their time on marketing and not enough on the ranch where they wanted to be. With the help of the Sonoran Institute, they revised their business plan. They decided to evolve beyond their own small business and grow a regional brand-and-distribution system geared toward giving ranchers a living wage and promoting synthetic-free and predator friendly standards. They recruited one of the country's best known conservation ranchers to help them tackle the complex undertaking of developing and implementing standards across widely varying range conditions throughout the Western states. While these standards will clearly be superior to conventional practices, some critics will no doubt challenge whether arid lands ranching is "good for the land" as the label proclaims—particularly public lands—or will merely be "less bad." Such an ecological critique may take a long time to earn popular currency in the ranching culture. In the meantime, Ervin's Natural Beef is pursuing its mission of supplying high-quality, cost-competitive products to market, brought to life by the stories of what these standards mean to the land and the people who practice them.

Which leads us back to the Mexican wolf reintroduction and former Department of Interior secretary Bruce Babbitt. When Babbitt heard the story that Will Holder's grandfather had shot the last wolf, the Secretary's staff contacted Holder to participate in the release ceremony. It was more than he imagined it would be.

"I was this cowboy, and you hear people from Phoenix talking about the wolf song," says Holder, rolling his eyes. "I was thinking this was going to be a big coyote, no big deal. But it was fairly dramatic when they let him go—the grace, the strength, the power, its eyes. The hair stood up on the back of my neck. It was truly one of the most powerful experiences of my life."

Ervin's Natural Beef is attempting to build an independent brand for chemical-free, predator friendly beef.

GETTING STARTED

Following such an impressive and inspiring range of examples, it is understandable perhaps to expect a template that defines what the ideal "wild farm" or ranch should look like. But as these preceding chapters have shown, we may only be at the beginning of a movement that is taking shape in different forms and in different regions across the country. Clearly absent in these farm profiles and photo spreads is all the hard work, long days, endless meetings, family struggles, and trials and tribulations that an engaged life on the land entails. We must continually remind ourselves that accomplishing ambitious conservation goals will require many involved, informed, successful farmers, ranchers, conservationists, and citizens who are committed to protecting the places where they live. This occurs at a time when economic survival is at stake for so many hard-working people.

Rather than providing a detailed blueprint for creating a "wild farm" then, this final section presents some of the best practices, core principles, and key resources discovered during the process of my research. There are sound reasons for offering a broad overview rather than a detailed manual. Farming and habitat conditions vary from property to property and from region to region, making generalizations difficult. What works for a certain farmer or rancher in central Montana may not directly translate to a given property in northern California and vice versa. Each farm also has unique management goals and varying levels of resources to pursue conservation strategies. And any single aspect of land management—wetland restoration, grass-finished grazing, landscaping with natives, natural systems farming, corridor design—would require an entire book to adequately address. In fact, many excellent resources are enumerated in the bibliography that follows.

In simple terms, a farm should be as wild as it possibly can be while simultaneously accomplishing its goals of agricultural production. At the same time, no farm should be able to break its social contract by degrading soils, polluting or depleting aquatic systems, or eliminating critical habitats upon which both the future of agriculture and biodiversity depend. As the examples in this book have demonstrated, individuals and groups around the country are increasingly finding numerous ways that farming and ranching operations and rural areas can directly benefit from the presence and proliferation of native species and habitat. No farm can be "too wild." Rather, a key management question in the very near future will be whether a farm is "wild enough." In other words, has the agricultural operation optimized the natural services of a healthy ecosystem that allow it to prosper? Pollinators and beneficial insects are absolutely critical for the long-term success of sustainable agriculture and are dependent on the presence of permanent vegetation. Barn owls, raptors, snakes, and other predators help to control rodents that can cause crop losses. Fire has proved to be a valuable management tool in reinvigorating and improving the nutritional quality of grasslands and pastures and in controlling shrubs and invasive weed species. Healthy riparian systems are essential for agriculture, protecting against flood events, providing stable banks, clean water, and habitat for fish and wildlife. Winter flooded fields can become migratory waterfowl habitat while also reducing weed pressures. These are merely a few examples.

Given agriculture's dominance on the landscape and the increasing imperilment of biodiversity and native ecosystems throughout most of the world, farming with the wild is an obvious and imperative direction for the future. The spirited stories documented in the preceding chapters have hopefully established a foundation of working models and methods. If we care about the future of small-scale agriculture that thrives within healthy rural regions, we will find ways to follow their leads, making new connections, and getting started, one farm, one household, one region at a time, on this challenging path.

SOME BASICS

1. Goal Setting

Can farming with the wild help to achieve farm objectives? The enhancement of wildlife habitat on the farm is a primary goal of many landowners. Increasing biodiversity can also work to accomplish personal and professional goals such as pollination and pest control, land and soil conservation, climate modification such as wind protection or shade, or recreational and aesthetic values.

2. Natural Resources Inventory

Understanding your site and the adjoining region can help to inform and direct on-farm management. Conducting a thorough natural resources inventory can help identify wooded areas, edge habitats, streams, field borders, remnant grasslands, marginal lands, or other potential habitat opportunities in or around the farm. An extensive inventory would include factors such as: land uses; topography; hydrology and drainage conditions; soils; plant and animal communities; cropped and non-cropped areas; places of historic or archeological interest, and so on.

3. Consultation and Economic Assistance

Consulting with experienced local landowners, wildlife resource specialists, and others during the planning process can serve to identify potential opportunities and challenges for specific projects. By seeking technical and financial assistance, landowners can more effectively install restoration projects and find cost-share programs to help fund them. Identifying ways to connect on-farm habitat enhancement projects to larger, regional wildway initiatives can greatly enhance the value to the broader ecosystem.

4. Assessing Benefits

Farming with the wild can offer various benefits to the landowner, from reduced long-term maintenance costs, to regulatory compliance, recreational or aesthetic enhancements, reduced operating costs, additional revenues, and more. Protecting and restoring marginally productive lands under a conservation easement can bring in additional funds, while planting structurally diverse native habitats adjacent to waterways can help to comply with federal and state endangered species and water quality regulations. In many countries, it is being recognized that conservation-based agricultural efforts also help to elevate the reputation and public perception of the farming profession.

ON-FARM BENEFITS

Enhanced wildlife habitat
Pollination
Biological pest control
Wind and snow protection
Erosion control and sediment filtration
Lower long-term maintenance costs
Aesthetic values
Predation reduction
Additional income
Farmland protection
Ecological values
Community interaction
Enhanced public image
Cost-share benefits
Better market perception
Increased land values

CHALLENGES

Short-term costs of resources and
  money
Time commitment
Can potentially host unwanted pests
  or weeds
Depending on the practices, may
  result in taking some land out of
  production
Need for technical expertise and scientific monitoring

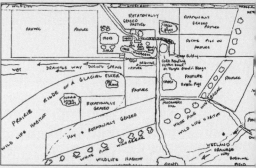

Top right, GIS mapping shows the diverse habitat types and residential uses of the Occidental Arts and Ecology Center. Bottom, a detail of a hand-rendered farm map.

FARM MAPPING

Most landowners find it extremely useful and satisfying to develop farm and project maps to better understand the uniqueness and essential characteristics of their farms. A wide variety of approaches and preferred techniques exist for farm mapping, ranging from GIS satellite overlays and aerial photographs to hand-drawn charts infused with humor and insight. Such maps should provide a complete property overview as well as adjacent properties.

Maps often include an inventory of habitat types, the presence and range of unique and common species, soil types, places of ecological concern for preservation or restoration, USDA winter hardiness zones, and other pertinent information. Complementary maps situating the farm within the watershed or bioregion can help identify the natural flow of water and paths of wildlife. Aerial and historical photos, as well as photographs that regularly document farm conditions over a long period of time can help to inform the land-use planning process.

The Occidental Arts and Ecology Center in Sonoma County, California, has used GIS imagery to identify the distribution of different vegetation communities and landmarks throughout its 80-acre property. (Previous page.) The maintenance and restoration of these unique plant associations as well as the plant and animal species that inhabit them is a key objective of OAEC's teaching gardens and ecological preserve.

The hand-rendered map of Four Winds Farm in River Falls, Wisconsin (previous page, bottom right), provides a detailed overview of the farm's many working areas as well as wild and restored habitats. The Four Winds map also shows how bordering lands affect habitat connectivity.

Landscape scale maps, such as those that identify wildlife corridors or other multi-property charts are essential to farming with the wild efforts. The Bootheel Fire Management Plan, for example, uses maps to carefully detail how wildfires interact with the grasslands of southern New Mexico. Landowners can elect to either allow burning across certain sections of their properties, to be consulted by agencies, or to have the fire immediately extinguished. This has created, in effect, a wildfire corridor that burns tens of thousands of acres annually under carefully monitored conditions, helping to restore grasslands toward pre-settlement conditions. Some of these fires even take place within safe proximity to roads and houses, with seasonal weather monitoring and regional mapping informing inter-agency management during fire events.

Landscape level maps can also show other dimensions of a landscape, such as temperature gradients or depths of the water table charted through numerous well sites.

The following list provides a framework for potential site mapping and planning:

● Survey for unique species, and consider working with a professional field biologist or local monitoring group to help you. Don't limit your list to migratory songbirds or waterfowl, but also attempt to include pollinators, insect predators, amphibia, native soil decomposers, large mammals, and others.

● Make a list of current and historical land uses on the property. Identify land use types such as forested hills, irrigated open lands, dryland pasture, prairie, range, wetlands, stream corridors, and so on.

● Generate a vegetative inventory of the property, including native plant species and communities, the distribution of introduced annuals and perennials, and how they got there. Consider plants and plant communities on neighboring properties as well. Also consider connectivity of habitat types, drainages, wetlands, and so on.

● Identify soil types of different zones on the property.

● Detail other important climactic influences, including USDA Winter Hardiness Zones, elevations, slopes and solar exposures, precipitation and wind patterns.

● Determine areas of natural processes such as flooding.

● Identify sloping lands, ranking slopes as highly erodable or in need of terracing or contours.

● Identify all areas of hydrological importance, such as riparian areas, ponds, seasonal or permanent wetlands, springs, shallow wet zones. and so on.

● Identify all farm edges, such as areas between fields, roadsides and ditches, and any odd-shaped patches where potential restoration plantings might take place.

● Plan according to distinct habitat types with the intent to maintain diverse habitat types and complex edges within corridors. Bigger setbacks from streams and wildlife corridors are better for wildlife.

● Strive for connectivity between habitat patches, wildlife areas, and corridors. Habitat patches that are linked are the most valuable to birds and wildlife.

● Attempt to allow for seasonal wildlife migrations through the property.

● Revisit the maps and documents on a regular basis as a means of analyzing long-term goals, and success of ongoing plans and efforts.

MANAGING FOR WILDLIFE

Planning and implementation can be done to varying degrees and can include a mix of both noncropped and cultivated areas. One primary emphasis should be placed on providing year-round sources of water and nectar, as well as diverse habitat types and cropping systems within the farm. Native vegetation around water bodies and riparian areas provides habitat and helps to protect water quality. One excellent book to help you get started is *Bring Farm Edges Back to Life!*, available from the Yolo County RCD office, *www.yolorcd.ca.gov*.

Biodiversity can take a number of forms. Structural diversity creates varied and changing plant communities across the landscape. Compositional diversity encompasses a wide range of species on the land. Functional diversity delivers numerous naturally provided on-farm services, such as the fixation of nitrogen; filtration of sediment; protection against soil erosion, wind, and weather; and sustaining of native habitat.

One of the difficulties of actively integrating conservation practices on the farm is that management efforts often favor certain species over others, or produce unintended consequences. While cultivation tillage techniques can greatly reduce soil loss, they also rely heavily on herbicides and increasingly on genetically modified crops. Expanded buffer strips—in combination with conventional chemical-intensive practices—may decrease sedimentation but pollute groundwater. The placement of wood duck houses in open marshes, rather than in the woods, has been found to drastically retard reproduction, as it can encourage females to competitively lay eggs in the same place rather than caring for their own clutches in the woods.

We are only beginning to understand this ecosystem-based approach to agriculture. The difficult task ahead lies in evolving ever-deeper ways in which the presence of native animals and plants can function as a benefit rather than a threat to agriculture. Adding to that challenge is the need for solutions to be cost effective and to fit appropriately within the hectic schedules of agricultural landowners. Finally, our regional conservation efforts now face the double charge of providing habitats for the most endangered species and plant and animal communities in a given region, while simultaneously benefiting the greatest distribution of species.

Wetland Enhancement and Restoration

In many states, where wetland loss is over 90 percent of pre-settlement conditions, even small drainage ponds and grassed waterways can provide critical habitat and resting areas for migratory waterfowl, and nesting and wintering habitat for others. Wetlands maintain water quality and help to recharge the water table. The ability to absorb and filter runoff can prevent flooding and avoid further land disturbance. Efforts to restore marginal lands and essential wetland habitat across the landscape must continue to be a top priority throughout this century.

Tailwater Ponds

Tailwater pond systems can be established in low-lying areas of furrow-irrigated fields to recycle irrigation water, trap and filter sediment and nutrients, catch winter runoff, and provide year-round wetland habitat for wildlife. Ponds can also be built simply to catch and store rainwater. Double pond systems can be designed to pre-filter and more effectively trap sediment (see illustration below). According to Sacramento Valley restoration farmer John Anderson, up to half of the volume of water that a small pond contains may recharge into the groundwater every time the pond is filled from seasonal storms or irrigation cycling. Recharge can occur numerous times throughout the season.

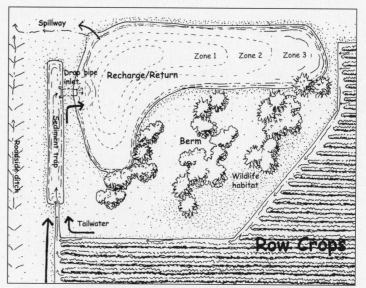

Tailwater pond diagram from the outstanding handbook, Bring Farm Edges Back to Life! *detailing sediment trap and reservoir design. Diagram by Paul Robins reprinted with permission.*

One of two tailwater ponds at Four Winds Farm in western Wisconsin, a grass-fed livestock operation that serves a growing local market.

Riparian Buffers/Filter Strips

Creek corridors are the single most important wildlife corridors according to California Fish and Game wildlife biologist Alan Buchman. They connect all other habitats and are at the heart of the ecosystem. Buchman, a career biologist who works closely with vineyard owners in Northern California counties, recommends the following management principles. Avoid breaks across creeks and riparian corridors. Do not fence wildlife out of creek corridors. Try to keep fences as close to field borders and as far away from wildlife corridors as possible. Avoid cultivating, grazing, or other activities in riparian areas that the majority of species use as invaluable corridors and habitat zones. Maximize shade and fallen debris to improve fish spawning areas. Vegetate buffers to stabilize stream banks, reduce erosion, and filter runoff. Swales in riparian buffers can increase percolation and sediment removal and are preferable to hardscaping (with cement, rock, or culverts). Keep riparian buffers as wide as possible to facilitate wildlife movement. Wide buffers can also serve as a deterrent against pest problems. Buchman recommends buffers of at least 100 feet in the wine-growing region of Northern California to prevent the infestation of the blue-green sharp-shooter, a vector for the vine-killing Pierce's disease.

Biological Engineering

According to Evan Engber, founder of Bioengineering Associates in Laytonville, California, traditional living systems techniques can be used to remediate rivers suffering from overdevelopment. Because rainfall no longer adequately percolates into groundwater, river velocities have greatly increased. Combined with heavy sediment loads and river channelization, severe streambank erosion has become both critical and commonplace.

Willow is a powerful rooting, pioneering, sun-loving plant that can be used to slow water velocity near the bank, allowing silt to deposit. Once established and the turbulence abated, oak, cottonwoods, and other succession species can be planted to create a natural shade canopy.

The four photos at right show the progress of a willow brush mattress project on an organic vineyard in Napa Valley, California. Work is best done prior to fall. Summer plantings must be irrigated. The project essentially followed these steps. A side channel was cut to move the gravel bar. The collapsing bank was bulldozed to create the proper slope. A boulder "toe" was formed at the base of the planting area. Willow branches were cut and kept moist prior to planting. Willow posts were made from thick material and driven into the bank in a grid pattern. Willow cuttings were planted end-down in trenches between posts. Branches were lashed laterally from post to post, keeping the mattress as thick as possible to provide minimum air space.
www.bioengineers.com

1. Collapsing streambank in dry season.
2. Bank resloped, posts arranged, footing dug for boulder toe base.
3. Willow mattress installed with boulder toe at base.
4. Revegetation after first wet season.

Ten Attributes of River Ecosystem Integrity

1. Spatially complex channel shape.

2. Variable streamflow patterns.

3. Frequently disturbed riverbed surface.

4. Periodic riverbed scour and fill.

5. Balanced fine and course sediment volumes.

6. Periodic channel migration and/or avulsion.

7. A functional floodplain.

8. Infrequent channel resetting floods.

9. Self-sustaining, diverse riparian corridor.

10. Naturally fluctuating groundwater table.

These core attributes of a dynamic, healthy, river ecosystem were based on a historical evaluation of the Tuolumne River hydrology and geomorphology. They were developed by the Tuolumne River Technical Advisory Committee as part of a habitat restoration plan for the Lower Tuolomne River Corridor to serve as measurable restoration objectives.

www.delta.dfg.ca.gov/afrp/watershed_links/ tuolplan.pdf

The riparian shelterbelt on Kenagy Family Farms includes a black walnut veneer wood crop with a perennial native grass seed crop of Bromus vulgaris.

Field Borders

Planting native vegetation in noncropped areas can become a cost-effective alternative to herbicide applications, discing, and mowing. Once established, borders of native perennial grasses can usually outcompete invasive weeds as well as supply valuable nectar sources, cover, and habitat for a number of species. A diversity of trees and shrubs, grass-legume mixtures, and other flowering plants can supply numerous agricultural as well as wildlife benefits throughout the year. Birds, beneficial insects, rodents, reptiles, and other wildlife use hedgerows and field borders as critical habitat zones. Trees and shrubs reduce drifting snow and block wind that can create erosion or harm crops. Larger field borders can serve as buffers or corridors that connect habitat throughout a region.

Windbreaks, Shelterbelts, and Living Snow Fences

Stands of trees and shrubs can limit soil erosion, provide passive solar heating, reduce livestock feeding costs, and conserve moisture on fields. By reducing wind damage, tree breaks can increase crop yields. Products obtained from windbreaks, riparian buffers, alley cropping, and woodlots have been valued in the billions of dollars. Edible nuts, fruits and berries, pulp, lumber and veneer wood, medicinal plants, native restoration plants, and more can be grown in structurally diverse buffer areas. (See photo top left.) Solar orientation should be taken into consideration when selecting tree species or crop types for shelterbelts. For example, tall trees on south- and west-facing field margins can eventually block valuable afternoon sun. According to a Wild Farm Alliance briefing paper, over 100 bird species are known to use windbreaks for foraging, nesting, and resting.

Pollinator Insectaries

Year-round sources of flowering plants can attract successive blooms of beneficial insects and pollinators. Pollinator gardens can be as small as an isolated patch or as large as a few acres.

Half-acre insectary amid the Benziger Winery in Glen Ellen, California, attracts pollinators and beneficial insects. It is irrigated and blooms throughout the growing season.

Hedgerows

Well-maintained field margins are an on-farm asset. Hedgerows should be designed with structural diversity in mind. Low level borders on the field edges or along roads and canals can be planted with native grasses. In a wider hedgerow plantings, shrubs, and taller trees can provide a variety of cover and nesting habitats. Choose plants according to your site, including soil types, height requirements, and other conditions. Select water-loving plants in wet areas and drought tolerant plants for arid zones. Try to select for a range of native species that will provide overlapping flowering for as long in the year as possible. Even roads within farms can be vegetated and regularly mowed to limit soil loss and stream sedimentation. A good field guide is *A Farmer's Guide to Hedgerow and Field Margin Management* published by Britain's Game Conservancy Trust at (44)01425-652381.

Wildlife-friendly Timing

Mowing, spraying, and other disruptive activities can be timed to minimize impacts during critical breeding periods–spring through early summer is optimal in many areas. However, according to Robert Bugg, early mowing is also sometimes done in February to mitigate against the "sink effect"– narrow patches of habitat that attract certain species but later fail to provide food or adequate protection due to predators, tilling, or mowing. High mowing or delayed mowing or grazing can be timed to respect the annual pulses of wildlife breeding, nesting, and so on. Delayed harvests can also accommodate the hatching period for ground-nesting birds. When considering harvest and mowing schedules, save fields closest to wetland and riparian areas for last, since they often maintain the highest nesting densities. Montana rancher Becky Weed suggests that sheep farmers can consider timing births for the fall to coincide with the Easter lamb market, rather than in the spring–coyote pup rearing season. Grazing can be conducted when undesirable annuals are seeding in order to promote perennials.

INSECTORY

Organic Baseline Standards

Studies have consistently demonstrated that diverse organic farm operations provide greater habitat values than conventional chemical-intensive, tillage-based agriculture. This is primarily a result of the absence of toxic chemicals on the farm. However, the same timing issues relating to tillage, mowing, and other habitat disturbances apply to organic farmers. Reduced-tillage systems have also been found to reduce impacts to wildlife, but reliance on herbicides can have adverse effects on birds, amphibians, and other species.

Adopting organic farming and livestock practices, or at a minimum using biologically integrated pest management or reduced insecticide applications can help maintain nonpest insect populations as forage for birds, and to decrease mortality to bees, fish, and other wildlife. Consult local agencies about what farm chemicals to avoid when working on restoration projects, particularly in riparian areas. Avoid planting Bt (*Bacillus thuringiensis*) genetically modified corn, because of its potential toxicity to soil organisms, nontarget moths, and butterflies.

Because of the less adverse and potentially positive habitat values of organic farm operations, some experts advocate zoning for organic agriculture near adjoining wetlands and other sensitive sites.

The Northwest Coalition for Alternatives to Pesticides has an informative website at *www.pesticide.org*.

Conservation Tillage

Conservation tillage practices—no-till, strip-till, and shallow tillage—that limit the cultivation of soil can help conserve soil biodiversity and moisture. The potential for soil erosion is drastically reduced by minimizing tillage and leaving dormant weed seeds undisturbed. Cover crops, crop stubble residues, and fallow fields provide much needed rest for fields, as well as food and shelter for birds, deer, and small mammals throughout the winter. Most no-till cropping systems, however, are still heavily dependent on herbicides to keep weeds in check. Further research is needed for minimizing or eliminating herbicide usage in no-till cropping systems.

Cover crops give fields rest and rotation, build soil fertility, reduce weeds, prevent soil erosion, build organic matter, and provide habitat. Planting strip crops of native plants can be used to break monocultures, generating food sources for birds and beneficial insects.

Consider experimenting with small plots of polycultures, such as drilling grain seed directly into a frost-killed leguminous cover crop, as is done in England. Keep abreast of the research being done in the United States in the field of perennial polycultures at the Land Institute (www.landinstitute.org) and at Washington State University (Professor Steve Jones).

Corn strip-tilled into the mulched mat of a winter-killed cover crop. The cover crop had been seeded directly into the stubble of a green bean field the season before.

Vegetated Waterways and Furrows

Waterways planted with grasses, sedges, or shrubs trap and filter sediment, reduce potential erosion and gullying, crowd out weedy species, and also provide forage and cover for birds and other wildlife. Ditches are sometimes referred to as "inverted hedgerows." At a minimum, most conservation guides suggest leaving at least one side of ditches vegetated to reduce runoff and provide habitat. Native sedges and grasses planted in the wet and dry zones in ditches and on the rims of ponds can reduce maintenance over the long term.

Low-impact Fencing

Fencing serves an obvious critical role in the protection and containment of fields, orchards, vineyards, and pastures. But fences can also seriously fragment the landscape, impeding the natural flow of certain wildlife, and in some cases, fatally ensnaring unsuspecting animals. From the conservation perspective, the less fencing, the better, particularly in well-traveled corridors, such as riparian areas, to which wildlife need direct access. Avoid fences that traverse creek crossings and keep fences at least 30 to 50 feet away from riparian areas to provide adequate passage. At the same time, fencing that excludes livestock from riparian areas, at least during certain times of the year or in priority areas, is becoming a key element of progressive grazing management. Fence only critical areas around home and landscape sites, garden areas, and agricultural areas to maximize open space. Low standing, portable or permanent electrical fencing can be used to fence out livestock yet still allow the passage of other wildlife both under and above the wire. Supplemental electric fencing can also be used to deter large animals and function as a viable alternative to lethal measures. Because fencing is such an expensive infrastructure cost, it is helpful to consider wildlife connectivity and exclusion prior to installation or upgrade.

Rotational Grass Farming

Low-input, grass-fed beef and dairy farms can essentially function as perennial systems of diverse grasses and vegetative communities. Particularly in areas with abundant summer rainfall, grass pasture livestock operations can offer an important opportunity to reduce dependence on the industrial corn, soybean, and feedlot system and the ecologically impoverished landscapes that accompany it.

When properly managed through intensive short-duration rotation systems, grass pastured meat and dairy farms can become self-sustaining, avoiding reliance on chemical fertilizers, herbicides, antibiotic and other medicinal treatments. Taller grass can shade the ground, helping to retain moisture. Improved grass management usually results in better grassland habitat types with benefits to greater numbers of species.

Rotational paddock systems allow for differences in topography and hydrology throughout the farm. When field edges, riparian borders, and forests are protected from grazing, these systems can improve forage for grazing wildlife, increase insect populations for birds and fish, and provide nesting cover. Permanent perennial forage cover reduces soil erosion. A good site on grass-fed meat and poultry is *www.eatwild.com*.

Flood-friendly farming

Since the early 1990s, farmers in the rice growing region of the Sacramento Valley have initiated the practice of winter flooding. Rather than burning the rice stubble after harvest as in previous years, the remaining fiber and grain are left in fields, which in turn are allowed to flood with winter rains, creating habitat for birds and helping to naturally suppress weeds and recycle nutrients.

Farther north, in California's Tule Lake National Wildlife Refuge, a unique research program is underway in marshlands that have been typically leased for agriculture. In this case, large plots rotate between actively farmed ground and either short-term marshes or long-term wetlands. Farmed fields are restored to seasonal marsh wetlands on a 3- to 5-year rotation, providing important habitat and offering weed and other pest (such as nematodes) suppression in the resting phase. Long-term wetland areas are allowed to develop substanital successional vegetation over a 15-year cycle. Those wetlands can eventually be burned, mowed, and/or disced prior to replanting. In an area where critical species declines and battles over water allocation for irrigation or conservation are escalating, this model should be carefully watched and studied. (A complete case history appears in the book *The Farm As Natural Habitat*.)

Fire Management Plans

Fires, both intentionally set and ignited by lightning, have historically been an integral element of certain North American grassland ecosystems. Fire can invigorate native grasses and forbs, enhance nesting cover for upland birds and other wildlife, improve the quality and nutritional content of pastures, and reduce invasive weeds and woody species.

Working with fires as a management tool typically requires consultation and coordination with numerous agencies and property owners. Each goal of a fire management plan often involves specific quantifiable management objectives. Weather conditions such as wind and humidity must be studied carefully for each specific area.

Support of long-term, science-based studies at the local level is needed to determine the effects of burning times to achieve specific management goals. These would include the control of certain insect pressures or the best effect in regenerating native grasses.

Bringing Back the Buffalo

Prior to the mid-1850s, some 60 million bison, or buffalo as they are commonly known, roamed North America in great herds from the Northern Rockies to the Atlantic coast. Scientists have divided those bison into three primary groups: wood, mountain, and plains buffalo. Only through desperate conservation measures did the bison survive the early 20th century. At the turn of the 21st century, however, efforts are underway to restore significant, if fragmented, populations of bison to North America. Presently, a more common approach has been to "cattle-ize" or treat them as a substitute for cattle in feedlots. On certain privately held ranches, federal lands and parks, and tribal territories, however, people are learning to reintroduce bison to semi-wild or wild conditions. The transformation is slowly taking root particularly in the Great Plains, where human populations have been declining for decades and where bison evolved with predators, prairie dogs, burrowing owls, and other members of grassland ecosystems. Restoring bison to Great Plains landscapes makes a great deal of sense. They are not attracted to riparian areas the way that beef cattle are, and therefore are far less impactful in those critical habitats. Grass-finished buffalo meat is found to be lean, healthy, and of high quality. Large yet fragmented areas seem to be the best short-term hope for the bison, which could help restore grasslands, improve ecotourism opportunities, and create a market for wild meat. An excellent account of a ranch conversion is *Buffalo for the Broken Heart* by Dan O'Brien.

Beyond Eradication

While one common argument against farming with the wild is an inevitable fear of crop losses, there are many examples of working with rather than against species on the farmscape. Adopting a non-lethal predator approach can limit human predation to specific, last resort measures.

Llamas. Studies at Iowa State University Extension have shown that the use of a single guard llama on sheep operations significantly minimizes flock losses to coyotes and dogs. In combination with proper fencing techniques, careful monitoring, scaring devices, and other nonlethal measures, ranchers can drastically reduce predation losses and save money. According to the study, a single gelded male llama can guard, on average, 250 to 300 sheep on 250 to 300 acres.

The Predator Conservation Alliance is in the process of creating a clearinghouse website for coexistence with predators at *www.predatorconservation.org*

Beavers. Rather than eradicating beavers from properties, some landowners are learning to work with them as valuable members of the landscape. Fencing around trunks with chicken wire is one way to prevent beavers from damaging wanted trees. A "beaver deceiver" is a fence constructed at an odd angle to a culvert opening to prevent blockage. It discourages beavers because they prefer to build dams at right angles to stream flow. Perforated pipes can be punched through existing dams to increase stream flow. The presence of beavers on a property can result in improvements in groundwater recharge (reducing irrigation needs) and greater habitat for other wildlife. According to Montana biologist and range specialist Lynn Burton, each acre of wetland acts as a safety valve for 69 acres of uplands by extending seasonal stream flow, filtering sediment and runoff, perpetuating streambank forests, and mediating floodwaters. Burton has even encouraged beavers to build a dam to protect a sloughing bank by placing a few rocks in the stream to get them started. Before large-scale trapping, an estimated 400 million beavers lived in North America, with ponds every 500 to 2,000 feet on nearly every stream on the continent.[1]

For more information on living with beavers, contact the Gallatin Wildlife Association in Bozeman, Montana.

Going Native and Perennial

Emphasize the use of natives and perennials on hedgerows, farm borders, and restoration projects. Native perennials can improve the appearance of the farmscape, reduce the need for maintenance in buffer areas, and provide habitat for beneficial pollinators and insects and other wildlife. Before working with native plants, consult with local nurseries about local plant types and availabilities. Local conservation agencies as well as sustainable agriculture and environmental organizations may have more detailed information about which plant types to emphasize or even avoid in agricultural settings. Studying remnant habitats and joining with regional restoration efforts can help understand appropriate plant communities and patterns for particular parts of your property.

Consider the height and distribution of plants in a restoration project. For example, use lower species along waterways, roadsides, and habitat borders, then increase plant height toward the center of wider habitat areas. In order to maximize chances for success, native vegetation must be actively farmed and managed for at least 3 to 5 years following installation. Make sure weeds are controlled before planting and in the spring and fall (at a minimum) at least through the first few years. Develop a

reliable irrigation system for the first 1 to 3 years after installation until plantings are established. Employ different strategies to control weeds that can outcompete slow-growing natives such as well-timed cultivation, burning, grazing before seed set, and so on.

Native perennial hedgerows, shelterbelts and restoration plantings are slowly becoming more common in farming areas. Wisconsin native seed farmer Sean Shotler of Gentian Farm is working to make prairie restoration more cost-effective. The Native Plant Society at www.nanps.org or 416-680-6280 can offer information on the native plant society nearest you.

Corridors, Connectivity, and Wildlands Networks

For at least the past decade, the concept of connectivity has been an urgent priority in the conservation community. Understanding the staggering toll that urban and agricultural development and other destructive practices have taken on river systems and landscapes, habitat connectivity should become a defining priority of the 21st century. Ideally, a national goal would be the establishment of a network of wildways throughout the continent—corridors that span through farmlands and managed forests and connect to cores of protected wildlands. In addition to benefiting wildlife, an integrated system of corridors would also help conserve resources such as soil, water, air, and plants. They can provide essential terrain for migratory songbirds as well as joggers, naturalists, and others. The Natural Resources Conservation Service has reported that throughout the country, however, corridors are in decline. Without enhancing and connecting existing corridors and habitat patches, wildlands will become increasingly fragmented. Animal and plant numbers will decline and gene pools will be further stressed.

The Vermont-based Wildlands Project identifies three primary elements of a wildlands network as being: core wilderness areas where natural processes direct the ebb and flow of life; compatible use lands that buffer core wild areas; and wildlife linkages that allow wide-ranging and migratory species to travel. (See their inspirational illustrated diagram at *www.wildlandsproject.org*.

Wildways on and through agricultural lands typically exist in riparian areas but can also be located in forested areas of farming regions as well. Wildlife corridors that provide linkages necessary to sustain large carnivores help to maintain ecologically viable food webs. Without large predators, such as cougars and bears that regulate populations of mid-sized mesopredators like raccoons, skunks, domestic cats, and so on, severe impacts can be dealt to nesting birds, reptiles, aquatic species, and others. According to Sara Scherr, a Senior Policy Analyst for Forest Trends in Washington, D.C., satellite images show that it's not just on marginal lands where connectivity is important. Even the most highly productive farm and forest lands must also provide essential ecosystem services.

Any successful corridor project that addresses connectivity across the landscape must begin with a concerned and engaged community. The Sky Islands region merits close study for how such landscape level efforts can be organized across diverse constituencies and even countries.

A number of excellent publications are available that address connectivity issues. The USDA NRCS has an on-line handbook titled: *Conservation Corridor Planning at the Landscape Level: Managing for Wildlife Habitat*, *www.ms.nrcs.usda.gov/whmi/corridors.htm*. The California Wilderness Coalition helped to coordinate and prepare a statewide document titled *Missing Linkages: Restoring Connectivity to the California Landscape*. The Sky Islands Wildlands Network reserve design is another potential resource.

Conservation Easements

Conservation easements are legal agreements commonly used to keep land in agriculture or open space by, among other things, limiting development and subdivision. The terms and restrictions of conservation easements range widely. Most are permanent, although some states allow for shorter-term arrangements. Conservation easements can help to provide extra income, reduce debt, decrease income and estate taxes, and ensure that land will be conserved for subsequent generations. Ongoing ways to measure biological goals can be included in an easement, as well as limits or outright bans on productive activities such as logging and excessive pesticide use.

Ideally, conservation easements are property and project specific rather than boiler plate agreements. GIS mapping and on-the-ground research studies can be included in the costs of easements to allow property owners to establish science-based priorities for long-term planning. From the landscape perspective, conservation easements can help to preserve unique areas and/or livelihoods, and to maximize habitat connectivity within a region. Once established, a well-executed conservation easement can have a domino effect, inspiring or putting pressure on neighboring landowners to contribute to a community effort.

Steve Hackett is a Northern California farmer and rancher who negotiated an easement on his 4,000-acre property in the Lower Eel River watershed with the Pacific Forest Trust. Since the late 19th century, the land had regularly been cleared and burned for timber production and sheep grazing. Hackett, a restorationist, worked carefully to craft a long-term plan to protect the property financially and to achieve measurable biological goals. Riparian corridors were identified with stream buffers designed according to soil type and other specific on-the-ground assessments. Production areas were established to continue dry-farmed hay farming, selective grazing, and selective forestry, with the right to log reduced to 25 percent per decade to encourage widespread late-seral forest characteristics. Development rights to 30 parcels were purchased. According to Greg Hendrickson, a San Francisco attorney with Coblentz, Patch, Duffy, and Bass, who specializes in conservation easements, Hackett's donation of half the value of the easement helped to seal the deal, which included participation from the Coastal Conservancy and the California Wildlife Conservation Board. California's Forest Legacy provided an early impetus to get this project off the ground. A number of adjacent landowners are following suit, and a broader regional easement initiative, Six Rivers to the Seas, has been formed to create a matrix of wildlife and production corridors.

For information on conservation easements or in locating the land trust nearest you, contact the Land Trust Alliance at *www.lta.org* or 202-638-4725.

Bringing Stewardship to the Table

As a modern saying goes, conservation starts at the breakfast table. In terms of farming with the wild, a day could start with certified shade-grown coffee and milk from a local grass-fed or organic producer, supporting songbird habitat throughout the Americas. (Not to mention grains, eggs, and fruits—each with their own local history.) Chef Alice Waters has written that our food purchases are serious choices that can create a different future for ourselves, our families, and the natural world. Developing a regional cuisine is probably the single most important step each and every one of us can take in attempting to shape on-the-ground change on the landscape. The power resides not only in individual households and restaurant kitchens but also at work and at conferences and events. Familiarity with local producers allows a direct connection with a product's history. Certification labels, such as organic, Salmon-Safe, and others provide market-based mechanisms for change. Chefs also wield enormous power, many of whom support not just local and organic foods, but also wild-caught and foraged ingredients. Gardening is one of our great pastimes. Using spare time to grow food and habitat is yet another way to cultivate a stewardship of the table.

Signage and Bilingual Education

It is important to keep workers and neighbors involved and informed of ongoing restoration goals. This can include road and field signage in English and Spanish, and careful instructions about places where mowing, discing, and other operations should be avoided or delayed. In the future, look for outreach programs specifically tailored toward involving farmworker communities in these efforts.

Monitoring

Monitoring ongoing conservation efforts on a farm or within a farm region can take a variety of forms. They can be done with or without assistance. One excellent resource for on-farm habitat monitoring is a handbook published by the Yolo County Resource Conservation District, titled *Monitoring on Your Farm: A Guide to Tracking and Understanding the Resources and Wildlife on Your Land* (530-662-2037; *www.yolorcd.gov*).

Certification groups, such as Salmon-Safe, Predator Friendly, and others provide formal monitoring arrangements with market-based goals. Other outside monitoring projects might include working with an extension office to evaluate the effectiveness of hedgerows in attracting certain agriculturally desirable and undesirable species, participating in annual bird and butterfly surveys, joining watershed and corridor connectivity initiatives.

The Vermont-based organization Keeping Track, Inc. provides instruction for citizen scientists to monitor wildlife movement across the landscape. By conducting workshops on how to read such signs as claw marks on trees, tufts of hair caught on a fence, and tracks in the snow, Keeping Track helps concerned citizens monitor the comings and goings of wildlife in communities. This in turn can assist in the crafting of strategies to preserve habitat, particularly for wide-ranging species like fisher, moose, black bear, and others that need connectivity to untrammeled areas. (*www.keepingtrack.org*; 802-434-7000)

This simple fabric fence and bucket trap helps monitor the presence of reptiles and amphibians on a Florida restoration site.

Landscape-Level Thinking: Reed Noss's Six Lessons of Thinking in Context

1. The integrity of any piece of land or water is ultimately dependent upon the integrity of the surrounding landscape.

2. Many species require areas well outside protected area boundaries. Whenever possible, work with regional planners to assure that key pieces of habitat are functionally connected, through habitat corridors or low-intensity intervening land use.

3. Ecological history is highly informative. Which habitats and species have prospered and which have declined as the extent and intensity of human activity increased?

4. Bigger scales are ultimately more meaningful for conservation of global biodiversity. Recognize that management may increase the number of species on one spatial scale while decreasing it on others.

5. Do not treat all species as equal. Focus attention on those most vulnerable to extinction as a result of human actions, those that have declined most, and those that are ecologically significant (including exotics and other opportunistic species that threaten native biodiversity).

6. Limit human activities around and within reserves and other natural areas. Surround sensitive areas of any size with transitional or buffer zones where the intensity of human uses increases with greater distance from the sensitive area.

Excerpted from leading conservation biologist Reed Noss's essay, "Context Matters: Considerations for Large-scale Conservation," published in *Conservation in Practice*, Summer 2002.

BIRD-FRIENDLY FARMING

Easy to see and hear, with long-term benchline studies available about their history in most areas, birds are essential indicators of ecosystem health. Understanding their cycles and habitat requirements for nesting is an important step in making a deeper relationship with the wild. The best way to begin helping birds is by leaving and enhancing the native vegetation in and around the farm or orchard. These include snags and dead limbs that may attract woodpeckers, bluebirds, and other cavity nesting species. Establishing a yearly regimen of observation and monitoring can help to nurture a deeper relationship with resident and migratory bird species on your farm. The following checklists can be used to develop a program of bird-friendly farming appropriate to your area.

Farmland Bird Protection Checklist

● Get to know the birds in and around your land;

● Make a list of local species; keep records;

● Survey your land at least once per year;

● Survey insects as well as birds;

● Involve citizen monitoring groups to help you better understand wildlife patterns;

● Emphasize native habitat;

● Provide roosting perches and nest boxes;

● Plant hedgerows of native plants along fields or orchards, irrigation ditches, and levees;

● Connect hedgerows to existing on-farm habitat since linked habitat patches are the most valuable to birds;

● Leave winter crop stubble and brush piles through the winter to provide ground cover;

● Plant cover crops to provide food and cover for native birds and to discourage foraging by Brown-headed cowbirds that prey on songbird nests;

● Maintain forested edges and hedges, with at least 20-foot riparian buffers;

● Diversify crops, use smaller fields, and minimize or eliminate pesticide and herbicide use;

● Time mowing, spraying, and other disturbance-related events to avoid critical breeding periods;

● Graze wisely;

● Get out of the truck and off the 4-wheeler whenever possible to increase observation time out in the fields; and,

● Help reduce feral cat populations, the cause of an estimated 4 million birds killed per day.

Food Plots

Food plots can be sown specifically to provide essential food supplies for wildlife. Grains, legumes, and other crops can provide winter food supplies as well as perform functions such as wind and snow protection and water and sediment filtration. Barley for Birds, sponsored by the Washington State Fish and Wildlife Department and Ducks Unlimited, provides cost-share funds for farmers who plant winter cereal grain crops such as barley, rye, oats, and wheat, which attract dabbling ducks, snow geese, swans, and other migratory species.

Snags

Snags or dead trees support birds and mammals with breeding and nesting habitats. At least three snags per acre is recommended in certain areas for proper woodland management. Leave snags, rock dens, wetlands, native vegetation, and woody debris for animal food and cover.

Cowbird Predation

Brown-headed cowbirds thrive in disturbed field margins and parasitize interior forest bird species by laying eggs in their nests. Planting groundcover crops in orchards and vineyards can minimize cowbird habitat. Reducing or eliminating grazing in riparian understory areas also discourages cowbird populations.

Important resources for national bird survey programs:

BREEDING BIRD SURVEYS
mbr.nbs.gov/bbs

PARTNERS IN FLIGHT
pwrc.nbs.gov/pif

CORNELL ORNITHOLOGY LAB
birds.cornell.edu/citsci

POINT REYES BIRD OBSERVATORY
prbo.org

AMERICAN BIRD CONSERVANCY
abcbirds.org

METHOW CONSERVANCY
methowconservancy.org

AUDUBON SOCIETY
audubon.org

Winter flooding of West Coast fields has become essential habitat for birds traveling on the Pacific Flyway. The photo far left is from the M&T Staten Island Ranch, a 10,000-acre working farm now managed by the Nature Conservancy of California.

Top left, snags and other debris provide valuable habitat for a variety of species.

Bottom row, far left, apple farmer Tim Bates no longer burns prunings but forms them into habitat rows.

Bottom center, steel tubular, bear-proof, solar-powered, bird feed disperser.

Photo directly below shows a watering station on the Turner Enterprise's Armendaris Ranch.

Three photos top-to-bottom in the row directly at right show three different custom-built bird shelters made by wildlife biologist Art Hawkins, who was a student of Aldo Leopold's.

Above, one of many barn owl houses at the Fetzer Bonterra vineyard south of Ukiah.

Bluebird houses, at right, have been designed for successful occupancy and ease of maintenance.

LANDOWNER INCENTIVE PROGRAMS

Incentives to participate in conservation programs range from financial support to technical assistance and help in cutting red tape. The following section profiles a number of programs across the country that with any luck, might inspire similar initiatives to facilitate wildlands connectivity in agricultural regions. For a policy-oriented overview of incentive programs, get a copy of *Wild Harvest*, a publication of the California Wilderness Society *(www.calwild.org.)*

Safe Harbor

A "Safe Harbor" agreement is an arrangement that attempts to protect a landowner in the event that restoration or conservation efforts might one day attract the presence of endangered species and subsequently, legal challenges. Across the country, regional chapters of Environmental Defense (EDF) have been working to establish "Safe Harbor" agreements to encourage landowners to restore ecosystems and natural processes that can increase habitat for endangered or threatened species. EDF essentially acts as an intermediary between landowners and the U.S. Fish and Wildlife Service. In Texas, for example, EDF identifies landowners whose property has habitat suitable for endangered species. Landowners are contacted and if agreeable, EDF arranges for a site visit with a field biologist. EDF can then help to restore habitat, secure financial incentives for the landowner, and maintain and monitor habitat throughout the contract period. In return, landowners retain the right to alter or develop the restored habitat at a later date, even if an endangered species has taken up residence there in the meantime. Since the program was introduced, more

than 2 million acres have been enrolled. Species benefiting include the red-cockaded woodpecker, northern aplomado falcon, gila topminnow, desert pupfish, Attwater's prairie-chicken, black-capped vireo, golden-cheeked warbler, San Joaquin kit fox, and the northern Idaho ground squirrel. Between 1994 and 2002 nearly 20,000 acres have been protected in East Texas for the golden-cheeked warbler and in West Texas for the red-capped vireo. The Nature Conservancy and the Peregrine Fund also work with the U.S. Fish and Wildlife Service on Safe Harbor agreements. Some conservationists have argued that Safe Harbor agreements and other habitat conservation plans can be used to circumvent rather than uphold important endangered species protection. Each should be scrutinized for design and enforcement, though it should be noted that as of this writing, these agreements remain uncontested in the courts. According to author and Yale University professor David Wilcove, Safe Harbor agreements are merely a temporary measure. Once habitats are restored, however, other events may be triggered, such as the reestablishment of species, the sale of the property to a conservation organization, or the donation of an easement. If nothing else, suggests Wilcove, they might help buy time for endangered species.[2]
www.environmentaldefense.org

Sustainable Conservation's Partners in Restoration Project

With the overarching goal of developing a critical mass of participation in improving water quality, enhancing wildlife habitat, and preserving agricultural resources, the San Francisco-based non-profit Sustainable Conservation established the Partners in Restoration Permit Coordination Project. The PIR Project is a regulatory streamlining process intended to create one-stop permit access for farmers and ranchers interested in implementing voluntary conservation projects to control erosion and sedimentation and enhance the natural resource values on their lands. The process starts with meetings that bring together all pertinent stakeholders in a given watershed, including the Natural Resource Conservation Service and Resource Conservation District. Regulatory road blocks and best management practices are identified with the end-goal being the establishment of watershed-based permits. In an attempt to avoid or mitigate future negative impacts on water quality, sensitive species, and important habitat, special conditions on the timing, location, and methods of installation are included in the farm's or ranch's plan. By making it easier for landowners to participate, PIR hopes to boost participation in watershed restoration efforts.

Sustainable Conservation's pilot project started in October of 1998 in the Elkhorn Slough Watershed in Monterey County, California, and has already succeeded in significantly reducing the amount of sediment delivered to Elkhorn Slough and in restoring large stretches of riparian areas in the watershed. Because of the interest expressed by regulatory agencies and community groups throughout the state, Sustainable Conservation and other partners are working to identify appropriate watersheds for a widespread expansion of the program. PIR is currently testing and replicating this regulatory coordination and permit streamlining program in the Morro Bay, Salinas River, Navarro River, and Coastal Marin watersheds.
www.suscon.org

California's Williamson Act

The Williamson Act, known officially as the California Land and Conservation Act, provides tax incentives to maintain land in agricultural status. Under this legislation, counties can designate agricultural preserves, within which farmland is assessed according to its agricultural value rather than its potential development value. In order to receive this tax relief, landowners agree to a ten-year contract that restricts land use to agriculture, wildlife habitat, scenic corridors, recreational use, or open space.
www.ceres.ca.gov/biodiversity/wwg.ht

Bailey Wildlife Foundation Wolf Compensation Trust

In cooperation with Defenders of Wildlife, the privately funded Bailey Wildlife

Foundation Wolf Compensation Fund was established to help livestock owners recoup losses due to predation from gray wolves, which were recently reintroduced in Yellowstone National Park and the northern Rockies. Compensation is intended to ease conflicts between ranchers that depend on the land for their livelihood and predators that play a key role in the western ecosystem.
www.defenders.org/wolfcomp.html

Florida Farm Stewardship Program

Developed in Florida to help protect the state's remnant population of Florida panthers and other imperiled species, the Farmland Stewardship Agreement is a privately funded program that compensates a landowner for managing critical wild habitats. This model includes the development of comprehensive management plans, monitoring protocols, and evaluation methods, and short- or long-term contracts. Hall's Tiger Bay Ranch was the first Florida farm to receive a contract, which provides native habitat for endangered species like the Florida panther and the red-cockaded woodpecker over a 4,500-acre natural area and 1,000 acres of improved pasture.
www.fl-stewardship.com

The Peregrine Fund

Restoration initiatives focused around urgently endangered species can be an important component of conservation efforts. For decades, the Boise, Idaho-based Peregrine Fund has developed integrated programs to conserve and restore habitat for raptor populations throughout the world.
www.peregrinefund.org

High Plains Partnership

This ten-state consortium brings together stakeholders around issues in the short-grass and mixed-grass prairies on the High Plains. The consortium works in partnership with private landowners and state and federal agencies with support from the Western Governors Association and the National Fish and Wildlife Foundation.
www.westgov.org/wga/initiatives/hppbroch.htm

Watershed Agricultural Program

Recognizing the value of clean sources of drinking water, New York City created the Watershed Agricultural Program to work with rural communities within its vast watershed. The WAP promotes voluntary participation in programs to stem streamside erosion and prevent runoff contamination from farming operations. Collaborating teams include employees from Cornell Cooperative Extension, Soil and Water Conservation District, and NRCS with other agency funding to offer cost-share on fencing, streamside plantings, and long-term rental payments. The Watershed Agricultural Program has established Whole Farm Planning Teams, a Nutrient Management Team primarily for dairy and livestock producers, as well as small farms outreach to promote best management principles and help farmers and landowners meet economic goals while adhering to high stewardship goals for the watershed.
www.nycwatershed.org

National Public Lands Grazing Campaign (NPLGC)

Grazing permits on public lands primarily in the arid West account for non-native animal impacts on nearly 300 million acres. Yet on that vast land base, less than 3 percent of the beef in the United States is produced, and it is subsidized by the federal government at costs far higher than market rates. The NPLGC advocates legislation to pay grazing permittees and lessees a set fee per Animal Unit Month to voluntarily retire their permit or lease to permanently end grazing on their associated allotment. This legislation, to be introduced in 2003 or thereafter, seeks to actively provide options for grazing permits or leases, in an effort to relieve public lands from continued livestock grazing. While a few voluntary grazing permit buyouts have been conducted with third-party funds, they are as yet just temporary easements. The NPLGC intends to launch the voluntary buyout program initially in Arizona, where preliminary research shows favorable support among the ranching community.
www.publiclandsranching.org

Skagit County Farm Legacy Program

For more than a century, Skagit County, two hours north of Seattle, has been a locus of agricultural production. It encompasses more than 100,000 acres of the most fertile farmland on the planet. Sprawl and urbanization have increasingly impacted this rural area over the past two decades, however, and efforts have been established to preserve farmland for the sake of agriculture, as well as a buffer for Nature. In 1996, Skagit County passed a Conservation Futures Ordinance, a small tax ($6.50 per $1,000 of assessed evaluation) to fund conservation easements. The Skagit County Farmland Legacy Program then uses those assessments to purchase perpetual development rights from willing farm owners, thereby limiting development and keeping the land in agriculture or conservation for future generations.
www.skagitonians.org

The Conservation Labels Project

The Land Conservancy of British Columbia works cooperatively with agricultural producers who voluntarily protect, restore, or enhance habitat on their properties. In recognition for these important efforts, producers can use an attractive Conservation Partners label to distinguish their products in the local market. The Land Conservancy supports the label project with an active education campaign. The goal is to increase public awareness about the importance of choosing products that support both ecological health and the local economy. In 2002, its start-up year, 18 growers entered the program with dozens of regional stores participating. According to the program director, Nichola Walden, enthusiasm is now spreading to adjoining properties in this region of predominantly organic growers with farms between 10 and 500 acres. The next step involves taking the campaign to the capital of the province.
www.conservancy.bc.ca

USDA CONSERVATION PROGRAMS

The Farm Security and Rural Investment Act of 2002 (Farm Bill) presents an important opportunity for funding and technical assistance for conservation programs throughout the country. Building on programs dating back to the mid-1980s, Farm Bill cost-share programs can help to prevent soil erosion, protect wetlands and wildlife habitat, and restore habitats within farmlands. The real challenge for agencies, landowners, and communities will be to identify programs that truly help to enhance regional wildlands initiatives throughout the country and to ensure that they receive assistance. Some of the major programs are outlined here. For more information on Farm Bill programs, contact your local USDA NRCS office or *www.nrcs.usda.gov/programs/farmbill/2002/.*

Conservation Reserve Program (CRP)

CRP provides annual rental payments and cost-share assistance to establish long-term, resource-conserving vegetative covers on eligible farmland. Practices also include converting cropland to native grasses and forbs, wetland restoration, shallow water development, and riparian buffers. Rental payments are based on the agricultural rental value of the land. Cost-share is provided for up to 50 percent of the participant's cost in establishing approved conservation practices. Rental agreement contracts are for 10 to 15 years.

Conservation Security Program (CSP)

This program was established by the 2002 Farm Bill and program details were under development at time of press. CSP's goal is to assist agricultural and forest landowners in implementing conservation practices applicable to their operations. CSP establishes three levels (tiers) of participation with corresponding increases in payments, based upon national land rental rates. This program is particularly important in supporting organic and diversified farm operations.

Environmental Quality Incentive Program (EQIP)

EQIP provides up to 75 percent of the costs of implementing conservation systems, which provide environmental protection and enhancement. Locally approved practices may include grassed waterways, filter strips, manure storage facilities, pesticide containment facilities, and capping abandoned wells. Producers may also receive incentive payments for applying best land management practices associated with nutrients, manure, irrigation water, wildlife, and integrated pest management.

Grassland Reserve Program (GRP)

GRP is a new program to protect and restore grassland, rangeland, and prairie. There are a variety of options available to landowners such as 30-year and permanent conservation easements as well as 10-year, 15-year, 20-year, and 30-year contracts coupled with restoration cost-share assistance. Specific details of the program were yet to be developed at time of press.

Wetlands Reserve Program (WRP)

WRP provides financial assistance to restore degraded wetlands. Landowners are offered three options: (1) permanent easements pay up to the agricultural value of the land and all the costs of restoring wetlands and uplands, (2) 30-year easements pay 75 percent of what would be paid for permanent easements and 75 percent of the restoration costs, and (3) restoration cost-share agreements pay 75 percent of the cost of restoring a wetland in exchange for a minimum 10-year agreement to maintain the restoration. No land use payment is provided.

Wildlife Habitat Incentive Program (WHIP)

WHIP encourages creation of high-quality wildlife habitats that support wildlife populations of National, State, Tribal and local significance. NRCS provides technical and financial assistance to landowners and others to develop upland, wetland, riparian, and aquatic habitat areas on their property. Participants voluntarily limit future use of the land for a period of time, but retain private ownership. NRCS works with the participant to develop a wildlife habitat development plan that becomes the basis of the cost-share agreement. Cost-share payments under these agreements are usually 5 to 10 years in duration, depending upon the practices to be installed. Greater cost-share assistance is provided to landowners who enter into agreements of 15 years or more for practices on essential plant and animal habitat.

WILD FARM ALLIANCE PLATFORM

Agriculture and the Biodiversity Crisis: Reconnecting our Food Systems and Ecosystems

The Wild Farm Alliance (WFA) was established by a national coalition of wildlands proponents and ecological farming advocates who share a concern for the land and its wild and human inhabitants. Our mission is to promote a healthy, viable agriculture that helps protect and restore wild Nature. To make our food systems sustainable in the 21st century, we envision a world in which community-based, ecologically managed farms and ranches are seamlessly integrated into landscapes that accommodate the full range of native species and ecological processes.

Wild Farm Alliance
406 Main Street, Suite 213
Watsonville, CA 95076
831-761-8408
831-761-8103 fax
wildfarms@earthlink.net
www.wildfarmalliance.org

Recognizing that:
- the current rate of species extinction signifies an unprecedented biodiversity crisis.
- industrial agriculture is a primary cause of species losses and a devastating threat to sustainable family-scale farms and ranches.
- protected and interconnected wildlands are essential to assuring biological diversity and sustaining healthy rural landscapes.

We believe:
- agriculture must be conducted in ways that are compatible with the preservation of native plants and animals.
- sustainable family farms and ranches nourish healthy human communities and help safeguard natural communities.
- the current biodiversity crisis calls for a new conservation ethic that promotes ecological recovery within agricultural lands and across the entire landscape.

We acknowledge:
- healthy ecosystems provide us with many life-giving services, including pollination, insect pest control, nutrient cycling, clean water, and erosion control.
- the need of farmers to succeed economically while farming ecologically.
- the right of farmers and indigenous peoples to maintain control over food production.
- the right of consumers to know how and where their food is grown and the responsibility of consumers to support ecologically sound agriculture.

We support:
- farming practices that accommodate wild habitat and native species, including large carnivores and wild fish.
- agricultural practices that strive to eliminate the use of environmentally toxic chemicals, and contamination of soil and water.
- locally adapted crops and animals that are not genetically engineered.
- local and regional food and fiber systems that boost rural economies.
- existing community-based efforts to establish a continental wildlands network in which large protected areas are connected by wildlife movement corridors and are complemented by ecologically managed farms and forests.

SUPPORTING ORGANIZATIONS

Resource directories, by their very nature, are ever-changing. Almost as soon as the ink dries on contact numbers, some detail or other seems to change. Still, we wanted to leave readers with a directory of some of the best organizations working on conservation-based approaches to agriculture. With assistance from the Wild Farm Alliance, we assembled a national list of organizations, agencies, companies, educational institutes, certifier and producer organizations, and others to help get you started. Many of these organizations will have their own directories of groups specific to their particular region and areas of expertise on their Web sites. Be sure to keep a listing of valuable resource groups and in the future, look toward the Watershed Media (www.watershedmedia.org) and Wild Farm Alliance (wildfarmalliance.org) Web sites for updated lists.

Conservation, Sustainable Agriculture, and Advocacy Organizations

Aldo Leopold Foundation
Programs include the restoration and protection of over 15,000 acres through partnerships with more than 30 organizations.
608-355-0279
Baraboo, WI
www.aldoleopold.org

The Adirondack Council
Dedicated to sustaining the natural and human communities of New York state's 6-million acre Adirondack Park by fostering protection of public wildland and good stewardship of private farms and ranches.
518-873-2240
Elizabethtown, NY
www.adirondackcouncil.org

American Bird Conservancy
Dedicated to the conservation of wild birds and their habitats in the Americas.
540-253-5780 or 888-247-3624
The Plains, VA
www.abcbirds.org

Animas Foundation/Gray Ranch
Supports biological diversity on ranchlands, researches the impacts of ranching methods, and monitors endangered species.
505-548-2622
Animas, NM
www.wnmu.edu/stewardship/organizationsac.htm

Applegate River Watershed Council
Works to develop economically viable farming and ranching practices that are compatible with the Applegate River watershed.
541-899-9982
Jacksonville, OR
www.arwc.org

Audubon California
Agricultural Habitat Program works to restore wildlife habitat on farms and ranches while preserving or enhancing economic conditions for agriculture.
530-795-2921
Winters, CA
www.audubon-ca.org

Arizona-Sonora Desert Museum
Bi-national research group whose projects include a migratory pollinator corridors campaign.
520-883-1380
Tucson, AZ
http://desertmuseum.org/conservation/mp/index.html

Bat Conservation International
Promotes bat conservation projects and research, and assists with bat restoration initiatives worldwide.
512-327-9721
Austin, TX
www.batcon.org

Biodiversity Legal Foundation
A nonprofit, science-based organization dedicated to the preservation of all native plants, animals, and naturally functioning ecosystems.
303-926-7606
Louisville, CO

Biodiversity Partnership/ Defenders of Wildlife
West Coast office of Defenders of Wildlife. Produced a directory of state government conservation incentives for farmers nationwide called "Conservation in America."
503-697-3222
West Linn, OR
www.biodiversitypartners.org

California Native Grass Association
Promotes native grasses and associated species for restoration and maintenance of California's grassland ecosystem as well as for use in urban and agricultural areas.
530-759-8458 or 866-456-CNGA
Davis, CA
www.cnga.org

California Native Plant Society
Provides support for the restoration and preservation of native flora and fauna of California.
916-447-2677
Sacramento, CA
www.cnps.org

California Wilderness Coalition
Published *Wild Harvest: Farming for Wildlife and Profitability*, a directory of conservation incentives available to farmers by both private and public funders within the state of California.
530-758-0380
Davis, CA
www.calwild.org

California Wildlife Defenders
Working to eradicate the prejudice toward predator animals, especially coyotes. Published a brochure "How to Coexist with Urban Wildlife."
323-663-1856
Los Angeles, CA
www.scced.org

Center for Biological Diversity
Pressures federal agencies to fulfill their obligation to protect native wildlife, watersheds, and ecosystems on public lands in the Southwest.
520-623-5252
Tucson, AZ
www.biologicaldiversity.org

Center for Food Safety
Provides leadership in legal, scientific, and grassroots efforts to address the increasing concerns about the impacts of our food production system.
202-547-9359
Washington, DC
www.centerforfoodsafety.org

Center for Rural Affairs

Works on agricultural policy that both strengthens opportunity for family farmers and ranchers and promotes sound stewardship of our natural resources.
402-846-5428
Walthill, NE
www.cfra.org

Chase Lake Prairie Project

Multi-county prairie pothole regional program with active easement acquisition, grassland restoration, and waterfowl production areas.
701-752-4218
Woodworth, ND

Chesapeake Conservation Seeds

Installs artificial wildlife nesting structures for various birds. Farm-scale wildlife habitat planning and management of woodland and agricultural systems to benefit upland birds and other wildlife.
410-822-5100
Easton, MD
www.cheswildlife.org

Community Alliance with Family Farmers

Dedicated to a movement that fosters socially, economically, and environmentally sustainable, family-scale agriculture. Provides technical assistance in installing native plant hedgerows and grassed waterways on farmlands.
530-756-8518
Davis, CA
www.caff.org

Cosumnes River Preserve

A nonprofit/public/agency partnership on one of California's only nondammed rivers, within an area of intensive agriculture and urban development.
916-684-2816
Galt, CA
www.cosumnes.org

Defenders of Wildlife

Leading organization in Farm Bill conservation research. Wolf Guardian Program organizes volunteers to keep wolves away from livestock and reimburses livestock producers for the occasional cases of predation.
202-682-9400
Washington, DC
www.defenders.org

Ducks Unlimited

Works to fulfill the annual life cycle needs of North American waterfowl by protecting, enhancing, restoring, and managing important wetlands and associated lands.
800-45DUCKS or 901-758-3825
Memphis, TN
www.ducks.org

Environmental Defense

Advocacy and research group of scientists, economists, engineers, and attorneys who seek practical solutions to a broad range of environmental and health problems.
212-505-2100
New York, NY
www.environmentaldefense.org

Florida Stewardship Foundation

Advances initiatives that will engender a thriving rural economy with an economically robust agriculture, a healthy natural environment, viable rural communities, and safe, abundant supplies of food and fiber. Farmland Stewardship Agreements provide habitat for endangered species.
Boca Raton, FL
www.fl-stewardship.com

Grassland Heritage Foundation

Conducts education regarding prairie ecology and restoration.
913-262-3506
Shawnee Mission, KS
www.grasslandheritage.org

Institute for Agriculture and Trade Policy

Promotes resilient family farms, rural communities, and ecosystems around the world through research, education, science, technology, and advocacy.
612-870-0453
Minneapolis, MN
www.iatp.org

International Wolf Center

Educates public about wolf issues; encourages research and distributes information on wolf-friendly ranching techniques.
218-365-4695
Ely, MN
www.wolf.org

Iowa Natural Heritage Foundation

INHF owns a handful of farms around the state that contain natural features–such as native, restored or reconstructed prairies; wetlands; woodlands; or oak savannahs.
515-288-1846
Des Moines, IA
www.inhf.org

The Kerr Center for Sustainable Agriculture

Offers progressive leadership and educational programs to all those interested in making farming and ranching environmentally friendly, socially equitable, and economically viable over the long term.
918-647-9123
Poteau, OK
www.kerrcenter.com

Land Stewardship Project

A private, nonprofit organization, fostering an ethic of stewardship for farmland, promoting sustainable agriculture, and developing sustainable communities.
507-523-3366
Lewiston, MN
www.landstewardshipproject.org

The Mountain Lion Foundation

"Living with Lions" program assists California 4-H farmers in protecting domestic animals from mountain lion predation.
916-442-2666 x102
Sacramento, CA
www.mountainlion.org

Malpai Borderlands Group

Encourages sustainable yet profitable ranching techniques, such as "grassbanking" and the establishment of conservation easements for habitat restoration.
Douglas, AZ
www.malpaiborderlandsgroup.org

National Public Lands Grazing Campaign

Promotes a voluntary buyout program for ranchers interested in retiring public lands livestock grazing leases.
www.publiclandsranching.org

Native Seed SEARCH

Seeks to preserve the crop seeds that connect Native American cultures to their lands.
520-622-5561
Tucson, AZ
www.nativeseeds.org

North American Pollinator Protection Campaign

Works to encourage the health of resident and migratory pollinating animals in North America.
415-362-1137
San Francisco, CA
www.nappc.org

Northern Prairie Wildlife Research Center

A USGS research center dedicated to the sound management and conservation of biological resources.
701-253-5500
Jamestown, ND
www.npwrc.usgs.gov

Partners in Flight

Works to protect North American landbirds by reversing species declines, stabilizing populations, and "keeping common birds common." Excellent resources.
www.pwrc.nbs.gov/pif
www.birds.cornell.edu/citsci

Pennsylvania Wildlands Recovery Project

New group working to establish wildlands connectivity throughout Pennsylvania.
www.wildpennsylvania.org

Peregrine Fund

Rehabilitates birds of prey populations around the world.
208-362-3716
Boise, ID
www.peregrinefund.org

Pheasants Forever

Protects and enhances pheasant and other wildlife populations through habitat improvement, land management, and education.
887-773-2070 or 651-773-2000
St. Paul, MN
www.pheasantsforever.org

Point Reyes Bird Observatory

Research institution focused on the conservation of bird habitat and populations.
415-868-0371
Stinson Beach, CA
www.prbo.org

Sky Island Alliance

Conducts scientific research and works toward the formation of national and international reserves to be integrated into a North American wildlands network.
520-624-7080
Tucson, AZ
www.skyislandalliance.org

Society for Conservation Biology

Actively engaged in ecologically-sensitive repair and management of ecosystems through a broad array of experience, knowledge sets, and cultural perspectives
520-622-5485
Seattle, WA
www.ser.org

Sonoran Institute

Conservation group working to promote strategies that preserve ecological integrity of protected lands and at the same time meet the economic aspirations of adjoining landowners and communities in the western U.S.
520-290-0828
Tucson, AZ
www.sonoran.org

Waterkeeper Alliance

Nationwide watershed alliance that has also initiated lawsuits targeting waste disposal at large confinement hog facilities.
914-674-0622
Tarrytown, NY
www.waterkeeper.org

White Earth Land Recovery Project

Dedicated to the social dignity, political transformation, economic self-sufficiency, environmental sustainability, and cultural integrity of the Anishinaabeg people.
218-573-3448
Ponsford, MN
www.nativeharvest.com

Wild Farm Alliance

A leading source of information and resources on wild farm practices. Promotes and supports efforts to make agriculture compatible with wild Nature.
831-761-8408
Watsonville, CA
www.wildfarmalliance.org

The Wildlands Project

Aims to protect and restore the natural heritage of North America, through the establishment of a connected system of wildlands. Publishes "Wild Earth."
802-434-4077 or 520-884-0875
Richmond, VT
www.twp.org

Xerces Society

Focuses on the conservation of insects and other invertebrates, especially butterflies.
503-232-6639
Portland, OR
www.xerces.org

Wildlife Damage Review

Brings public attention to the USDA's Animal Damage Control (Wildlife Services) program which kills wildlife for private interests such as agriculture and ranching.
Tucson, AZ
www.Azstarnet.com/~WDR

Wild Futures

Excellent research on large carnivore conservation.
206-780-9718
Bainbridge Island, WA

Y-2-Y Conservation Initiative

Linking wildways between Yellowstone and the Yukon.
406-327-8512
Missoula, MT
www.rockies.ca/y2y

Land Trusts, Agencies, Cost-share Programs, and Other Supporting Organizations

American Farmland Trust

Works to stop the loss of productive farmland and to promote farming practices that lead to a healthy environment.
202-331-7300
Washington, DC
www.farmland.org

Bluegrass Conservancy

A nonprofit regional land trust focused on the conservation and preservation of the Inner Bluegrass region.
859-255-4552
Lexington, KY
www.bluegrassconservancy.org

The Land Trust Alliance

Provides direct grants to land trusts, and offers training programs and conferences. A leader in the conservation easement movement.
202-638-4725
Washington, DC
www.lta.org

Methow Conservancy

Provides conservation easements to help families keep their farms and ranches. Provides landowners with alternatives to subdivision. Helps the community to preserve open space.
509-996-2870
Winthrop, WA
www.methowconservancy.org

National Fish and Wildlife Foundation

A federally funded foundation that works to support healthy populations of fish, wildlife, and plants, on land and sea, through creative partnerships.
202-857-0166
Washington, DC
www.nfwf.org

Natural Resource Conservation Service

Administers Farm Bill 2002, funded conservation programs such as EQIP, WHIP, WRP, CRP and Grassland Reserve Program.
202-720-7246
Washington, DC
www.nrcs.usda.gov

New York Watershed Agricultural Council

Works with farms and forests within New York City water supply watersheds to ensure a thriving rural economy and long-term water quality protection.
607-865-7790
Walton, NY
www.nycwatershed.org

Skagitonians to Preserve Farmland

Conducts efforts to encourage ecologically sound agricultural practices in one of the world's most productive farming regions.
360-336-3974
Mount Vernon, WA
www.skagitonians.org

Sustainable Conservation

Provides project management and documents streamlining processes to facilitate watershed restoration projects between private landowners and local NRCS and RCD agencies in California.
415-977-0380
San Francisco, CA
www.suscon.org

Western Prairie Habitat Restoration Area

Working to protect and restore up to 20,000 acres of grasslands in Western Wisconsin, from Osceola to River Falls through the tallgrass prairie.
715-386-9644
Hudson, WI
www.prairie.pressenter.com

Educational Centers, Monitoring Organizations

Alternative Farming Information Center

One of several topic-oriented Information Centers at the USDA's National Agricultural Library (NAL) specializing in accessing information about alternative cropping systems including sustainable and organic agriculture.
301-504-6559 or 301-504-6856
Beltsville, MD
www.nal.usda.gov/afsic

Appropriate Technology Transfer for Rural Areas

ATTRA, run by the National Center for Appropriate Technology, provides technical assistance to farmers, extension agents, market gardeners, agricultural researchers, and other agricultural professionals in all 50 states.
800-346-9140
Fayetteville, AR
www.attra.org

Center for Agroecology and Sustainable Food Systems

Operates a 25-acre organic farm/research, education, and training facility.
831-459-4140
Santa Cruz, CA
www.zzyx.ucsc.edu/casfs

Center for Sustainable Environments at Northern Arizona University

Brings together scientists, educators, independent scholars, business leaders, government agencies, nonprofits, students, and community members to seek creative solutions to environmental problems through initiatives that safeguard natural and cultural values and resources.
928-523-0637
Flagstaff, AZ
www.environment.nau.edu

The Forest School

Teaches and promotes forest management practices that include the propagation of a variety of crops, such as herbs, medicinal plants, fruits, and mushrooms. Horse logging of high-value timber products as an alternative to high-till, low-return commodity agriculture.
270-862-4459
Constantine, KY

International Forum on Food and Agriculture

Addresses global concerns regarding the consequences of the rapid global conversion to industrial agriculture. Develops international cooperative strategies to counter this dangerous trend and articulates successful alternative models.
415-561-7650
San Francisco, CA
www.ifg.org/IFA/ifa.htm

Keeping Track

Trains and assists volunteers in establishing wildlife habitat monitoring programs in their areas. Trains youths and citizen scientists with the skills to track wildlife and assess habitats.
802-434-7000
Huntington, VT
www.keepingtrackinc.org

The Land Institute

Strives to develop an agricultural system with the ecological stability of the prairie and a perennial grain yield comparable to that from annual crops.
785-823-5376
Salina, KS
www.landinstitute.org

Leopold Center for Sustainable Agriculture

An organization whose mission is to identify and reduce the negative impacts of agriculture on natural resources and rural communities.
515-294-3711
Ames, IO
www.ag.iastate.edu/centers/leopold

Long Branch Environmental Education Center, Inc.

A small educational center dedicated to sharing positive strategies of local self-reliance, wildlife protection, and improved environmental quality.
828-683-3662
Leicester, NC
www.main.nc.us/LBEEC/

Occidental Arts & Ecology Center

Offers training programs in whole-systems ecology; permaculture; biodiversity and seed saving; social, economic and environmental justice; fine arts; natural building; and sustainable living skills.
707-874-1557
Occidental, CA
www.oaec.org

UC Sustainable Agriculture Research and Education Program (SAREP)

Leading scientific research and education program in agriculture and food systems that conserve natural resources and biodiversity.
530-752-7556
Davis, CA
www.sarep.ucdavis.edu

Wild Futures

Develops materials on nonlethal predator controls and other environmental education.
206-780-9718
Bainbridge Island, WA
snegri@igc.org

Wildlife Habitat Management Institute

Develops scientifically based technical materials to promote conservation stewardship of fish and wildlife.
601-607-3131
Madison MS
www.ms.nrcs.usda.gov/whmi

Certification and Producer Organizations

Conservation Beef
Provides premiums for ranchers who are willing to implement land stewardship plans that support wild ecosystems on their land through the Conservation Beef certification program.
877-749-7177
Helena, MT
www.conservationbeef.org

Demeter Association, Inc.
The Biodynamic or Close to Biodynamic labels incorporate guiding principles that include cosmic rhythm (i.e. timing of the sun and moon phases); food grown from healthy, living soil; specific biodynamic preparations for fertilizing; and consumer connection with farmers.
315-364-5617
Aurora, NY
www.demeter-usa.org

eatwild.com
Provides an overview of the human and animal health, environmental, and farm benefits of pasture-raised livestock.
www.eatwild.com

Ervin's Natural Beef
A ranching company that values wildlife conservation and ecological health. Does not use hormones/antibiotics, cows are grass-fed and free-range, and predators are not shot/trapped.
Safford, AZ
www.ervins.com

International Federation of Organic Agricultural Movements
The worldwide umbrella organization of the organic agriculture movement, with about 750 member organizations and institutions in about 100 countries all over the world.
(+49) 6853-919890
Theley, Germany
www.ifoam.org

The Food Alliance
The Food Alliance seal of approval represents food produced in environmentally and socially responsible ways, including the provision of wildlife habitat on farms.
503-493-1066
Portland, OR
www.thefoodalliance.org

Great Plains Buffalo Association
Dedicated to promoting the raising and feeding of buffalo on grass pastures while advocating principles of sound grassland management.
www.gpbuffalo.org

Intertribal Bison Association
A nonprofit organization of 51 member tribes in a 16-state region that practices buffalo herd management, land restoration, and marketing of meat products.
605-394-9730
Rapid City, SD
www.intertribalbison.org

The Land Conservancy of British Columbia
Works to protect ecologically sensitive wild areas within British Columbia. They also have an ecolabel program called Conservation Labels Program.
250-479-8053
Victoria, British Columbia
www.conservancy.bc.ca

National Wildlife Federation
Backyard Wildlife Habitat Program certifies school, home, and community gardens that meet the requirements for healthy wildlife habitat.
703-438-6000
Reston, VA
www.nwf.org

Organic Farming Research Foundation
Institute that funds organic and sustainable farming research, including a Bat Conservation International project to install 45 bat houses at 10 organic farms in central California.
831-426-6606
Santa Cruz, CA
www.ofrf.org

Predator Conservation Alliance
Works with land management agencies, tribal groups, and land owners to restore predator habitat through their Grassland Predator and Living with Predators programs.
406-587-3389
Bozeman, MT
www.predatorconservation.org

Predator Friendly, Inc.
Certifies "Predator Friendly" products produced by ranchers who use only nonlethal methods to protect their livestock from native predators.
406-222-7825
Livingston, MT

Quivira Coalition
Teaches ranchers, environmentalists, public land managers, and other members of the public that ecologically healthy rangeland and economically robust ranches can be compatible.
505-820-2544
Santa Fe, NM
www.quiviracoaliton.org

Rainforest Alliance
Better Banana and Eco-OK labels certify farmers who grow bananas, cocoa, coffee, juice oranges using environmentally sound pest and disease management practices, soil and water conservation, and fair labor practices.
212-677-1900
New York, NY
www.rainforestalliance.org

Smithsonian Migratory Bird Center
Bird Friendly ecolabel verifies that coffee has been grown using shade management practices. The program goal is to foster conditions on coffee plantations that provide sound bird habitats.
202-673-4908
Washington, DC
www.si.edu/smbc

Salmon-Safe, Inc.
Salmon-Safe is a non-profit organization working to restore the agricultural and urban watersheds of the Pacific Northwest.
503-232-3750
Portland, OR
www.salmonsafe.org

Sinapu
Dedicated to the recovery of native carnivores of the Southern Rocky Mountains and to the restoration of wild habitat in which all species flourish. Promotes Predator Friendly certification, as well as a coalition called AGRO, which works to end aerial gunning of wildlife.
303-447-8655
Boulder, CO
www.sinapu.org

Wild Idea Buffalo Company
Ecologically sensitive ranching company thta sells buffalo meat.
866-658-6137
Rapid City, SD
www.wildideabuffalo.com

Selected Farms, Ranches, Supporting Businesses and Organizations

Bioengineering Associates
Uses natural vegetative systems to restore watersheds, stabilize stream banks, control erosion and sediment, and repair damaged lands and river courses.
707-984-7334
Laytonville, CA
www.bioengineers.com

Central Coast Vineyard Team
Identifies and promotes the most environmentally safe, viticulturally and economically sustainable farming methods.
805-434-4848
Templeton, CA
www.vineyardteam.org

Circuit Rider Productions
A non-profit organization with a long track record and excellent reputation in ecological restoration work.
707-838-6641
Windsor, CA

Forest Agricultural Enterprises
Agroforestry and permaculture farm design for the Midwest. Specializes in "agricultural savannas" that mimic the savanna ecosystem and use harvestable woody species such as chestnuts and American hazelnut.
608-627-TREE or 608-627-1772
Viola, WI

Fungi Perfecti
Leading group in working with edible, medicinal, and other fungi as part of farming and restoring the landscape.
360-426-9292
Olympia, WA
www.fungiperfecti.com

Hedgerow Farms
Produces seeds of native grasses, sedges, and forbs. Also performs consulting on farmland habitat restoration, erosion control, and landscaping.
530-662-4570
Winters, CA
www.hedgerowfarms.com

Kenagy Family Farm
Producers of grains, beans, vegetables, as well as native plants for restoratoin projects in the Willamette Valley.
541-926-8038
Albany, OR

Kevin Erwin Consulting Ecologist
Wetland restoration specialists, wildlife monitoring and consultants and training.
239-337-1505
Ft. Meyers, FL
www.environment.com

Kirschenmann Farms
Producers of organic and biodynamically grown grains and grass-fed beef.
701-486-3578
Windsor, ND

Mayberry Centre Bat Homes
Manufacturer of various bat house structures.
903-645-2028
Daingerfield, TX
www.mayberrybat.com

Morris Grass-fed Beef
Morris Grass-fed Beef produces grass-pastured, chemical-free meats on the coast of central California. They are committed to developing an agricultural system carefully integrated to their locale.
831-623-2933
San Juan Bautista, CA
www.morrisgrassfed.com

Polyface Farm
Polyface Farm produces a variety of grass-pastured, chemical-free meats and poultry. They sell a number of books about successful grass-finished livestock production, including *Salad Bar Beef* and *Pastured Poultry Profits*.
540-885-3590
Swoope, VA

Rana Creek Habitat Restoration
Rana Creek is an active, sustainable agricultural center for environmental consultation and restoration, specializing in native plant and seed products.
831-659-3820
Carmel Valley, CA
www.ranacreek.com

Rincon-Vitova Insectaries, Inc.
Rincon-Vitova is an insectary that offers knowledge, organisms, and other resources to control pests biologically and naturally in safe ways for people and the environment.
800-248-2847
Ventura, CA
www.rinconvitova.com

Shoulder to Shoulder Farm
Producers of Wild Garden Seed heirloom lettuces, herbs, and vegetables selected and bred for organic growing conditions.
541-929-4068
Philomath, OR

Thirteen Mile Lamb & Wool Co.
Produces lamb, wool, and beef with the "Predator Friendly Wool" label. Do not use lethal predator control in their organically certified sheep and beef ranching operation.
406-388-4945
Belgrade, MT
www.lambandwool.com

SELECTED BIBLIOGRAPHY AND RECOMMENDED READING

Altieri, Miguel, *AGROECOLOGY: THE SCIENCE OF SUSTAINABLE AGRICULTURE*. Westview Press, 1995.

Barbato, Joseph, and Lisa Weinerman, editors, *HEART OF THE LAND: ESSAYS ON LAST GREAT PLACES*. Vintage, 1994.

Berry, Wendell, *THE UNSETTLING OF AMERICA: CULTURE AND AGRICULTURE*. Sierra Club Books, 1977.

Bill, Katherine, *GOOD NEIGHBOR HANDBOOK: A GUIDE FOR LANDOWNERS IN THE METHOW VALLEY*. Methow Conservancy, October 2000.

Brody, Hugh, *THE OTHER SIDE OF EDEN: HUNTERS, FARMERS, AND THE SHAPING OF THE WORLD*. North Point Press, 2000.

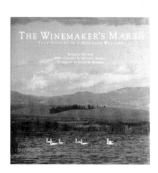

Brower, Kenneth, *THE WINEMAKER'S MARSH: FOUR SEASONS IN A RESTORED WETLAND*. Sierra Club Books, 2001.

Callenbach, Ernest, *BRING BACK THE BUFFALO: A SUSTAINABLE FUTURE FOR THE GREAT PLAINS*. University of California, 2000.

Clark, Jeanne, and Glenn Rollins, et al., *FARMING FOR WILDLIFE: VOLUNTARY PRACTICES FOR ATTRACTING WILDLIFE TO YOUR FARM*. Multiple agencies and organizations, April 1997.

Coleman, Eliot, *THE NEW ORGANIC GROWER: A MASTER'S MANUAL OF TOOLS AND TECHNIQUES FOR THE HOME AND MARKET GARDENER*. Chelsea Green, 1989.

Coleman, Eliot, *THE WINTER-HARVEST MANUAL: FARMING THE BACK SIDE OF THE CALENDAR*. Self-published, 1998. Available from Four Season Farm, RR Box 14, Harborside, ME 04642, $15 per copy.

CREATING NATIVE LANDSCAPES IN THE NORTHERN GREAT PLAINS AND ROCKY MOUNTAINS, Montana Association of Conservation Districts, 406-443-5711.

Diamond, Jared, *GUNS, GERMS, AND STEEL: THE FATES OF HUMAN SOCIETIES*. Norton, 1997.

Faulkner, Edward, *PLOWMAN'S FOLLY*. University of Oklahoma Press, 1994.

Freyfogle, Eric T., editor, *THE NEW AGRARIANISM: LAND, CULTURE, AND THE COMMUNITY OF LIFE*. Island Press, 2001.

Grumbine, Ed, *GHOST BEARS: EXPLORING THE BIODIVERSITY CRISIS*. Island Press, 1993.

Hoffman, Leslie, publisher, *SUSTAINABLE CUISINE WHITE PAPERS*. Earth Pledge Foundation, 1999.

House, Freeman, *TOTEM SALMON: LIFE LESSONS FROM ANOTHER SPECIES*. Beacon, 1999.

Howard, Sir Albert, *AN AGRICULTURAL TESTAMENT*. Oxford University Press, 1943.

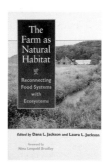

Jackson, Dana, and Laura Jackson, editors, *THE FARM AS NATURAL HABITAT: RECONNECTING FOOD SYSTEMS WITH ECOSYSTEMS*. Island Press, 2002.

Jackson, Wes, Wendell Berry, and Bruce Colman, editors, *MEETING THE EXPECTATIONS OF THE LAND: ESSAYS IN SUSTAINABLE AGRICULTURE AND STEWARD-SHIP*. North Point Press, 1984.

Kimbrell, Andrew, editor, *FATAL HARVEST: THE TRAGEDY OF INDUSTRIAL AGRICULTURE*. Island Press, 2002.

LaDuke, Winona, *ALL OUR RELATIONS*. Consortium Books, 1999.

Leopold, Aldo, *A SAND COUNTY ALMANAC AND SKETCHES HERE AND THERE*. Oxford University Press, 1949. (See also a new edition with introduction by

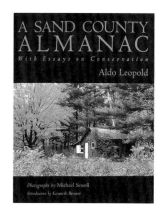

Leopold, Aldo, edited by Susan L. Flader and J. Baird Callicott, *THE RIVER OF THE MOTHER OF GOD AND OTHER ESSAYS*. University of Wisconsin Press, 1991.

Lev, Esther, *HEROIC TALES OF WETLAND RESTORATION*. The Wetland Conservancy, 2001.

Logsdon, Gene, *THE CONTRARY FARMER*. Chelsea Green, 1994.

Manning, Richard, *GRASSLAND: THE HISTORY, BIOLOGY, POLITICS, AND PROMISE OF THE AMERICAN PRAIRIE*. Penguin, 1995.

Margolin, Malcolm, *EARTH MANUAL: HOW TO WORK THE LAND WITHOUT TAMING IT*. Heydey Books, 1995 (reissue).

Margolin, Malcolm, *THE OHLONE WAY: INDIAN LIFE IN THE SAN FRANCISCO-MONTEREY BAY AREA.* Heydey Books, 2002, (25th Anniversary Edition).

Margoluis, Richard, Vance Russell, et. al., *MAXIMUM YIELD? SUSTAINABLE AGRICULTURE AS A TOOL FOR CONSERVATION.* Biodiversity Support Program, 2001.

Matthiessen, Peter, *WILDLIFE IN AMERICA.* Viking, 1957.

McNeely, Jeffrey, and Sara Scherr, *ECOAGRICULTURE: STRATEGIES TO FEED THE WORLD AND SAVE WILD BIODVIERSITY.* Island Press, 2003.

Nabhan, Gary Paul, and Stephen Buchmann, *THE FORGOTTEN POLLINATORS.* Island Press, 1996.

Nabhan, Gary Paul, and Jim Donovan, editors, *NECTAR TRAILS FOR POLLINATORS: DESIGNING CORRIDORS FOR CONSERVATION.* Arizona-Sonora Desert Museum Technical Papers, 2000.

Noss, Reed, and Alan Cooperrider, *SAVING NATURE'S LEGACY: PROTECTING AND RESTORING BIODIVERSITY.* Island Press, 1994.

O'Brien, Dan, *BUFFALO FOR THE BROKEN HEART,* Random House. 2001.

Pickett, C. H,. and Robert Bugg, *ENHANCING BIOLOGICAL CONTROL: HABITAT MANAGEMENT TO PROMOTE NATURAL ENEMIES OF AGRICULTURAL PESTS.* University of California Press, 1998.

Pollan, Michael, *THE BOTANY OF DESIRE: A PLANT'S-EYE VIEW OF THE WORLD.* Random House, 2001.

Quaamen, David, *SONG OF THE DODO: ISLAND BIOGEOGRAPHY IN AN AGE OF EXTINCTIONS.* Touchstone Books, 1997.

Rothenberg, David, and Marta Ulvaeus, editors, *THE WORLD AND THE WILD: EXPANDING WILDERNESS CONSERVATION BEYOND ITS AMERICAN ROOTS.* University of Arizona Press, 2001.

Salatin, Joel, *PASTURED POULTRY PROFITS.* Polyface Farms Inc. (distributed by Chelsea Green).

Salatin, Joel, *SALAD BAR BEEF.* Polyface Farms Inc. (distributed by Chelsea Green).

Sayre, Nathan, *THE NEW RANCH HANDBOOK: A GUIDE TO RESTORING WESTERN RANGELANDS.* Quivira Coalition, 2001.

Schell, Orville, *MODERN MEAT: ANTIBIOTICS, HORMONES, AND THE PHARMACEUTICAL FARM.* Vintage, 1984.

Schlosser, Eric, *FAST FOOD NATION: THE DARK SIDE OF THE ALL-AMERICAN MEAL.* Houghton Mifflin, 2001.

Sloane, Eric, *OUR VANISHING LANDSCAPE.* Wilfred Funk, 1955.

Sotherton, Nick, and Robin Page, *A FARMER'S GUIDE TO HEDGEROW AND FIELD MARGIN MANAGEMENT.* Game Conservancy Limited, 1998.

Smith, J. Russell, *TREE CROPS: A PERMANENT AGRICULTURE.* Island Press/Devin-Adair, 1950.

Snyder, Gary, *THE PRACTICE OF THE WILD.* North Point Press, 1990.

Soule, Michael and John Terborgh, *CONTINENTAL CONSERVATION: SCIENTIFIC FOUNDATIONS FOR REGIONAL RESERVE NETWORKS.* Wildlands Project, 1999.

Stegner, Wallace, *BEYOND THE HUNDREDTH MERIDIAN: JOHN WESLEY POWELL AND THE SECOND OPENING OF THE WEST.* Penguin, 1953.

Steinberg, Ted, *DOWN TO EARTH: NATURE'S ROLE IN AMERICAN HISTORY.* Oxford, 2002.

Thrupp, Lori Ann, *CULTIVATING DIVERSITY: AGROBIODIVERSITY AND FOOD SECURITY.* World Resources Institute, 1998.

Wrysinski, Jeanette, *MONITORING ON YOUR FARM: A GUIDE TO TRACKING AND UNDERSTANDING THE RESOURCES AND WILDLIFE ON YOUR LAND.* Yolo County Resource Conservation District, 2002.

Wallace, Ben, *WILD HARVEST: FARMING FOR WILDLIFE AND PROFITABILITY,* California Wilderness Coalition, 2002.

Weaver, William, and Danny Hagans, *HANDBOOK FOR FOREST AND RANCH ROADS: A GUIDE FOR PLANNING, DESIGNING, CONSTRUCTING, RECONSTRUCTING, MAINTAINING, AND CLOSING WILDLANDS ROADS.* Mendocino County Resource Conservation District, 1994, 707-468-9223.

Wilcove, David, *THE CONDOR'S SHADOW: THE LOSS AND RECOVERY OF WILDLIFE IN AMERICA.* Freeman, 1999.

Wilson, Edward O., *THE DIVERSITY OF LIFE.* Norton, 1992.

Wuerthner, George, editor, *WELFARE RANCHING: SUBSIDIZED DESTRUCTION OF THE AMERICAN WEST.* Island Press, 2002.

Yana-Shapiro, Howard, and John Harrisson, *GARDENING FOR THE FUTURE OF THE EARTH.* Seeds of Change/Bantam 2000.

Yolo County Resource Conservation District, *BRING FARM EDGES BACK TO LIFE!* Yolo County RCD, 2001.

END NOTES

Foreword, by Fred Kirschenmann

1 Aldo Leopold, *A Sand County Almanac*. (Oxford University Press, 1949).
2 Richard Lewontin, *The Triple Helix*. (Harvard University Press, 2000).
3 David Abrams, *The Spell of the Sensuous*. (Vintage Books, 1996).

The Case for Farming with the Wild

1 Jared Diamond, *Guns, Germs, and Steel*. (Norton, 1997), p. 132.
2 Michael Pollan, *The Botany of Desire: A Plant's-Eye View of the World*. (Random House, 2001), p. xxiii.
3 Diamond, *Guns, Germs, and Steel*. p. 132.
4 Yvonne Baskin, "Reuniting Pangea: A Crowded World Connected not by Geology but by Human Commerce," *Wild Earth*, Summer 2002, p. 26.
5 USDA, *America's Private Land: A Geography of Hope*, (USDA Government Printing Office, 1999), p. 54.
6 Amy Vickers, *Handbook of Water Use and Conservation: Homes, Landscapes, Businesses, Industries, Farms*. (Waterplow Press, 2001), cited from Wild Farm Alliance White Paper.
7 Paula MacKay, "Farming with the Wild: Reconnecting Food Systems with Ecosystems," *Wild Earth*, Summer 2001, p. 53.
8 The Decline of Freshwater Ecosystems. (World Resources Institute 1998-99), available from *www.wri.org/wr-98-99/freshwat.htm*.
9 Stanley Wood, Kate Sebastian, Sara Scherr, "Pilot Analysis of Global Ecosystems: Agroecosystems," International Food Policy Research and World Resources Institute, 2000.
10 Vickers, *Ibid*.
11 B.A. Stein, L.S. Kutner, A. Jonathan, *Precious Heritage: The Status of Biodiversity in the United States*. (Oxford University Press, 2000).
12 Judith Soulé and Jon Piper, *Farming in Nature's Image*. (Island Press, 1992), cited in Wild Farm Alliance White Paper.
13 Laura Jackson, *The Farm as Natural Habitat: Reconnecting Food Systems with Ecosystems*. (Island Press, 2002,) p. 45.
14 Anne Platt-McGinn, "Blue Revolution: The Promises and Pitfalls of Fish Farming, *World Watch*, March-April 1998, p. 15.

15 Personal communication from Fred Kirschenmann to the Wild Farm Alliance.
16 Michael Pollan, "When A Crop Becomes King," *New York Times*, July 19, 2002.
17 Robert F. Kennedy Jr., "I Do Not Like Green Eggs and Ham," *Sustainable Cuisine White Papers*. (Earth Pledge Foundation, 1999), p. 66.
18 Linda Baker, "The Not-so-sweet Success of Organic Farming," *Salon.com Magazine*, July 30, 2002.
19 David Gould and Fred Kirschenmann, "Tame and Wild: Organic Agriculture and Wildness, unpublished paper, 2000.
20 Wendell Berry, "For Love of the Land: A Farmer and Conservationist is Tired of Being on Two Losing Sides," *Sierra*, May-June 2002, p. 50.
21 As paraphrased by Steve Talbott, "Ecological Conversations," Netfuture, January 10, 2002, *www.netfuture.org/*.

The Sky Islands

1 "An Extraordinary Plan for a Place Beyond Compare," Sky Islands Wildlands Network brochure.
2 Aldo Leopold, "Conservationist in Mexico (1937)," in *The River of the Mother of God and Other Essays*, (Universtiy of Wisconsin Press, 1991), p. 240.
3 According to personal correspondence from Field Program Director Matt Skroch of the Sky Island Alliance, the figure breaks down as follows: 339,000 acres of wilderness in the Coronado National Forest; 75,780 acres of wilderness on BLM lands; 81,690 acres of wilderness in National Park lands (Saguaro and Chiricahua); and 62,000 acres of study area in the Mt. Graham Wilderness Study area.
4 Tony Povlitis, "Toward Grassland Recovery in the Sky Islands Region," *Wild Earth*, Fall-Winter 2001-2002, pp. 57–59.
5 Jake Page, "A Quiet Revolution in the Borderlands," *Smithsonian*, June 1997, p. 53.
6 Drummond Hadley, "Seeding Open Space: The Origin and the Future of the Grassbank," *Orion Afield*, Winter 1998/99, p. 34.
7 *Ibid*, p. 36.

8 Gary Paul Nabhan, "On the Nectar Trail," *Audubon*, March-April 2001, p. 83.
9 Gary Paul Nabhan, "Nectar Trails of Migratory Pollinators: Restoring Corridors on Private Lands," *Conservation Biology in Practice*, 2 No. 1, (Winter 2001), p.21-27.
10 Jack Hitt,"One Nation Under Ted," *Outside Magazine*, December 2001, p. 78.

The Sacramento Valley

1 Jane Braxton Little, "Sowing New Wildlife Habitat, Seed by Seed," *Audubon*, January-February 2001, p. 100.
2 *Ibid*.
3 Elaine Acker, "Going to Bats for Bug Control," *The Furrow*, Spring 2001, pp. 15-16.
4 Bats and Integrated Pest Management, Bat Conservation International brochure.
5 Mark and Selena Kiser, "Bat Houses for Integrated Pest Management: Benefits for Bats and Organic Farmers: Phase 1," Final Report, submitted to Organic Farming and Research Foundation, January 2002, p. 2.
6 Glen Martin, "Reclaiming a River: Wetlands, Birds and Salmon Returning to the Sacramento," *San Francisco Chronicle*, February 22, 2000, p. A1.
7 *Ibid.*, p. A6.

Building a Matrix of Wildland Habitat

1 Carolyn Lochhead, "California to Lose Out in Massive Farm Bill: Measure Assailed on Environment, Market Grounds," *San Francisco Chronicle*, Thursday May 2, 2202, p. A1.
2 *Ibid*.
3 Aldo Leopold, "The Land Ethic," *A Sand County Almanac*, (Oxford University Press, 1949), p. 208.
4 Richard Manning, *Grassland: The History, Biology, Politics, and Promise of the American Prairie*, (Penguin, 1995), p. 31.
5 George Boody, "Agriculture as Public Good," in *The Farm as Natural Habitat: Reconnecting Food Systems with Ecosystems*, (Island Press, 2002), p. 267.
6 Lisa Gaumnitz, "Restoring Life to a Watershed," *Wisconsin Natural Resources*, (February 2002), p. 7.
7 *Ibid.*, p. 8.
8 Glen Martin, "Where the Buffalo Roam, Humans Are now Plains' Vanishing Species," *San Francisco Chronicle*, April 22, 2001, pp A1, 18, 19.
9 "The Grains of Wrath," *Organic Style*, 2000, p. 72.

10 Elizabeth Becker, "Prairie Farmers Reap Conservation Rewards," *New York Times*, Monday, August 27, 2001, A-1 & 12.
11 "The Prairie Pothole Venture: Cultivating Cooperation for Wildlife and Agriculture," Prairie Pothole Venture general information pamphlet, June 1996.
12 According to correspondence from Mick Erickson, wetland losses thorugh out Prairie Pothole states include: Montana: -27%; N. Dakota: -49%; S. Dakota: -35%; Minnesota: -75%; Iowa: -98%. Grassland losses include: Montana: -50%; No. Dakota: -67%; S. Dakota: -53%; Minnesota: -53%; Iowa: -89%.

Natural Systems Farming

1 Fred Kirschenmann, "Agriculture's Uncertain Future: Unfortunate Demise or Timely Opportunity," a speech delivered to the University of Florida's Institute of Food and Agricultural Sciences.
2 *Ibid*.
3 Miguel Altieri, "Agroecological Principles for Sustainable Agriculture," in *Agroecological Innovations*, edited by N. Uphoff, (Earthscan, London, 2002), pp.40-46.
4 *Ibid*.
5 *Ibid*.
6 Janine Benyus, *Biomimicry: Innovation Inspired by Nature*. (Quill, 1997), p. 43.
7 Gene Logsdon, "Marrying Grain and Pasture," *The Land Report*, The Land Institute, No. 72, (Spring 2002), pp. 14.
8 Benyus, *Biomimicry*, p. 47.
9 Howard-Yana Shapiro and John Harisson, *Gardening for the Future of the Earth*. (Bantam Paperback, 2000), p.196.
10 Lee DeHaan and Scott Bontz, "Breeding Wheat to Hold its Own and the Soil, *The Land Report*, Number 72, (Spring 2002), p. 9.
11 Shapiro and Harrison, *Gardening for the Future of the Earth*, p. 201.
12 Benyus, *Biomimicry*, p. 47.
13 Eliot Coleman, *The Winter Harvest Manual: Farming the Backside of the Calendar*, February 1998. Available from Four Season Farm, RR Box 14, Harborside, ME 04642, $15 per copy.

Corridors, Wildways, and Citizen Monitoring Programs

1 Rachael Freeman Long, Corin G. Pease, and M. Irene Wibawa, "Insects Associated with Hedgerows of Flowering Shrubs," p. 4.
2 Nabhan, "On the Nectar Trail," p. 83.
3 Craig Johnson, Gary Bentrop, Dick Rol, *Conservation Corridor Planning at the Landscape Level: Managing for Wildlife*. (USDA NRCS, 1999), p 1-1.3

4 Gary Nabhan and Jim Donovan, editors, *Nectar Trails for Pollinators: Designing Corridors for Conservation, Restoring Connectivity for Migrant Wildlife through Wildlands and Adjacent Croplands to Ensure Nature's Services: A Case Study from the Binational Rio Santa Cruz*. (Arizona-Sonora Desert Museum, June 2000), p. 16.
5 Paul Spitler, Editor, *Missing Linkages: Restoring Connectivity to the California Landscape*. Produced by the California Wilderness Coalition, The Nature Conservancy, The US Geological Survey, The Zoological Society of San Diego, The South Coast Wildlands Project, the Talon Association, and the California State Parks Commission.
6 Johnson, Bentrop, and Rol, *Conservation Corridor Planning*, 5-2.

Wild Garden Farmers

1 Correspondence from Gary Anderson of the Forest School, Inc. to Foundation for Deep Ecology.
2 Winona LaDuke, "Under the Wild Rice Moon," *Natural Home*, January-February 2002, p.65.

Ecoloabels and Local Marketing Inititatives

1 Ted Williams, "Living with Wolves," *Audubon*, November-December 2000, web edition.
2 Ted Williams, "Red Baiting," *Audubon*, November-December 2001, p. 32.
3 Jonathan Gold, "A Woman of Sustenance," *Gourmet*, October 2001, pp. 224 and 272.
4 Mari Szatkowski, "Thirteen Mile Farm: Couple Out Front with Ideas That Blend Agriculture with Practices Friendly to the Environment," *FenceLines*, February 2001.
5 Peter Friederici, "When Control Means Kill: Activists Combat Compound 1080," *Orion Afield*, Winter 1998/99, p. 15.
6 Mike Finkel, "The Ultimate Survivor," *Audubon*, May-June 1999, p. 54.
7 Mari Szatkowski, "Thirteen Mile Farm."
8 Gregory Digum and Nina Luttinger, *The Coffee Book: Anatomy of an Industry from Crop to the Last Drop*. (The New Press, 1999), p. 38.
9 *Ibid*.

Getting Started

1 Scott McMillon, "Wild Work Crew," *Bozeman Daily Chronicle*, June 16, 2002, D1.
2 David Wilcove, "From Pugilist to Pragmatist," *Society for Conservation Biology Newsletter*, February 2002, on-line edition.

INDEX

PHOTO CREDITS

Anderson, John — Back cover and 8 (slough), 47 (all but portrait and dragonfly), 49 (tomatoes), 159 (winter shelterbelt)

Austin, Jho — 26 (muddy creek)

Carra, Roberto — Front cover (apple picking), 3, 8, 11, 13, 31, 32, 33, 36-37 (all), 40-41, 42, 46 (portait), 49 (portrait, water), 51, 57, 58, 65, 70-71, 73, 75, 85-87, 92, 117, 119, 125, 127, 134-135, 136, 149 (portrait), 157, 159, 161, 162, 163, 174, 175

Clark, Jack K. — 47 (dragonfly)

Crabtree, Rob — 15 (coyote in Snare)

Damrosch, Barbara — 95 (Four Season Farm greenhouse farming operations)

Eaton, Mike (TNC) — 54 (egrets at Cougar Wetland)

Engber, Evan — 155 (restoration photos)

Erickson, Mick — 67 (white pelican photos)

Evans, Terry — 76 (Land Institute aerial), 81-82 (crop close-ups)

Glenn, Warner — (jaguar)

Gosling, Doug — Back cover (tree frog), 122-123 (tree frog, lettuces, potatoes, child), 161 (salad servers)

Greaves, Ed — 54 (California quail, northern flicker, loggerhead shrike), 57 (yellow billed cuckoo)

Guenther, Dan — 148-149 (CSA box and hayride)

Hilty, Jody — Front cover (mountain lion)

Hollett, Willy — 26 (2 photos of baby Sonoran mud turtles)

Hunter, Rich — 152 (GIS map of OAEC)

Imhoff, Dan — 20, 57, 63, 89, 99, 107, 109, 111, 131, 141-142, 152 (map), 154 (pond), 156, 158, 159, 163

Jakobs, Lynn — 15 (hawk on barbed wire)

Karlin, Lynn — 95 (Eliot Coleman and Barbara Damrosch)

Lonsdale, Sandy — 15 (coyote carcasses)

McGrath, Dan — 156 (riparian shelterbelt)

Morton, Karen — 129 (all Shoulder to Shoulder Farm photos)

O'Brien, Pat — Back cover (bison), 40-41 (pronghorn, prairie dog, Texas horned lizard, bison herding, wolf)

Payne, Robert — Front cover and 54 (sandhill cranes in rice field)

Porter, Pam — 30, 31 (Gray Ranch grasslands, full moon and fire, cowboys)

Randorff, Gary — Back cover and 100 (hayfield), 105 (owl, landscapes, portrait)

Robbins, Paul — 154 (tailwater pond illustration)

Skagitonians to Preserve Farmland — 111 (winter stubble)

Smith, Steve — Front cover (fire)

Snyder, Noel — 27 (thick-billed parrot)

Tompkins, Doug — 113 (Conservation Land Trust)

Tuttle, Merlin D. — (Bat Conservation International) 51 (bat)

USDA — 11 (corn, hay, crop duster), 13 (Central Valley, manure lagoon), 15 (feedlot, hog operation), 63 (archive)

Valenzuela, Pablo — 113 (aerial view of farm)

Wildlands Project — 33 (Mexican wolf)

Wolpert, Adam — 114 (painting)

PRODUCTION TEAM

Writing & Research	Daniel Imhoff
Graphic Design	Roberto Carra
Project Editor	Jo Ann Baumgartner
Associate Editors	John Davis
	Sam Earnshaw
	Ellen Smith
	Janet Reed Blake
Indexing	Ellen Davenport
Graphics Assistance	Claudia Carra
Project Coordination	Watershed Media
Research Assistant	Autumn Turpin

ABOUT WATERSHED MEDIA

Watershed Media is a 501(c)3 communications organization that produces strategically tailored projects with leading advocacy organizations to catalyze change around urgent and often under-reported environmental issues. Watershed Media was founded by a research, writing, and graphic design team who have been collaboating on environmental and social issues communciations topics for over a decade and who believe that visually dynamic, concisely written, audience-specific tools can not only increase education, but also influence behavior in moving us toward a more sustainable society. To date, their primary projects include the Wood Reduction Trilogy (paper, building materials, and packaging) and *Farming with the Wild*.

Daniel Imhoff is a writer and researcher on issues related to food, the environment, and design. His articles and essays have appeared in *Saveur, Sierra, Whole Earth, Orion Afield* as well as many other magazines and books. Imhoff is the co-host of a monthly Farm and Garden radio program on Mendocino County Public Broadcasting where he regularly interviews leading activists in the world of sustainable agriculture. He received a B.A. in International Relations from Allegheny College and an M.A. in International Affairs from the Maxwell School of Public Affairs at Syracuse University. He lives with his wife and two children; they divide their time between Healdsburg and a small homestead in California's Anderson Valley.

Roberto Carra is an internationally renowned photographer, graphic designer, and art director. Born in Parma, Italy, Roberto Carra's still-life photography significantly influenced commercial communication during the 1980s and '90s when he worked for the Esprit image studio. A classically trained graphic artist, Carra works in a broad range of visual communication media. He is a widely published editorial photographer as well as a freelance art director whose work appears in books and magazines throughout the world.

Watershed Media
451 Hudson Street, Healdsburg, CA 95448
www.watershedmedia.org
707-431-2936

BUILDING WITH VISION: OPTIMIZING AND FINDING ALTERNATIVES TO WOOD
(ISBN 0-9709500-0-4)
136 pages
Written by Daniel Imhoff
Photography and graphic design by Roberto Carra
Preface by Randy Hayes, of Rainforest Action Network
Introduction by Sim Van der Ryn, Van der Ryn Architects

"A lens into the future of building."
Zahid Sardar, *San Francisco Chronicle*

"A rare mix of philosophy, practical information on building materials and practices, and superb visual presentation."
Alex Wilson, *Enviornmental Building News*

THE GUIDE TO TREE-FREE, RECYCLED AND CERTIFIED PAPERS
(ISBN 0-9673788-0-X)
80 pages
Written by Daniel Imhoff
Designed by Roberto Carra

"If a green future is to come, it must be aesthetically pleasing, and this is the best access for paper consumers to find beauty in their quest to print books and minimize harm to forests and soils."
Peter Warshall, *Whole Earth Review*

"Compiles the best alternatives to wood-based, nonrecycled, chlorine-bleached papers."
Orion Afield